THE SHERIFF'S CATCH

PART ONE

of

THE SASSANA STONE

Pentalogy

JAMES VELLA-BARDON

To Donna Madden

'...apprehend and execute all Spaniards found there, of what quality soever. Torture may be used...'

– Sir William FitzWilliam, Lord Deputy of Ireland

I

WILLEBROEK, THE SPANISH NETHERLANDS

17- August 1585

As we walked along the street, we drew closer to the church of Saint Nicholas. Arm in arm we hesitantly approached its solitary bell-tower, which rose above the rest of the village. The scrape of our footsteps ended when we reached the high wooden doors, as Elsien clutched my hand tightly.

'To think that we were married here over six months ago.'

'Indeed,' I replied, for it seemed incredible that the time had passed so quickly.

I could well remember the day. I had been as nervous and fidgety then as I was now, a man bracing himself for a fight. The ceremony had been sombre and muted. It had also rained hard throughout, and few villagers had attended a wedding between one of their daughters and a hated Spaniard.

A vicious war had raged in the Netherlands for years, after Protestant rebels rose up against the reign of King Philip II of Spain who sent his best troops to crush them. The fighting had ruined the once prosperous Low Countries, as it raged on for nineteen years, with the struggle seeming to have no end in sight. As chaos grew in the provinces, even the Catholic Netherlanders had come to hate the sight of the Spanish soldier.

In the midst of all this strife, our company was sent to the Duchy of Brabant, where we secured some of the villages which lay along the banks of the river Scheldt. It was a vital watercourse running on to Antwerp, which had been Europe's financial centre before the war. This great city still withstood a fierce siege by Spanish troops which had lasted for over a year, and it was barely ten miles north of Willebroek, where I was barracked.

Despite the unwelcome presence of Spanish soldiers in her village, Elsien had somehow fallen in love with me. Our growing dalliances had been strictly forbidden by her wealthy father Reynier, who was the local miller, yet two months later he had been shocked to discover that she was with child.

'Penniless bastard,' he had growled at me, upon learning the news, 'you'll rob me of my daughter, but not of her honour!'

Having long been a generous contributor to the local parish, Reynier had been quick to coax the village priest to overlook any lengthy formalities, so that within the week Elsien and I were brought together at Willebroek's parish church. The old miller had glared at me throughout the rite, with his knotted white brows closely bunched together in outrage. Yet the two younger brothers of my betrothed had grinned openly at our union, as had a few of her other family members. Meanwhile my fearsome army comrades had stood watch at the church door, to ensure that no trouble ensued during the unpopular ceremony.

It had been a pure and sacred chapter during years spent serving Spain in countless horrific war theatres. As Elsien and I stared on at the church door, I found myself smiling at the memory, perhaps the only fond one from my decades in the army. It slowly dawned upon me that I was as happy as I had ever been in Willebroek, despite the day-to-day sufferings inflicted by the war.

'Your father was so angry with me,' I said, 'I think he would have killed me on that day if he could have.'

Elsien cleared her throat awkwardly.

'I doubt it, Abel. You saved his life remember? Deep down papa loves you, but he hates surprises.'

'Certainly a few of those,' I muttered, as I looked down the street towards the houses to our right. 'To think that I saved his neck on that very corner. Those debtors were giving him a merciless kicking.'

'And then you appeared out of the night,' Elsien said with a broad grin, 'a Spanish God-fearing hero sent to save the day. Papa has recounted it so many times now.'

'Has he?' I stuttered, turning red in the face. 'It was certainly a close thing. Corporal Salva told me not to bother, but I couldn't bear to see an old man suffer like that. It was below me to stand idly by.'

'Well it's just as well you did something,' she said, grasping my arm tightly against hers and leaning over to plant a soft kiss on my cheek, 'otherwise we'd never have met.'

'I wonder how he feels about that now.'

'Oh!' she exclaimed, so that I turned towards her as she leant over and clutched at her swollen belly. 'Oh! Oh!'

'What is the matter?' I gasped, fearing that she might already be due.

'Can you feel it?' she asked me with a growing smile. 'Can you?'

Elsien took my wrist and held my hand to her belly. The slightest kick could be felt against my palm, which changed the scowl on my face into a rueful grin. A contented glow grew within me, at the repeated thuds, until I raised my eyes and met my wife's gaze. In the light of dawn, she was as radiant as she had ever been, with her blue eyes dancing above her high cheekbones, and the single blonde lock falling across her forehead.

'A strong child,' I said.

'A love child,' she replied, with a mischievous grin.

'Don't call it that,' I frowned, then gave her a kiss on the mouth which was as lengthy as it was heartfelt. When at last I pulled my head back, she uttered the plea which I had dreaded for days.

'Don't leave us. Papa is so ill, and the boys both look up to you.'

With a sigh, I curled my arm around her olive-coloured kirtle, holding her tightly against the gunpowder charges which hung from the bandolier on my breast. My rifle dangled sideways as I held her chin and stared back at her silently. Her mention of her father and brothers left me feeling moved, for in recent months they had become the closest family I had ever had.

'Do not fret, woman. I'll not be gone long.'

Her hands formed into fists as she punched me gently on the chest.

'I hate the thought of you leaving us. Can you not find another to replace you?'

'You know I would, if only I could. Yet the sergeant has insisted. And your father still owes him protection money.'

'To hell with your sergeant,' she snapped, as she pushed me away with a dark scowl, 'Papa only owes him a month's pay. Still better than your king, who has not paid a single one of you in two years.'

'*Your* king too,' I cut in sternly, holding her by the shoulders and raising an eyebrow, 'so have a care how you refer to him. As for Sergeant Ramos, only a fool would not fear him.'

My words were followed by a low peal from Saint Nicholas' belfry, which left me startled that it was already seven o'clock.

''Tis the hour of our gathering,' I gasped. 'Quick, begone, for the others will soon be here!'

She stared back at me defiantly, with her lips showing the slightest twitch of unease.

'I do not fear them,' she said curtly, with her eyes blazing, 'and in any event, it is too late.'

'Certainly your father's daughter,' I sighed. My head was by then turned towards the other end of the street, where I could see the first Spaniards making their way towards the church.

They were hardly a sight for sore eyes, for most went unshaven and wore tattered collars. None of them had been paid in years, so that morale was in the gutter. In the heat of summer many wore loose-fitting shirts, with strips of red cloth tied around their arms or with a saltire sewn on their breasts, to mark them out as Spanish soldiers. Pieces of rusted armour could also be seen, and all were armed to the teeth.

The men resembled a gathering of shabby street cats as they assembled before the church, and I could not help thinking what a blight they were upon the civilised and hard-working villagers of Willebroek. Yet despite their low spirits, the soldiers were each very haughty of bearing, although their sallow complexions betrayed poor nourishment. Two years spent rotting in the village without pay had weighed heavily upon them, and rumours of mutiny had grown by the day. I could only hope that any loot to be had from the impending ambush might help to cool their general resentment.

'Go,' I urged my wife, gently pushing her away, 'this is no place for a woman.'

'Why if it isn't the Lynx of Haarlem,' called a half-crooning voice from across the street.

I cringed at the sound of it, before turning to see my sergeant, Curro Ramos, who walked over towards us wearing his red sash across his breastplate, and bearing a halberd carried by officers of his rank. It was an axe with a long handle and a cruel spike at its end, which I had often seen the sergeant use at close quarters with devastating effect.

'Would that I were truly as keen of sight as a lynx,' I replied disconsolately, 'that I might see a way out of this mess.'

Ramos approached us with our three other comrades, who like him were hated and feared by both Spaniards and Netherlanders. They walked close to each other in the middle of the street, with Ramos flanked to his right by the tall and lanky Corporal Salvador Ortiz. As always, the right side of Salva's face twitched uncontrollably, because of a thrashing he had received as a boy. His trusted *partesana* was held out before him, a long staff with a knife-like blade at its end that was only borne by corporals.

To the sergeant's left was the sinister Gabriel de Andrés, the fastest-thinking swordsman I knew. He was also no mean shot, and I curiously noted the crossbow which hung from his belt, for I had never seen him carry it before. At Gabri's back, taking long ponderous steps, strode the towering pikeman Tomé de Cristóbal, otherwise known as Cristó. He was a hulking monster as broad as two of his comrades, with huge arms like iron levers. As always, he trod behind his trusted companion Gabri, with his long pike resting upon his broad shoulder.

As my four comrades drew nearer, they stared at us with narrowed eyes, as wicked smiles grew on their weathered faces. At their approach Elsien finally made to leave, squeezing my hand once before the scrape of her soles could be heard upon the ground.

'Why *beste mevrouw*,' called Ramos to her in a voice that was as mocking as it was unnerving, 'will you not also bid us farewell? We are, after all, your husband's brothers-in-arms, part of a comradeship sworn to protect one another.'

The glare Elsien returned could not have been more hateful, while the rattle and clank of arms against armour ceased when the foursome stopped a few feet away from us. They left me feeling as if we were being eyed by a pack of wolves, as some of the other Spaniards also thronged around them, amused by the spectacle of my wife trading glares with the notorious sergeant.

'Farewell, Sergeant Ramos,' she said in accented Spanish, 'may you be triumphant in your endeavour. If only to return my husband to me safe and unharmed.'

'Ah, don't you worry about our pretty little Abelito,' exclaimed Ramos as he stepped towards us, pinching my left cheek between two fingers, and shaking my head from side to side, 'he is a big boy, who can look after himself. He has, after all, survived many worse conflicts.'

So saying, he next fixed his attentions to her, with his voice suddenly harder and dripping with malice.

'I would worry more about your father's lot,' he continued, as I jerked my head away from his hand, 'for he is more than two months behind in his payments to us, and we have faithfully protected him from his debtors.'

'Not in the last month,' I cut in angrily, feeling annoyed by his deviousness.

Ramos' head slowly turned towards me, as a look of outrage grew on his bearded face.

'There you go, Abelito, always standing up for the local heretics! Why don't you ever spare a thought for your own kin?'

'For the last time,' I hissed between gritted teeth, 'they are not heretics. Not all Brabantians are heretics.'

'Whatever you say!' he exclaimed, mockingly raising his arms before me. 'Need you get so agitated when defending people who are but our subjects? And do you not realise that this woman's father is in our debt? A man who is said to have many stashes of silver hidden across the village?'

'It is a lie!' cried Elsien. 'He has not so much wealth!'

'Ah, but some of it, to be sure!' exclaimed Ramos furiously, drawing a knife from his belt, which he pointed towards her. 'And the sooner he parts with it, the safer your home will be!'

'Do you threaten us, Sergeant?' asked Elsien sternly, as she pulled her woollen partlet closely about her and drew away from his blade.

'Well, that depends,' replied Ramos, meeting her stare, 'if you consider a promise to burn your house down to be a threat... then maybe, yes.'

'That's enough,' I said.

'What's enough?' he snapped. 'Will you just stand there and allow your wife to insult your sergeant? Always so ready to belittle me, Abelito, yet one of these days you might regret it.'

'What do you mean?' I asked hesitantly, taken aback, and wondering whether he had just threatened me too.

'We'll see,' he said, clearly struggling to not speak his thoughts, 'we'll see.'

Meanwhile Elsien's face had assumed a hue of scarlet, and in her anger, she seemed ignorant of the many other Spanish soldiers who had gathered about us. For a moment I feared that she might insult Ramos before them, when an order was barked from the church door, announcing the presence of Captain Arturo Fernández. The captain was a brave and honourable man who was well liked by the troops. He was also known for his pragmatism and loyalty to the men, which made him the natural leader for our raid.

'Gather round whoresons, stay your idle chatter. We have a good stretch to cover before midday and must soon begin our march. I see forty volunteers gathered before me, brave souls who will all get rich pickings. But know before we leave that half of everything we take goes to the sergeant-major, who sanctioned this venture at great personal risk.'

'What personal risk?' snorted a soldier behind us, scratching at lice behind his ear. 'What men don't return shall just be dead-pays, leaving him to pocket their salary.'

'Whenever that is paid,' shot back the captain, 'hence the risk.'

A ripple of laughter ran through the men, as Fernández lived up to his fame for jokes which poked fun at authority. His irreverent humour in the face of our misery was always warmly welcomed, although word of it had probably cost him many promotions. Yet Fernández had always remained close and committed to his men, and he allowed our laughter to subside before resuming his address.

'Our scouts were despatched at dawn, and we will meet them at the agreed place. No drums, pipes, or banners, for we require stealth. My subalterns will be the sergeants *El Perro* and Curro Ramos, whose fellowship includes Abelardo de Santiago, the Lynx of Haarlem.'

Fernández paused to seek me out among the small crowd, then nodded once when his eyes fell upon me. It was at the captain's specific request that Ramos had insisted that I partake of the ambush, since Fernández believed that my inclusion would raise morale.

'The men we fight are all low-born mercenaries,' continued Fernández, 'so none need be spared. They number at least sixty, but we have the element of surprise. Otherwise you know what to do. Now kneel for the blessing.'

He stepped aside, standing along the edge of the doorway as our company's chaplain appeared alongside him, Bible in hand, to recite a holy missive which we received on bended knee. Few of those present understood Latin, but a defiant clamour rose among us when the final imprecation to the Lord was delivered. As the rumbling subsided, we next proceeded to check our weapons, which were also inspected by the sergeants and the captain.

'Farewell,' I whispered, holding Elsien tightly.

She silently returned my embrace, then held her hand to her eyes as she turned away from the mustering. A pang of guilt ran through me as she trudged off, and I felt that I ought to make it up to her somehow. I decided to reveal the secret crib to her, which I had made in recent months while on sentry duty.

'Ask your brothers to show you what I made,' I called out to her. 'For the baby!'

'What?' she asked, trying to hear me above the din of barked orders.

'Marti and Pieter!' I called back. 'Ask them to show you what I made for the baby!'

She nodded back at me and waved when Ramos butted me with his shoulder as he hurried past.

'Fall in line, lovebird,' he grunted, and I stepped among the dozen men in his charge. Before we knew it, we were marching through the houses, as silently as could be managed to avoid waking villagers and spreading rumour of our advance. A backward glance afforded me a last glimpse of Elsien, whose cheeks glistened in the sunlight as we hurried out of the village.

It was then that I saw the members of her family standing behind her, and my jaw dropped at the realisation that they had gathered to see me off. Elsien's brothers Maerten and Pieter stood alongside her, watching on in silent farewell with their Aunt Margareta just behind them. A few other cousins and relatives were also among their number, and I felt deeply moved by their appearance, raising my hand to them in a silent goodbye.

'Very moving,' sneered Ramos ahead of me, having noticed my gesture in the corner of his eye.

We wrinkled our nostrils at the stench of the open rubbish pits beyond the edge of the village, where we found ourselves striking the open country. Before long we entered the first copse which lay in our path, keeping to a narrow trail between the trees. We travelled light, as we did before every ambush, with our rolled-up blankets bouncing on our shoulders. There were five miles left to cover until the larger forest, which was a short distance for Spanish troops who were used to marching over forty miles in a day.

'I wish we were headed to bloody Antwerp instead,' said Cristó, raising the well-worn topic that the men always talked about, ever since we had been barracked in Willebroek. I had known the huge pikeman for years, and still marvelled at his size and height. No one in our company even reached his shoulder.

'How we ended up posted in Willebroek is beyond me,' replied Salva, with his eyes widening and his face twisting sideways due to his spasm. 'Fancy travelling so far from home to be left to rot in a little hole by the river. We'll never make a bean in that forsaken place.'

Each of my comrades wanted to leave Willebroek and be posted to Antwerp instead, to stand a chance of sacking the city when it finally fell. Word had long circled among our company that we would soon be sent towards the city to swell the ranks of its besiegers. This rumour excited the men, for memories of the infamous 'Spanish fury' lingered from nine years earlier, when Antwerp's first siege had been broken. I had myself partaken of the horror of the three-day sacking which followed, when not a single nail had been left on a wall.

'Can you imagine the fair daughters to be had,' said Cristó with an evil grin.

'Not to mention the fountains of ale,' added Salva whimsically. 'It shall be a plunderer's paradise.'

'That wretched city will never fall,' whispered Gabri behind us, with his wide-brimmed hat pulled so low over his eyes that it seemed to have a voice. 'The heretics will hold out to the last man.'

'Not that you can blame them,' I reasoned, then instantly regretted it.

'There he goes again,' sneered Ramos, 'good old Abelito. Always quick to defend our enemies. It's just as well you're of use to us in a fight, or I'd shove that rifle up your backside.'

'Indeed,' I replied as calmly as I could manage, knowing it to be the best tone with which to frustrate him, 'yet after years of fighting, don't you even ask yourself why we are here?'

'To root out heresy and rebellion,' said Salva, assuming a highborn officer's voice, 'before they spread to Spain. We bring the Low Countries both lawfulness and salvation.'

Both Cristó and Ramos chuckled openly at the corporal's affected accent, but I was not impressed.

'We bring them only ruin and the sword,' I said, 'and Spain is far away. We should not even be here.'

'Then where else would you be?' asked Ramos, as he cast me a dark look over his shoulder. 'On a street corner back home, hiring your blade out for a handful of coppers?'

'At least you admit that we're only here for plunder.'

'Perhaps,' said the sergeant, after a few moments, 'which is why I'm grateful to be part of the winning side.'

The smugness of his words annoyed me, although it was true that the soldiers of Spain were feared across Europe and beyond, given that they were always triumphant in battle. All other kingdoms trembled before the stamp of the Spanish tercios' boots, and not since the legions of Rome had an army inspired so much dread and loathing among its rivals. I therefore chose to let the matter lie, rather than trade any more words of anger with Ramos.

We were also halfway towards the forest, so that I was distracted by the large Empress tree which had appeared on our left. I felt a twinge of longing as we passed its wide trunk, where I had first met secretly with Elsien, whispering sweet nothings in her ear which had in time become deep somethings.

'Why me?' I had often asked her as my hand slid behind her waist, while she held me by the shoulder. Elsien would look at me with large, trembling eyes, and her grin filled me with a happiness I had once given up on.

'So many rich villagers and burghers from afar covet your hand,' I continued. 'Why a soldier with no future?'

'Because I feel safe with you,' she said, reaching out to stroke my scarred cheek, 'and you are a good man, although you have forgotten it. And not bad to look at, either.'

Each time her words had left me feeling bewildered and full of disbelief. Almost as if I had stepped into some vision by accident, one which belonged to another. Each time I saw her sharp, handsome features staring back at me expectantly, and each time I buried my face in hers, in case it was truly all a dream from which I might stir.

With a sigh, I realised that I missed those carefree days of first love, when we were merely delighted by each other's company. Yet the passing of months as a married couple meant that we also had to think of our future, which clearly did not lie with the army or in the war-torn Netherlands.

'If only I had the means to get us away from here,' I said to her only the previous week, 'that we might venture to the New World and leave this ravaged, weary continent behind.'

'We have the means,' she had replied firmly, but would not say another word when I pressed her on it.

'There is no point speaking of it,' she told me. 'For what you do not know can't hurt you. And besides, we are not going anywhere while father still lives. He will never give up on his home.'

A low cheer from the men returned my thoughts to the march. Two of them gestured across the plain towards the forest which had come into sight. It appeared an endless cluster of trees, which spread so far and wide that it obscured our view of the city of Mechelen. The wood was home to all manner of lawless bandits and wild beasts, and a grim silence fell among us as to a man we each wondered if we would leave it alive.

As we drew nearer to the nameless wood, I realised that I did not, in fact, want to take part in the impending ambush or even the siege of Antwerp. I was sick of years spent fighting Spain's enemies, and felt reluctant to leave Elsien's family, who had provided me with both a hearth and a home. They were things I had not known since I was a youth when I had fled my uncle's protection to enlist with the Spanish army.

'Slowly,' growled Ramos as I stepped on a sundried branch, causing a cracking sound just as we entered the cover of forest.

A few more disgusted looks were cast at me before we made our way through the trees that became ever more tightly clustered together. The August warmth hindered our progress throughout, for dried twigs and leaves were strewn in our path, yet we had faced similar terrains for years, and learned how to travel over them softly and silently. In each instant, we were aware of the importance of stealth, for the slightest sound might alert hidden pickets or brigands to our whereabouts.

At last, we reached a part of the forest where the ground sank before us towards a gully, which ran as far as the eye could see to both our left and our right. Two men stood before us, with muskets in one hand and their other arms raised in greeting. They were part of a small group of scouts who had been despatched by Fernández the previous day.

'We can set up camp here,' called one of them, 'there is no one around for miles.'

At the captain's order, we fell out of line and laid our blankets and jackets across the forest floor. Some of us returned to sleep while others spoke in muted voices. With a reluctant sigh, I threw myself to the ground alongside my comrades, while Salva pulled a side of tainted mutton from his pack, which was to be our dinner that evening. As he set about picking the maggots out of it, I realised that we were close enough to Fernández and his subalterns to overhear their talk with our scouts.

'How far are they?' asked the captain impatiently.

'We spotted their pickets over an hour ago. They seem to know their business, yet the militia's a slovenly bunch and appears to be in no haste.'

'Humph,' grunted a sergeant, whose drooping cheeks had earned him the nickname of *El Perro*, 'and we are certain that they are heading here?'

'Our informer is convinced,' replied the scout nervously, 'that their direction is the northern provinces, and that De Groote prefers the cover of forest. In any event, we have men at the eastern edge of the wood, who shall notify us when they appear.'

'And is their booty worth all this hassle?' snapped Ramos, his voice filled with irritation.

'We have been assured that it is.'

Fernández proceeded to dismiss his scouts and withdrew with his sergeants deeper into the woods, where they walked about and spoke in hushed tones.

'Sounds like the usual,' whispered Salva.

'It does,' said Gabri, from beneath his hat, 'should be a straightforward affair, unless it's a trap.'

'Isn't it always a trap?' I asked disconsolately.

'Not always,' snapped Salva, then glared at me with suspicion as the left side of his face twitched furiously.

A loud snore from Cristó interrupted our talk, so that Gabri booted him awake, for only he would get away with it, given his close bond with the hulking pikeman.

'Is it time?' gasped Cristó, his eyes widening as his hands fell to his weapons.

'Not for a while yet, you big oaf,' snapped Gabri, 'now turn on your side and stop snoring!'

The giant pikeman issued a loud grunt before he obliged the musketeer, and I checked my rifle and all my gear a last time before getting some rest myself. It was less than two hours later when one of our scouts could be seen running through the wood, calling out to the prostrate Fernández between ragged pants of breath.

'Picket sighted, less than an hour away.'

'Time to rouse the men,' said the captain, rolling onto his knees and snatching up his rifle. 'We must take cover.'

Ramos and *El Perro* quickly followed his lead, running between soldiers and booting them to their feet. Quick plans were next laid between the officers before they scattered around the defile with their men at their heels, hiding behind trees and lying low in the plants among them. Ramos swiftly led his men through the ravine and back up the other side.

'Draw the crossbow,' he whispered. 'We're to take out their pickets if we think they've seen us.'

His orders were quickly followed, with Gabri cranking up the windlass he had brought from the village, while the rest of us loaded our guns. In minutes our weapons were all primed and ready, with Ramos hissing his last orders to us as he pulled out a ramrod from one of his pistols.

'Now all of you pick a target. And when Abelito here takes out De Groote, we'll let them have a volley. I'll take over from there.'

The sergeant's men were all seasoned veterans, used to taking cover and keeping position. We had partaken of many skirmishes and night raids over the years, and each of us could lie as still as a statue, barely breathing for hours on end.

'You,' hissed Ramos, grabbing me by the shoulder and shoving me towards a nearby elm, 'get up there and do what you do best.'

Within moments I was hauling myself up towards the tree's highest boughs, which would afford me the best vantage of the ground below. I stopped at the last sturdy branch which offered enough concealment, and which grew a few feet from the top of the tree. I slowly rose to full height upon the bough, finding it strong enough to bear me at a dizzying distance from the ground.

My comrades below me were still working on their concealment. Gabri could be seen pouring some water from his skin onto the ground, then rubbing the damp earth between his hands and spreading it upon his face. Ramos and Salva were nestled deep in a bush, with their backs barely visible to me, with Cristó having vanished beneath the leaves he had pulled onto himself, save for the back of a huge boot which I could make out close to the gully.

I crouched low in the leaves upon spotting two men stealthily making towards our direction, peering about like hawks. Both carried snaplock rifles, and their jerkins of padded leather hung loose around their breasts. They were fair-skinned Netherlanders who walked barefooted through the gully, never making a sound and ready to fly at the first hint of peril.

As the pair of pickets passed along the defile, I slowly exhaled a sigh of relief, when one of them suddenly pointed at the ground, silently beckoning to his fellow who hurried alongside him. A look of alarm was traded as they made to turn back the way they came, when the twang of crossbows was heard. Three bolts were released from different directions, with one picket being struck clean through the throat while the other was hit in both his thigh and stomach.

'Stop him!' hissed Ramos as the second picket tried to reach for his rifle, in the hope of firing a warning shot to De Groote's men. As always Gabri was the first to react, having already sprung from his hiding place with his dagger drawn. Within moments he had kicked the rifle away, then jerked the pickets' heads back and slit them both from ear to ear.

The dying pair hissed like drowning cats as they were next grabbed by the heel, with Gabri swiftly dragging them behind him before Salva ran over to help him. After the bodies were buried beneath a pile of leaves, my two comrades used dried branches to brush away the pickets' prints, before scurrying back to their hiding places.

From the movement of the sun behind the rim of trees, I could tell that at least another hour had passed. During this time, I readied my rifle, slowly sliding it out of its leather sheath. It was a beautiful gun, a princely gift which had been awarded to me by the High Command following my exploits at the siege of Haarlem. The signature of the Spanish gunsmith Salado could be made out on the lockplate, alongside the lion mark that was embossed on it.

As always, my fingers itched to load the weapon, as I released a charge from my bandolier and poured powder through its bore, then spat an iron ball down it. I used the ramrod to shove them both down hard, then filled the pan with my priming flask. Finally, the spanner that hung from my neck was used to turn the wheel shaft, and I sat back against the bark of the tree, seeking out the first sign of the enemy.

When I swung the doghead onto the pan the first telltale rustle was heard to my right, and the leading mercenaries crashed through the trees, cursing and spitting as they marched towards their end. From their accents and tongues I recognised soldiers who mainly hailed from various Protestant nations, and included Englishmen, Scots, Germans, Swedes and Netherlanders.

They were one of many motley militias raised to fight for their Calvinist masters against Spain. Men who had turned rogue when they were no longer paid. Like most soldiers of fortune, they carried their spoils on their person, with bands of gold and silver glistening upon their ragged clothing.

'Mother of mercy,' I gasped at the sight of them, for there were at least eighty men on foot even though we had been told there were sixty.

Although we Spaniards were known to beat twice our number in battle, we had not accounted for the ten horsemen who appeared behind the footmen. A man in black armour rode before them, with his wheellock pistol held at the ready. Behind him rode other armoured riders, yet I could tell from his red beard that my target had finally appeared.

As the rifle was raised to my shoulder, I made out De Groote passing right before me, leaving me in no doubt that my shot would pass clean through his steel helmet. His head was caught in my sights as I hastily mouthed my usual sniper's threnody from the book of Samuel, to steady both my nerves and my hand.

> *This day will the Lord deliver thee into mine hand;*
> *and I will smite thee,*
> *and take thy head from thee*

A slight billow of smoke left the pan as I jerked back the hair trigger. Acrid smoke blinded me when the rifle was fired, with the gun's kick throwing me back against the tree trunk. As I waved away the smoke, I could see De Groote toppling from his horse, with blood spurting out of his helmet. His ambushed force froze as a dozen lit grenades were flung at their feet, followed by a loud volley of musket fire.

'*Spanjaarden!*' screamed one of De Groote's men.

He swiftly drew his sword, only to be hurled off his feet by the blast of a grenade. Behind him mercenaries dropped to their knees amid cries in various tongues. Over half their number were stricken by the second fusillade when a roar from Captain Fernández echoed across the gully, scattering more birds from the trees.

'Go Santiagoooooo!'

It was the cry used by Spaniards before every raid, and below me Ramos could already be seen bursting from the trees, running at the trapped militia with his men at his heels. A mountain of leaves rose from the ground and fell away as Cristó also stood up, raising his pike before him as he raced towards the fray. His pike caught the first enemy clean through the waist, with passing straight through the screaming man and ripping out of his back. The skewered man was whisked off his feet as Cristó's step never faltered, with his spear point also passing clean through another man's throat.

'For Saint James!'

Yet another of De Groote's men was lanced by the roaring Cristó, leaving three enemies dangling from his bloodied pikestaff. With this butchery accomplished, the pikeman hurled his spear to the ground and drew his two-handed broadsword.

Their howls pierced the air as he brought endless strokes down upon the impaled men, a monstrous sight which chilled both friend and foe.

I quickly refilled the rifle's pan with my powder flask, then plucked another ampoule from my bandolier and emptied it down the bore. As the rifle was reloaded, I studied the ground beneath me, until I spotted Ramos hacking a stout hireling in the neck with his halberd. To his right the deft strokes from Salva's *partesana* and Gabri's sword cut down those who offered resistance, and behind them I spotted a wounded mercenary raising a pistol towards their backs. I instantly picked him off, a clean shot to the head, then set about reloading my rifle again. As the stinking smoke around me cleared, I made out Captain Fernández, who was held in the grip of a burly axeman.

'Steady,' I whispered to myself as I fixed my sights on the nape of the attacker's neck, then jerked back the trigger so that I was once more shrouded in smoke.

Although blinded by the fog I loaded the rifle swiftly, having done it so many times before that a blindfold would not have stopped me. Another three heretics were felled by my fire, until I could make out the men led by the captain and Ramos cutting down the last of their foes. I turned my attention to *El Perro's* band, who were still locked in a desperate hand-tohand struggle.

Two more of De Groote's men were hit by my shots, which had swung the fight firmly in our favour. The ambush quickly deteriorated into a rout, with the heretics cut down without mercy. I could already see Elsien standing before her father's house, smiling at my return. The thought was quickly banished as I returned my attentions to the fight.

Yet it was an instant of distraction that would cost me dear, and I never saw the crossbow bolt until it struck my rifle. The shaft sent both the Salado and the ramrod flying from my hands before it slammed into the bark behind me. I lost my balance amid the loud thud of wood and the cry of battle, clawing thin air as I fell over. My ribs struck the next branch below, knocking the wind out of me before I fell feet first towards the ground.

My forehead was opened by yet another branch before I crashed into the tree roots, feeling a momentary burst of agony through my ankle as I lay dazed and winded on the forest floor. Someone was calling out to me, yet it was hard to tell who it was. The sound of fighting lingered a moment longer before everything turned into darkness.

II

Willebroek, The Spanish Netherlands

17-20 August 1585

When I stirred again a deep hunger tore through my belly, and my ears were filled with the howl of a wolf. Darkness engulfed me as I moved from side to side, causing a rustle of leaves. I found myself pushing even more leaves and brushwood away as I rose out of a small ditch, and above me a new moon shone in the middle of a star-filled sky, which was clear and without shadow.

'What in Christ's name?' I muttered, spitting leaves from my mouth as I crawled out from the hole. 'Who did this to me?'

Someone had dragged me away from the foot of the tree, before covering me as best they could. Whoever it was must have been in haste, for my sword still hung from my side and nothing had been taken from my person. Yet I had no time to dwell on the matter, since low growling could be heard a few feet away from me, as well as the shredding of clothes and flesh. I got onto my right foot, then fell over with a loud curse as a burst of pain ran through its ankle.

'Holy host of the Madonna!'

The growls ahead of me subsided somewhat, and I froze as countless shining orbs appeared before me. After a few moments, I reached for the knife chained at my hip, then drew it from its sheath and held it before me. Two by two the orbs slowly vanished from view, as the wolves returned to the scavengers' bounty which had been provided by the ambush.

'Where is everyone?' I muttered, then slowly crawled ahead until I made out a large oak in the moonlight.

After repeated attempts, I managed to climb it using only my arms and one leg. I hugged one of its boughs for dear life for the rest of the night, while rats scuttled through the branches above my head and the curs below gorged themselves on human flesh. My shock at being abandoned slowly turned to bafflement and then bitterness, for I could not believe that someone had concealed me while I was unconscious.

The growling beneath me subsided towards dawn, when the wolves retired from the defile to their lairs. I scrambled back down the oak, feeling drowsy from the gash to my head and the sleepless night. A terrible fear was also upon me, that I might be found by bandits or other mercenaries. I slowly crawled towards the elm I had fallen from the previous day, desperate to find my Salado rifle. I spent close to two hours searching for it, all the while seeking to ignore the thick smell of blood and flesh which lingered in the air. At last, I found the gun near the roots of a nearby tree, and I would have cried out in delight had I not been in such danger.

With the search for the rifle finally over, I crawled back towards the corpses which had been dumped in the gully. The stench of torn bodies was almost intolerable as I cast my eyes over them, seeking to identify some other weapon that I might use. Yet the dead had been picked clean of everything before the wolves had got to them, and I moved further along the defile before crossing it, wishing to be free of the smell and sight of torn bodies.

'What happened?' I kept whispering to myself as I limped and crawled towards the direction of Willebroek, keeping all senses alert for the slightest noise from any other being.

It was at a snail's pace that I hobbled along, always wondering if I was heading the right way. At last, my head was so light that I climbed back into another tree to gain some rest. I slept through the whole afternoon and night, rising again with a start at mid-morning.

'Curse it,' I groaned, holding my aching belly, 'I need to find something to eat.'

After abandoning the tree, my slow journey resumed, and I limped on step by painful step, always throwing myself to the ground whenever I heard a distant sound. A small feed of roots and earthworms followed, which slightly reduced my hunger as I made through the dells and sunbursts, wishing to leave the wood behind me.

I lay spent on the forest floor for long stretches, staring at the ring on my finger while I prayed that I might see Elsien again. Despite my huge weariness, it was the image of her that kept me trudging onwards, hoping all the while that I might soon come upon Willebroek. Yet another night was once more spent in the trees, followed by another day of crawling, as I was slowly overcome by despair.

'Why did they leave me?' I sighed, although a slight suspicion had begun to form in my mind, which I tried to cast aside, dismissing it because of my desperate predicament.

'Surely he wouldn't have. Surely not.'

I shivered upon hearing the sudden sound of hooves, and my skin crawled at the thought of an approaching band of Protestants. I rolled over behind a tree, afraid that they might discover me, before nailing me to the closest tree or beating me to death. It was then that I saw Elsien's younger brother riding through the bursts of daylight between the trunks, atop a fine black Frisian and leading another behind him. I blinked at the sight in disbelief before calling out.

'Marti, stop! Whither do you ride Marti?'

I heard a cry of relief from him when he spotted me, turning his mount around and reining it in alongside me.

'How did you find me? I croaked, limping towards him, and gratefully drinking from a water flask he held out to me.

'Sheer luck, it would seem,' he replied with a hesitant smile, 'but it's just as well I did find you, or Elsi would have murdered me.'

He dismounted and passed me some fruit rinds which I quickly wolfed down. Maerten then held his hand out to me and helped me up onto my good leg, and to climb atop the second horse.

'Your head is a mess,' he said, 'and what's with the ankle?'

'I fell, got knocked out by a branch,' I grunted, having a care to only pass my left foot through its stirrup.

We nudged our steeds back towards the village. As we passed beneath the cover of trees a deep guilt gnawed at my conscience, which was already well worn from years of fighting and savagery.

'You should never have left them.'

Maerten looked at me in surprise. He greatly resembled his sister, so that the frown beneath his locks reminded me of Elsien.

'They are your family,' I insisted, ignoring the jolt of pain as I kicked my horse into a faster trot when the path through the trees widened.

'It's your fault, for marching off to that ambush,' he replied, 'it is what forced me to have to leave them in the first place. You'd have been skinned alive if I'd not found you first, and we're not out of the woods yet.'

'I would have survived,' I lied, 'I was a soldier before you were even born...'

My words were broken off by a loud snort. At first, I thought it was from one of the horses, before realising that it had been produced by Maerten.

'Nonsense, Abel,' he said angrily, 'your ankle is the size of a goose egg. You'd still be crawling through the thicket on all fours without a horse.'

He had spoken the truth of it, and I dared not think what might have befallen me had he not found me first.

'What was I supposed to do?' I said at last, over the loud clop of hooves. 'It was sergeant's orders.'

'Ah yes,' replied Maerten, issuing yet another snort of disgust, 'your beloved Sergeant Ramos. Where was he when you were passed out? And what of Corporal Salva and those two other scoundrels that you hang around with the whole time?

So much for your unbreakable *camarada* and your oath of loyal comradeship!'

The youth's words cut close to the bone, for I was myself furious at having been abandoned by my four comrades. For years I had rescued them during numerous scraps and battles, shooting down any rebel who crept up from behind them. Yet the one time I had needed them, they had left me unconscious at the foot of a tree. It made no sense to me at all.

'Don't speak ill of them,' I muttered, feeling both perplexed and hurt, 'something must have happened. Other rebels must have turned up, or else they were cut off...'

'Really?' replied Maerten with a sarcastic grin, and clearly delighting in my feelings of betrayal. 'They did not seem too worried upon their return to Willebroek.'

'Did they not even mention me?'

'Ramos said you must have been captured or killed. I asked him how that was even possible, given that you're a sniper and always well away from the real fighting.'

The words of my brother-in-law left me flustered, and for a moment I clenched my reins in a rage at his insolence. Yet Ramos' abandonment stung me worse, and I was baffled by how my sergeant had explained my absence.

'Is that all they said?' I asked again, as our mounts veered to the left. 'Are you sure?'

'Yes,' said Maerten, sounding somewhat smug about it, 'that's all. So I obtained two horses and came looking for you. I had to leave Papa and Elsi behind, at the mercy of our debtors and the other Spaniards.'

'Elsi' was Maerten's nickname for Elsien, the sister he had always looked up to. His mother had died giving birth to his younger brother Pieter, so that throughout his life Elsien had been as much a parent to him as she had been his older sibling. The two of them shared an especially close bond. I could not forget Maerten's delight eight months earlier, upon discovering that his sister was with child.

I winced at the thought of my pregnant wife, overcome by guilt at the hazards which might have befallen her and her father while Maerten was away searching for me in the forest. Yet I pushed all dark thoughts to one side, choosing not to be burdened by them.

'None would dare lay a finger on your family,' I said defiantly, 'for they are now also my relations through marriage. The relations of a soldier of Spain.'

'You still have too high an opinion of your comrades,' he replied.

A shrill wind then rustled through the leaves that surrounded us, and I bent over to avoid a low-hanging branch. As always, the boy's outspoken nature irritated me, with the warning of his words having left me feeling more worried.

'You should not have done it,' I muttered again anxiously. 'I told you to stay with them until my return.'

'Would that I had been left with a choice!' he shouted, finally losing his cool and whirling his horse around to face me. His cheeks were flushed with anger as his tattered cloak fluttered about him, so that I pulled my own mount up in surprise.

'Elsi wouldn't stop nagging me!' he yelled. 'Kept telling me you're the father of her child and my brother by marriage! Finally even Papa had enough of her whining, sick as he was in bed. He forgave most of the mayor's debt so that I could borrow these horses.'

I fell silent at his outburst, lowering my eyes to the black Friesian he rode, which puffed spurts of mist and kicked the ground impatiently. It was a fine, well-built stallion, just like my own mount. Prized, invaluable possessions from a time when peace and plenty had reigned in the Low Countries before the troubles with Spain had begun. One could not have asked for a better horse in the Netherlands, or indeed the whole world.

My attention then returned to my brother-in-law's sparsely bearded face. He grunted aloud in annoyance as he wheeled his horse around, kicking it back along the path towards Willebroek. With a grimace I also spurred my own steed on again, ignoring the pain in my ankle. For a while thereafter we rode on in brooding silence, which was only broken by the twitter of birds and the crunch of sun-dried August leaves underfoot. Together we wended our way through the forest at a brisk canter, but slow enough to allow us to draw our weapons at the first sign of danger.

My right hand rested upon my sword pommel throughout our ride, with my prized wheellock hanging off my shoulder, ready to be snatched up at need. I soon recognised different parts of our wooded surroundings, stretching before us beneath the clear sky overhead. Familiar landmarks came into view, with a reddened oak followed by a clump of tall firs last seen three days earlier, when marching with my comrades towards the ambush.

I smiled faintly when the last trees of the forest were left behind us, feeling relieved that I was soon to be reunited with Elsien. After a time, we sighted the Empress tree, and I realised that I had been away from her and her family for close to three days. Too short a time for them to have endured much torment, I kept telling myself.

'I wonder how we shall find the village,' I mused aloud after a time, keen to distract myself from my brooding thoughts through idle talk. I also hoped that my attempt at conversation might show Maerten that I had left our latest argument behind us.

'You've not been away that long,' he muttered after a time, sounding relieved that the heavy silence between us had been broken. 'It will be as boring as ever, with the usual resentment towards anything Spanish.'

'Which now includes your sister,' was my dry reply, and he turned to serve me with a rueful grin.

'How's the foot?' he asked.

'Aches but a little,' I lied, for the ankle bit harder than the devil, having been badly sprained after my fall.

'And your head?'

Despite the crusted gash on my brow the aching in my head had passed, and Maerten nodded when I mentioned this.

'Hopefully your tumble's knocked some sense into you,' he said.

'How is your father?' I asked, keen to avoid another argument.

'He is stable,' was all Maerten said, in a voice tinged with sadness.

In recent weeks, the tough old miller had been taken badly ill, weighed down as he was by the many problems which the war had caused him. He had once been his village's wealthiest son, yet only five of Willebroek's forty-five barns still held wheat, with the rest being long filled with billeted Spanish soldiers. The constantly reduced amount of wheat that reached his watermill also meant that he enjoyed less and less profit. It had been a hard blow to his fortunes.

To make matters worse, many were those who could no longer repay their debts to him, with several angry locals demanding that he extend them more loans. Of late Reynier had even found himself threatened with violence by those very same Spaniards he had hired to protect him, against my wishes. As Reynier fell behind in his payments to them, I often found myself having to fend off my own comrades' advances in the doorway of the miller's house.

'My patience is wearing thin!' Ramos had often yelled in my face. 'Your girl's father had best honour his debts soon!'

'He will pay,' I replied, 'and if not, then I will make good on his debts.'

'*You?*' Ramos would scoff, 'How? You are but a penniless flea-ridden whoreson like the rest of us.'

Elsien and her brothers had often heard my remonstrations with the sergeant while they sat in silence inside their house. Meanwhile Salva, Gabri and Cristó would watch my arguments with Ramos with a keen interest, toying with the ends of their daggers, and ever ready to do their master's bidding.

I kicked my horse's flanks in frustration at these memories, as Maerten also spurred on his mount. My teeth were gritted from the jabs of pain in my ankle, while I pondered my lot in life. The army had reduced me to a starving bag of bones without a copper coin to spit on, the sworn servant of a bankrupt king. So miserable was my predicament, that I could not even guarantee my family's safety from my own comrades.

My thoughts returned to the path as the trees around us became sparser. In the distance I could already make out the shimmering canal, with the small cluster of dwellings along-side it that was Willebroek.

It was the height of summer and, although spared from a blazing heat, it was still warm enough for Maerten to remove his cloak from his back and roll it up. In following his lead, I also took off my cloak and called out to him.

'Bring on the autumn, brother.'

'But a few weeks now, Abel,' he called back over his shoulder.

'Indeed, uncle Maerten,' I added, hoping to give him some cheer, and make good for any upset I had caused him earlier.

After a few moments, he slowly nodded his head.

'It will be a boy.'

We both laughed at his words, which had been spoken in jest. For the van der Molens were both a learned and progressive family, and Reynier's late wife had been a respected schoolteacher. The selftaught miller shared my fondness for the writings of moderate humanists like Erasmus and had a respectable collection of books. Reynier had always been interested to listen to my accounts of my travels with the army and was enough of a pragmatist to encourage me to speak Spanish with his children while he helped me to recover my Latin.

Reynier had raised my wife in almost the exact same way as her brothers, and a daughter would have been as warmly welcomed into our family as a son. Elsien had prepared for both outcomes, having insisted that we also choose the names of girls in advance. Many spirited discussions were held about this, with my wife insisting on something Brabantian-sounding, with my own preference being Spanish or Italian.

My trials following the ambush had made these arguments seem trifling, so that I dismissed the recollections from my mind as we reached the small copse near the village. We spurred our mounts on faster into a furious gallop, tearing around the edge of some trees before almost running down a lonely traveller. We frantically drew rein and hauled our rearing horses away from the fellow, who hopped out of our path with a grunt. His hat fell off his head before he turned to glare at us, shaking his axe before him.

'Have a care on the path!' he growled, as we recognised an old woodsman from the village, who eked out an existence by trading the wood that he cut for scraps of food.

With their fortunes fast reversed by the conflict, the locals had become ever more reliant on barter, and the woodsman's ragged appearance spoke of every hardship endured by the locals during the war.

'Our pardon, *Geachte Heer* Thielman,' replied Maerten, as he frantically patted the neck of his distressed horse, 'we are in haste to return home.'

'*Geachte Heer* Maerten,' said the woodsman frigidly with the slightest of nods, before snatching up his hat and serving me with a hard stare.

'You are too late, Spaniard,' he said in his heavily accented dialect, 'your company is already gone.'

We regarded old Thielman in surprise, as we took in the tidings he had just shared. The man's wizened face crinkled further as his lips curled in justified contempt, while he seemed torn over whether to speak further.

'What do you mean, gone?' asked Maerten. 'Have they been ordered on to Antwerp?'

One of the old woodsman's bushy brows was raised as he glared back at us in contempt.

'Antwerp has fallen,' he said at last, then turned on his heel and abandoned the path, marching on through the trees instead.

Elsien's brother and I exchanged a look of shock, for we were overcome by dread as the consequences of the city's fall sank in. My mouth went dry at the thought of the grim outcome which might have befallen the villagers of Willebroek, while Maerten beheld the woodsman who crunched his way through the trees, with his barrow bouncing off the roots he stepped over.

'What news from the village?' cried my brother-inlaw at the vanishing form.

'Nothing of joy,' called back Thielman as he vanished through the leaves, 'yet I'll not be the bearer of ill tidings.'

No sooner had the woodsman replied than a deep groan of dismay left my throat, as I slammed both ankles against my mount's flanks, ignoring the mindsplitting pain from the injured ankle as I hurtled on towards the direction of Willebroek. The remaining distance was covered at a desperate charge, with the lighter figure of Maerten gaining on me as the village grew before our rapid advance. Together we approached it without ever trading a word, with the same fear growing in both our minds.

Only weeks earlier, a nearby village had been torched by unpaid and starving Spanish troops who had been ordered on to Antwerp. These departing soldiers had made a last demand for the protection money they claimed from the stricken villagers, and when this request was not met, the villagers' houses were torched by the very same soldiers of Spain who had been tasked with their protection.

'Surely not,' I kept on telling myself, as we galloped through the blur of trees around us, 'surely not. Not the family of a fellow soldier.'

I was astonished by the hollow ring of my own reassurances, when the single tower of Saint Nicholas came into view, rising above the cluster of houses and cabins. The sight of the steeple once brought back happy wedding memories, yet it only filled me with dread as we thundered on. A dozen soldiers were seen gathering before a log cabin as we drew closer, holding up their muskets as their leader raised a hand towards us.

'Who goes there?' croaked the scrawny officer, who I recognised as the leader of the small village militia that were partly entrusted with sentry duty.

'It is the miller's son,' said one of the men, before proceeding to drop his musket and take a step back, 'with Santiago the sniper.'

The other men also lowered their guns as we tugged at our reins to slow our mounts to a canter. I was about to ask them about the goings-on in the village when I noticed the hesitant frowns upon their faces. They looked away as I opened my mouth to address them and seemed openly disturbed and confused by my appearance. Behind them I could see unknown Spanish soldiers outside the barns along the periphery of the village, along with the spirited chatter of new recruits.

An orderly air also hung over the edge of Willebroek, with none of the usual veterans loafing about the street, playing cards or dice. Nor could I see any of the clothes and armour which were usually left lying about on the ground.

'The woodsman spoke true,' I muttered to myself, as my head turned from left to right, 'they are gone...'

Maerten had hardly reined in his mount to address the guards when I spurred my horse on again, already fearing the worst. The black Friesian made like a lightning bolt in the direction of the watermill, with my hat falling backwards as my hair fluttered wildly behind me. Despite its blistering charge, I rose in my saddle and lashed the horse's withers with its reins, leaving it to skid around the local militia's stableyard before thundering on towards the bridge.

At the sight of the first burned house my breathing grew faster, with the horse's shoes ringing against the stone cobbles like a smith's hammer upon the anvil. Linen-clad locals hurled themselves aside as I reached the wooden bridge and dashed across it, howling at any bystanders who appeared before me.

'Make way! Stand aside!'

After making the crossing I heard the thud of wooden boards behind me, with Maerten repeating my cries. A startled Spanish patrol sprang aside as I charged on down the road, with scowls appearing on their proud, youthful faces as I passed the blackened remains of too many houses along the canal. My heart sank at the sight of the ruins, although a few dwellings had either been partly burned or left intact. The sight of them left me hoping that Reynier's house had also been spared.

Two dogs and a girl were nearly trampled beneath me before the charred ends of the waterwheel came into view. A shudder of dread ran through me as I hauled at the reins, so that my horse slowed to a standstill, snorting and stamping alongside the mill's adjoining house where I had hoped to meet a smiling Elsien with outstretched arms. The clatter of Maerten's horse could be heard behind me when he also reined in his Friesian, and together we gazed at the blackened walls of his home in horror.

'Mother of God,' I finally exclaimed as I threw myself off my horse, forgetting the injury to my ankle.

As it burst with pain I fell to one knee with a groan, before proceeding to unsling my rifle off my back. I used the gun like a crutch as I pushed myself back onto my feet, just as Maerten flung himself off his mount. I seized his shoulder for support and hobbled as fast as I could, as we made our way towards the burnt-out dwelling whose roof had collapsed.

'Elsi!' cried my wife's brother, as he pushed at the sagging scrap of front door which fell aside at the touch.

We entered the house in growing horror, staring in fear at the burned wood and charred furniture around us. Together we crossed the parlour where I beheld the books beneath the fallen rafters, with each of the priceless tomes having been burned to a crisp. The sight tore at my soul, as did that of the ravaged book cabinet. Maerten and I proceeded to crunch our way over the collapsed beams towards the bedchambers, pushing aside the debris and rubble that still smouldered, and pulling our hands away whenever our fingertips were singed.

'Please Lord,' I found myself whispering beneath my breath, 'spare them, spare them. Spare them, I implore you.'

A glare from Maerten made me refrain from my pitiful gibbering until we had cleared away enough of the rubble to enter the first room. At last, her bed appeared before us, browned and yellowed from the flames, with the crib also blackened by the fire which had raged through the house. My heart quailed at the sight, yet we found no bodies. For a moment I dared to think that I had perhaps been overly concerned, and that the houses had been burned without any lives being claimed.

'They would not dare endanger the life of a Spanish soldier's wife,' I told myself again. 'These things only happen to the Netherlanders.'

I pushed the shameful thought from my mind as my eyes met Maerten's, and in unspoken agreement we tottered in the direction of his father's room.

'Papa!' called Maerten with a hint of fear in his young voice. 'Papa?!'

A heavy beam lay across the doorway to Reynier's bedroom, and we each seized an end to move it aside. The wood smouldered as it was raised, then broke in two, revealing red embers at its core. We entered Reynier's bedchamber, finding only the charred remains of his bedstead and other furniture. Through the tattered pieces of curtain and the broken window I could see the canal gently flowing downstream, leaving me to wonder if the shrewd old miller had somehow made it to the water while his house burned down.

'Where are they?' cried Maerten as he rifled through the warped remains of his father's wardrobe, where Reynier's fine clothes were reduced to a pile of ash.

The youth's face was black from the soot on his face and hands, and I cringed at the misery of our plight, which was as bitter as the cinders on my lips. After leaving Reynier's room we searched through the rest of the house, breaking the burned remains of cupboards open and hauling debris away with sticks and hands.

'No sign of Pieter, either.'

After more fruitless and frantic searching we staggered back towards the main doorway, with our hair crinkled and our eyes watering. We were still coughing up ashes when we emerged onto the cobbled road, taking in breaths of fresh air. I fell against the outside wall of the house, then slid towards the ground as I tried to ignore the searing pain in my ankle.

'Where are they?' I gasped, as I shielded my eyes from the lowering sun overhead. 'Where in the Lord's name are they?'

Maerten made as if to reply, then turned towards the road and stared at it in surprise. I jerked my head in the direction of his gaze, and suddenly saw the boy who stood before us.

He was not yet ten, with a pair of blue eyes that observed us fearfully. Pieter, Elsien's youngest brother, was a timid, shy lad who caused little bother and said even less. The boy peered at us beneath his scruffy brown curls as Maerten called out to him in a rasping voice.

'Pieter!' croaked the youth, his voice full of soot and relief. 'Where are Papa and Elsi?'

'Y-you have come...' stuttered Pieter, as if seeing us for the first time, 'y-you are here...'

'Yes, we are,' cried Maerten, as he ran over to his younger brother and wrapped him in a huge embrace.

'What happened here?'

The boy's face paled at the question and for a few moments he appeared unable to speak. In his impatience Maerten seized his brother by the shoulders and gave him a good shake.

'Speak up brother! Where are they?'

'I-I will take you to them...' gasped Pieter, keeping his eyes upon the ground as he wrested his shoulders free of Maerten's grasp. He then hurried off down the road along the canal, leaving us to exchange glances of puzzlement before we scrambled after him. The boy's pace grew as he made past the houses along the eastern edge of Willebroek, and we had barely passed the last one when he turned left towards the stretch of grass that lay between the village and the beginnings of a nearby wood.

As I limped behind him my feet felt heavier, for already I knew that our destination was the village cemetery. Maerten brushed past me as I hobbled by the crosses that sprouted from the ground, making for the small gathering who stood ahead of us. At Pieter's approach, they each turned towards us, and it was then that we saw the two bodies covered with white sheets.

Our young guide ran into the arms of his aunt Margareta, when an untimely northern wind rippled the grass around the coverings, exposing a long slender arm.

'Elsi,' Maerten barely uttered, then he burst into tears and fell upon his knees beside her, seizing up her hand.

'Elsi! Elsi!'

He next pulled the sheet away from her face as I hurried towards him as best I could. The first pangs of shock left me reeling as I also fell alongside her. Her sapphire eyes stared into nothing, having lost the glow of life. She was as beautiful in death as she had been when I last saw her. The gaunt, scrawny onlookers took a step back at my low moan of dismay, their faces bereft of hope or sentiment after the years of suffering they had endured because of the war.

'Elsien,' I whispered, as her hair brushed my face, while Maerten turned to bend over the body of his father. Reynier looked as severe in death as he had in life. The man who had taken me into his home, received me at his hearth and shared everything with me. His face was once corpulent and flushed, yet his sunken, gaunt cheeks now rendered it as thin as a shrivelled stick.

'A terrible tragedy,' were the words offered by the kindly old priest who had wed us but months earlier. 'She was a good woman, both gentle and kind.'

I regarded him in disbelief, only to see his eyes become fixed on his shoes. My whole world had just crashed down about me, so that I was already changed although I did not yet know it. In silence I beheld the limp corpse of the woman who had once been so full of laughter and life. She who had lifted my spirits whenever they were dashed, who had eased my fears whenever the days seemed darkest.

A couple of others also spoke kind words, while the undertaker stood by, shovel in hand. Yet I was deaf to all of them as my head reeled, trying to take in the hard truth that pierced my breast like a cruel, twisting spear. When my lips met her forehead, my hair stood on end, for the warm flesh had long been replaced by a slab of ice. I recoiled at the touch, as the ground around me seemed to rise and fall, rise and fall.

Not a hint of life was left in her although I sought for it in vain, hoping that everyone else was wrong with their words of condolence. Just like people were wrong when they told me that Spanish soldiers were barracked in a village to keep the peace, or to preserve the one true faith.

'What happened?' I whispered.

I was met by faces that watched me without reply, some wearing expressions of outrage, and others of pity.

'Don't just stand there,' cried Maerten. 'Who did this? Tell us!'

'The boy said it was Abel's own comrades,' blurted a portly villager, who I recognised as uncle Amant, Margareta's husband. He then seized his face with both hands, weeping aloud at the atrocity which had been committed.

'The fire-tax?' Maerten asked, in disbelief, with Amant nodding back at him as he dabbed at his eyes with a tattered sleeve.

'And Sergeant Ramos...' I muttered, '... did he not try to stop them?'

'He was the one who set off the blaze!' yelled Amant in outrage, and my jaw dropped in horror as the chilling dread of realisation ran through me. I remembered the arguments with Ramos outside the house, when he had insisted on receiving the protection money he was owed. Suddenly my abandonment made terrible sense.

'We found her by the doorway,' said Frans, the local smith. 'Her breathing was already faint. She somehow dragged Reynier all the way to the door, but they took in too much of the smoke.'

His words went ignored as Ramos's cruelty left me feeling more lost than before, with the whole core of my being having been crushed to dust. I stared in disbelief at my wife's face.

'Beautiful as a saint,' muttered a bystander, 'just like her mother was.'

I leant over towards Elsien, only just refraining from the soul-rending act of kissing her ice-cold forehead again, with my hand reaching for her swollen belly. The tips of my fingers met a rock-hard lump, which flung my mind further over the edge.

'I always said taking up with Spaniards would bring trouble.' The gruff voice belonged to Amant. 'Reynier should never have spoken to them,' he went on. 'Now let us begone from this place.'

'He had no choice!' cried Maerten angrily.

The youth was furious and desperate for someone to blame, and, in that moment, I feared that he was capable of anything. As he lifted himself to his feet, I held my hand out towards him, calling out halfheartedly.

'Don't Marti...'

He was too angry to pay me any heed. As my eyes fell back to Elsien, he pointed an accusing finger at his barrel-chested uncle, who bristled at the approach of his nephew. Because of the ongoing burden of the war, tempers in the village were short at the best of times, with the recent tragedy of the fire-tax pushing the locals to their wits' end.

'You accuse him of cavorting with Spaniards,' spat Maerten, 'yet in life he always bailed you out of trouble, you old soak!'

'Get out of my way lad,' bellowed Amant, 'or I'll deal you a blow you shan't forget.'

'Come on then!' cried Elsien's brother.

There followed the sound of a lot of pushing and shoving, with the women protesting aloud, and other villagers trying to separate the two quarrelling kinsmen. Yet I had no mind for their scrap, lost as I was in my feelings of loss and betrayal which had left my head swirling. Of a sudden my mind was overwhelmed by memories of the ambush, of how Ramos had insisted that I join him, and how I had woken up alone at the foot of the tree.

'Hey, you there!' called someone in Spanish, interrupting my thoughts. 'What is the meaning of all this stir?!'

The villagers fell silent as they turned towards the sharp, cocksure voice, before the sound of many footfalls announced the approach of the soldiers who I had seen at the bridge. I tore my stare away from my wife, long enough to spot six lean, youthful *bisoños*. They were recruits both young and wet behind the ears, who had served their first two years in an Italian garrison before being sent north to see some real action. They were always annoyingly keen.

As was typical of their kind, they strutted towards us with their chests puffed out and a spring in their step, their defiance as yet untempered by the horrors of battle. The sight of the haughty, arrogant band somewhat reminded me of my own *camarada*, for their domed helmets lent their sneering faces an evil cast, and they inspired as much dread and hate as every other Spanish fellowship.

'My name is Hernán de Vargas,' snapped their leader, 'ensign in the service of His Majesty the King. I demand that you explain this din!'

He studied us closely with a hand rested upon his sword pommel, before gesturing to his comrades to halt with an affected outstretching of his arm.

'But a small argument, Ensign de Vargas sire,' said Amant in broken Spanish, quickly wiping away the blood that trickled off the edge of his cheek, and releasing Maerten's crumpled shirt, 'all resolved now.'

Maerten's uncle had barely spoken when he drew his breath in sharply, as his hot-headed nephew turned towards the Spaniards and shook his fist at them.

'I'll tell you what this noise is about, de Vargas. Your whoreson comrades burned my house down! And killed my father and sister!'

His face was flushed scarlet as he cried out his accusation, and the six soldiers took a step back at his outburst while drawing their blades. After a few moments, the ensign spoke up again in a voice that bristled with menace.

'These are serious accusations against the king's men, boy. Do you have any proof to back them up?'

'Never mind the boy,' said Amant, as he reached for Maerten's shoulder, 'he speaks out of grief, understandably...'

Yet another intake of breath was heard from onlookers, as my brother-in-law shrugged his uncle's hand away and pointed at the trembling Pieter, who had wrapped himself in his aunt's skirt.

'My brother saw Sergeant Curro Ramos setting fire to my house. Together with the three whoresons known as Salva, Gabri and Cristó!'

De Vargas observed Maerten's outburst with an expression that was in turn both pitiful and amused, taken as he was by his own sense of self-importance.

'I am afraid, boy, that your brother is but a child and cannot be a witness at law. You could, I suppose, submit a complaint with the High Command, requesting that you be served with justice. Yet these are spurious allegations that you bring against worthy men of the king, and ones that must, at a minimum, be backed by more than the foolish words of a child.'

The remark was delivered in a tone that was both doubtful and mocking, so that Maerten's reddened face next turned a hue of purple. Elsien's brother walked up to the six Spaniards, with his hands forming fists as he growled beneath his breath.

'I'm no boy to you, popinjay, for you've not a single whisker upon your lips either. If you'll not help me obtain justice then I shall hunt down those king's worthy men myself.'

'Halt!' declared the haughty ensign, bringing the point of his sword to rest upon Maerten's chest and serving him with a defiant stare. 'Not another step or it will be your last.'

Maerten briefly looked down at the sword blade. Then he smacked it aside and crashed his forehead into the officer's face. Some of the onlooking villagers howled, before they all scattered and made away from the cemetery as fast as they could. Meanwhile de Vargas' five Spaniards had already un-slung their muskets, using the butts to beat Maerten down to his knees while their leader returned to his feet. The ensign's nose was a bloody mess, and his eyes looked like they might bulge out of his sallow, aquiline face.

'Tosspot!' he screeched, kicking Maerten again and again while the youth received cracking blows across his body, 'I'll give you your justice with a noose round your neck!'

The vicious assault on Maerten lingered on for a few moments after he had curled into a ball, before the Spaniards angrily hoisted him to his feet. De Vargas punched Elsien's brother in the stomach before hauling his head back by the hair.

'You'll pay for this,' he said, attempting to wipe his bleeding nose against his sleeve before jerking his face away. 'You've gone and broken it you cur.'

So saying, he paused to pick his helmet up from the grass, before seizing Maerten's collar and hauling him back towards the village. Two of his men seized the arms of their Brabantian prisoner, while the remaining trio jabbed the youth in the back with their swords.

'Leave him alone,' I sighed.

De Vargas and his men turned their heads in surprise towards me, having not previously noticed my presence. A few moments of disbelief passed between them, before the young ensign shoved his captive away and stepped towards me.

'Who are you?' he asked, as he slowly drew his sword again from its scabbard.

'Abelardo de Santiago,' I replied without emotion and as matter-of-factly as I could manage, before staring him straight in the eye.

The young ensign slowly raised his head at my words, before speaking again.

'Santiago the sniper?'

'Yes,' I replied, hoping that any disagreement might end there.

De Vargas regarded me for a few moments as he summed up the dangers and consequences that I presented. Then a smug grin appeared on his bloodied face when he returned his blade to its scabbard. He next cast a quick look over his shoulder towards his men, who stared back at him expectantly. Between them, Maerten's face was bloodied and bruised, and the youth's head sagged sideways as he peered at us through eyes that were all but swollen shut.

'The Lynx of Haarlem,' said the ensign at last. 'Your reputation precedes you, but marksmen don't scare me.'

A hawking sound was heard from his throat before he gobbed spittle at me, which landed a handspan away from Elsien's shoulder. The insolent act caused the blood to rise to my head, where a vein at my temple throbbed furiously. It took me a few moments to regain some composure, as I reminded myself that de Vargas was but a young, stupid recruit who had just committed his last stupid act. Another sigh left me as I turned my back on him, returning my attentions to my dead wife.

'Courtesy without rival,' sneered the ensign behind me, 'to turn your back on an officer. But never fear, Santiago. I'll deal with you once I'm done with this footpad.'

'Abel,' groaned Maerten, as the Spaniards led him off again, dragging him away from his slain family members, 'Abel!'

'Where are they taking him?' whimpered Pieter behind me, although none replied to him.

For a time thereafter I did not stir, as my hand came to rest upon the cheek of Elsien's angelic face, which might have been carved by the hand of Michelangelo himself. Already she seemed as distant and remote as a statue, yet I somehow still hoped that at any instant she might return a familiar stare, or that her eyes might regain their crisp blue glow, and her sunken cheeks break into the grin I remembered so fondly, creasing her handsome features.

'Elsien,' I muttered, resting my fingers against her slender arm that felt more rigid than a rifle bore, as the tears welled up in my eyes and I stared at her in a reverent trance.

'Abel!' yelled her brother far behind me, having clearly regained some awareness, while realising the trouble he was in, 'Abel!'

Yet I could not turn my face away from his sister as I treasured my last moments by her side. No longer would the warmth of her hand caress my grizzled features, with all our hopes of life in another world having been cruelly snatched from us by those I had myself protected so many times before.

'Abel!' called Maerten again, before a dull blow was followed by loud shouting from de Vargas, as the men reached the houses across from the graveyard. The sounds went ignored as I lowered my face back towards Elsien's, as if seeking an answer to what I should do. An answer she had provided so many times before, whenever I had been torn between duty and conscience.

'Why did you bother with me?' I whispered, as a tear slid down my cheek. 'I told you I'd only bring you grief.'

Another untimely northerly rippled the grass around both bodies, and I imagined her staring back at me with that all-knowing look, almost hearing her voice upon the wind that rustled my hair.

'Because you are a good man, although you have forgotten it.'

I slowly nodded my head at the memory, then drew the knife chained behind my back, while caressing the edge of her cheek with my other hand. All the things I had taken for granted about her came back to me more resoundingly than ever before.

'Farewell,' I whispered, as another irksome tear crept down my nose, and I cut a length of her beautiful blonde hair with the edge of my blade. There was felt another sharp jab of sorrow as I gently pulled the wedding ring off her finger, a silver band which her father had procured for me on credit.

As I got to my feet the northern gale still blew strong, causing my white shirt to flutter around me as her ring was slipped into my pouch. I next proceeded to remove the Salado rifle from my shoulder while pulling a powder charge off the belt slung across my chest, and as the gun was loaded and armed, I felt a strange comfort in the sequence I had followed for years on end.

Ahead of me Maerten's hair was seized in the rough grasp of a young recruit, while yet another had seized him by the throat. My arm was outstretched towards them, and my thumb raised like a painter's as I gauged the distance of the six bisoños from me, before I brought the butt of the rifle to my right shoulder, placing the point of de Vargas' helmet in between my sights as I mouthed those words again:

This day will the Lord deliver thee into my own hand;
and I will smite thee,
and take thy head from thee

A deafening shot was heard when my forefinger jerked back the hair trigger, with the sound reverberating across all corners of the cemetery. As I hobbled out of the cloud of stinking smoke, I could see birds scattering from along the banks of the canal, while the band of plucky Spaniards had in the meantime frozen to a standstill, with the bareheaded de Vargas seen rising to his feet. His helmet was nowhere to be seen, and he turned to shake his fist at me while I used the rifle to hobble in his direction.

'Whoreson!' he roared across the grass, as I raised my thumb again and calmly studied the distance between us. After gauging that he was less than a musket shot away, I stopped in my tracks again.

'Hey, Santiago!' shouted the ensign. 'What in Christ's name is passing through your thick head?!'

His cries went ignored as already my fingers readied the gun. There was no one faster than me at loading a rifle, and in moments it was armed again.

'Lost your tongue, coward?' screamed de Vargas, as I swung back the doghead and raised the Salado to my shoulder, never feeling a thing as I brought my eye to the sights once more.

'What are you doing?' cried the ensign in disbelief, with the cockiness having vanished from his voice. 'Are you going to shoot me before my own men?'

My threnody had already been mouthed as I did just that, jerking back the hair trigger as the pain in my ankle went ignored.

'You wouldn't dare-'

I had slain men from three times that distance, so de Vargas' squeals were quickly cut off by the roar of my rifle. It was an act of the highest insubordination, for officers were not even slain in mutinies. It was an act that sealed my exit from the Spanish army, after decades of loyal service. Yet I felt nothing as I stepped out of the smoke, using the Salado as a crutch again as I hobbled on towards the houses.

The ensign's body lay before his startled men, who quietly observed their fallen leader, whose head resembled a burst melon. Maerten fell to his knees as they let go of him and fled before my approach, howling bloody murder as they reached the street and ran on towards the bridge with their hands waving above their heads.

With the composure of a funeral priest, I used my rifle to reach Elsien's dazed brother, before sliding it back into its sheath, and swinging it over my shoulder. My bruised brother-in-law watched me in silence before I stared back at him askance. In an instant he was forcing himself onto his feet, allowing me to rest upon his shoulder as we made our way back towards the pair of Friesians that grazed along the edge of Reynier's house.

A couple of neighbours could be seen peering at us from behind their window, while Maerten ran off to dig up his father's hidden stash of silver by the water, before hurrying back to me with the sack over his shoulder. After mounting the Friesians, we abandoned the scene of so much despair and death, making away at a gallop, intent on quenching the gaping loss that consumed us with blood and justice.

When we had almost reached the bridge, only one of de Vargas' men dared to stand in our path, with his musket shot going well wide as we charged him down. His screams could still be heard as we rumbled across the wooden planks above the water, two shadow riders in the growing dusk. Together we charged back towards the perilous path through the forest, intent on taking up the long, hard road to vengeance.

III

SEVILLE

21 May 1587

The squelch of boots could be heard ahead of me. Through the thin bandage over my eyes, I could just make out an obscure figure running towards me.

'For the love of Christ, stop that awful din!'

The boy shouted right in my face, leaving me to shudder before his plea, which went ignored. I started strumming the strings again with my thumb, although I knew not how to play a single note. Years firing rifles had rendered me almost deaf in one ear, and I had always been tone-deaf before that.

'Mercy sire, I beseech you. I have no other means to make ends meet.'

'I'd give you a sack of gold doubloons if I could,' he groaned, 'if only to end that racket. You're murdering that godforsaken guitar.'

'Easy lad,' said someone behind him, 'can't you see he's just a blind old war veteran?'

'And who are you? The good Samaritan?'

There followed a heated debate between the two speakers as they trod heavily down the stinking *Calle de las Armas.* They left me to resume my cacophony upon the guitar, disguised as a blind minstrel until Maerten's return. The fingers on my left hand seized the instrument's neck like a drowning man's, wrapping and unwrapping themselves around it so that my strumming was largely muted. A deep humming from my throat accompanied my fevered scratching, which made me sound like a strangulation victim, so that I started at the sound of coppers thrown into the hat between my feet. It was a generous gesture, which left me to marvel at how much money I had made for slaying the ears of passers-by for well over an hour.

'God bless you, sire,' I called out to the fading footsteps.

'Very well, you can stop now,' called someone to my right.

'Marti?' I asked, pausing from my playing at the sound of my brother-in-law's arrival.

'Who else?'

'Is there anyone else about?' I asked nervously.

'Wait, just the one... very well, he's gone now.'

I lifted the bandage above my right eye, so that the blind minstrel I played at was of a sudden only half blind.

'Another soul approaches,' I muttered, 'quick, help me up.'

'Excuse me?'

'Help me up!' I snapped, seizing my headstrong companion by the elbow, and heaving myself onto my feet. I next picked up the wooden guitar case I had been sitting on, which contained my rifle and other gear.

'It's just as well you're not too heavy,' he said sarcastically, as I leant awkwardly upon his shoulder, pretending to be guided by him.

'Refrain from your bleating – have you seen them?'

'Yes,' he shot back, of a sudden serious and with his mind clearly bent on the task at hand, 'but a few corners away from here.'

'Good,' I said, 'now to be rid of this disguise.'

I flung the old guitar into a dark alleyway, and it landed upon the cobbles with a loud clatter, causing a street cat to yowl amid the scrabble of frightened rats. I then shoved Maerten away as we turned right into another street.

'That's enough loving embraces for one evening.'

'Loving?' he snorted, as we stopped along a dark corner of the street, where I could ready my weapons and put on my gear.

The bandolier, priming flask and ball bag were slung over my shoulders, before two pistols were snatched out of the guitar case. I primed their pans and fed their bores powder and ball, then shoved them through the holsters at my hips. I next readied the long Salado rifle, ramming the scouring stick down it a few times before slinging the weapon over my back.

'I can scarce believe that their hour is at hand,' whispered Maerten nervously.

'Believe it,' was my terse reply, as I unfurled a thin cape and threw it over my shoulders to conceal my guns.

'You're quite a sight,' he said, staring at me in awe, 'let's hope you still shoot better than you sing.'

'Are you sure you saw all of them?' I asked, ignoring his jest.

'They were all four together when last I saw them.'

'Good,' I replied, 'we might be returning for Pieter sooner than I thought.'

I shoved my way past him and walked on down the street, keen to reach the *Taberna de San Pablo*. It was almost dusk, that time of day when all sorts of mischief would be unleashed across the city. Despite myself, I secretly hoped that other murders might also be afoot, so that my acts of revenge might go unnoticed.

Then again, I thought to myself, *it's not every day you get someone killing four men in one night.*

The realisation did not deter my brisk step as we approached the inn. I was the picture of cold and calm resolve, readying to slay my former comrades. A stir of excitement was suppressed when I saw the sword-nicked tankard above the tavern doorway, which held a faded image of the apostle Paul. As I drew closer, I whispered final instructions to Maerten, with my hands falling to the pistols at my belt.

'Now stay here and wait in silence. I mean it, Marti. If I don't come back out, you must use the last of the silver to bring your brother to Spain and set sail with him for the New World. It was your sister's dream for you both.'

'You will come back out,' he said, as he withdrew into a dark doorway, then called out: 'Good luck Abel, and may God be with you.'

I walked stealthily towards the tavern, as I bristled with rage and anticipation. Maerten and I had stalked the men for over twenty months, so that it hardly seemed possible that they were finally within my grasp. In those terse instants, most of the episodes which had followed Elsien's killing flashed through my mind, so that I remembered how we had fled from

Willebroek, before obtaining a passport from an army officer in a neighbouring village. In return for a few pieces of silver he had happily drawn up the document, to help me rejoin my company, and no sooner had he provided it to us than we were galloping off again, to avoid word of the ensign's murder catching up with us. The signed letter had been worth its hefty price, since it had allowed us to get through most checkpoints and borders on our ride south unhindered.

We had kept to the Spanish road for most of our journey, which was the route used by soldiers travelling from Spain to the Netherlands and back again. Our progress had been delayed by scrapes with bandits, as well as my falling badly ill. Yet our travels to the port town of Genoa had been completed in just over a month, only to find that Ramos and his men had eluded us again.

To my chagrin we discovered that they had boarded a galley to Barcelona. Great storms had delayed our own departure for over three months, by which time the sailing season was over. We next spent close to another three months wallowing in the Italian port, during which time the pair of fine Friesians were sold for a handsome price, while we assumed false names and acquired newly forged passports.

The days dragged on as we lay low in a peripheral district, until the morning finally arrived when we boarded a ship to cross the Ligurian and Balearic seas for Barcelona. Upon reaching land we swiftly made our way across the Spanish peninsula, hiring horses from inns until we arrived in Seville, streaked in dust and sweat. We had spent weeks seeking out Ramos's whereabouts, while keeping to our false names to avoid notice from anyone.

'And now,' I muttered to myself, 'now you'll all pay for our loss.'

The street was poorly lit by lanterns as I closed in on the entrance to the inn, with my hands passed beneath my cloak and resting on both pistol butts. I shoved myself back into the shadows when the tavern door was kicked open, slamming into the sidewall as a hulking figure emerged onto the street, holding a woman by the arm. The man's identity was instantly recognisable from his stature, for it was none other than Tomé de Cristóbal.

'It's Cristó!' hissed Maerten from the street corner behind me, causing me to bite my lower lip in frustration.

Cristó's lot in life had certainly improved, for apart from the silken shirt that he wore, he also had a brocaded jacket folded over one arm. In recent weeks, I had come to learn that few had done better out of Seville than Ramos and his men. Upon arriving in the city, they had forged a fearsome reputation, and their swift rise in Seville's underworld had made them the agents of nobles and crime lords alike. In eighteen months, the ruthless foursome had dug their fingers into many illicit pies with typical ruthlessness, building a strong circle of influence both in the underworld and with those in authority.

I bristled with anger at the thought of their ill-gotten fortunes, which had been so easily achieved without me. This seething rage all but overwhelmed me as I drew the pistols from my belt, before turning the wheel shafts on them with the spanners which hung from a chain around my neck. Upon arming the guns, I held them down at my sides, with my long cape falling back over them and concealing them from view once more.

'Come on, brother,' bellowed Cristó towards the inn, 'let's take her in an alley!'

It was then that Gabriel de Andrés could be seen stepping through the tavern door as silently as a shadow. He was still a furtive and slinky cat, and doubtlessly twice as dangerous if cornered. For a moment I wondered which of the two men I feared more. They had always formed an unlikely yet effective pairing, with the musketeer providing the brains, while the huge pikeman supplied the brawn.

'You go, brother,' whispered Gabri as he stood before Cristó, 'I have not the mind for women tonight.'

'What's the matter with you?' roared his towering comrade. 'Wine got to your head already?'

The scar-faced maiden tried to twist her wrist free of his grasp. Her vain efforts to pull herself away from the brute met with the tightening of his grip on her arm, which left her squealing aloud.

'Where are the others?' I hissed over my shoulder, as I waited for Ramos and Salva to emerge too. 'Damn their souls, where are they?'

'I swear they were there before,' whispered Maerten. 'They must still be inside...'

Gabri then said something to Cristó that we couldn't hear, which led the latter to sound distraught as he drew himself up to his full height.

'So you're all leaving me alone tonight, just because of one cudgelling and a double murder? 'Tis but a normal day's work!'

Meanwhile the wench finally managed to wrest her arm free, yet he leant over and seized her by the shoulder as she tried to run away from him.

'Stop that!' roared my former comrade, serving her with a slap which left her sprawling across the street, 'I'm in no mood for games tonight!'

At the sight of her mistreatment the blood slowly rose to my head again, so that I reached for the two wedding rings at my neck which hung upon my guns' spanners, and slowly pressed them to my lips. A murderous mood had seized me, and I whispered a last imprecation before venturing upon an act of lunacy.

'Tonight, my love. For you, or with you...'

The bands were dropped as I jerked the dogheads back on both pistols, then strode across the street towards my former comrades.

'Abel...don't...' whispered Maerten behind me, surprised by my sudden movement.

The plea went ignored since my temples were pounding with wrath. Cristó's act of violence had sparked off a mad fury within me, at the memory of Elsien's end at the hands of my former comrades. A small group of hangers-on had gathered around the dangerous pair, chuckling raucously at the ill treatment which was being meted out to the woman. The huge pikeman rested his foot heavily on her back, pinning her to the ground, and her low groans and squirming drew all the onlookers' attentions, so that none spotted me until I reached Cristó.

'Who are you?' he snapped, suddenly noticing my presence.

I silently raised the pistol in my right hand, resting its mouth upon his cheek. With a curse, he roughly seized my forearm, causing the hood of my cloak to fall backwards as his eyes widened in disbelief.

'Santi?'

'For Elsien,' I whispered, pulling the trigger back hard.

The pistol shot echoed across the street, as I was blinded by gun smoke. His grip on my hand was released, followed by a scrape of boots and an almighty thud upon the ground. My second pistol was swiftly raised and swung towards Gabri, who as always had been first to react. As my finger drew the trigger his cloak was flung towards me, so that he foiled my next shot which resounded across the *calle*.

'Fool,' I spat, scolding myself, then flung the garment off my arm.

He was already running down the street as fast as he could, leaving me to shove both pistols back in my belt and reach for the loaded rifle upon my back. To save time I ignored the ramrod and instead tapped the gun's butt hard against the ground, then seized the spanner and turned the wheel shaft. The gun's peep sights were raised to my eyes and trained on the vanishing shadow which was but a few feet away from the street corner.

Behind me the voices of the bystanders arose in outrage, and Cristó's boots kicked the ground as blood spurted from his face. Yet my gaze remained fixed upon Gabri, who was sprinting for the end of the street as if the devil himself were on his tail. His form became blurry despite the lamplights, and the voices around me grew as other patrons emerged onto the street to see what had happened.

'The Lord will deliver thee,' I whispered quickly, 'and I will smite thee.'

Gabri had all but vanished into the darkness, yet on an impulse I instead turned the rifle's sights upon the street corner, which was far from the closest lamplight and barely visible. When the faint glow on the wall was further darkened by shadow, I jerked back the trigger, which released the scream of a third gunshot. It also drew a piercing howl from the other end of the street, which was followed by cries of shock and fear from the bystanders.

'This is an outrage,' cried one of them, 'summon the *hermandades*!'

I stepped out of the acrid gun smoke, already refilling the pan as I swung my head from left to right. Men and wenches cowered against the walls, and some fled amid cries of fear and distress. On the ground, I could see that Cristó had drawn his last breath, with bits of bone also visible along the blackened skin around his wound. It was a disturbing sight, yet one that filled me with a certain comfort.

'Where are you Mar—?' I cried, only just refraining from saying his name.

'I'm here,' he called out, as I saw him running out of the tavern. He then paused to kick and spit on Cristó's corpse.

'Are the others in there?'

'No,' he said, with a face like a thundercloud, 'it appears they left before our arrival.'

'Are you sure of it?' I snapped in disappointment.

'I am, unless the innkeeper is lying.'

'Then let's at least finish off half of them tonight,' I replied.

No sooner had I spoken, than the youth tore past me towards the direction of Gabri.

'Wait!' I cried, hurrying after him. 'Don't be hasty.'

As I ran, I shoved more powder from a charge down the rifle, then spat a ball after it. The ramrod was drawn and jammed hard down the bore, before the wheel plate was shifted into place and the doghead flicked back onto it. Upon reaching the wall at the street corner I could see that its edge was slightly chipped, with a few flecks of rubble littering the ground. A trail of fresh blood could also be made out along the cobbles.

'Your shot was true!' cried Maerten excitedly.

I ignored his exclamation as I rested my back against the wall and slid along its edge, then carefully peered over my shoulder and made out the slightest flicker of movement along the next *calle*, when an obscure figure vanished into a street on the left. As I made after it, Elsien's brother soon caught up with me, and I angrily snapped a warning at him.

'Keep close and don't run ahead of me! Remember, the cornered beast is the most dangerous of all!'

'I shan't,' he replied, although I did not believe him.

Ever since we had left Willebroek, Maerten had developed a strong-headed nature, as well as a stoic resolve to do anything to avenge his late sister. Yet his keenness to help had at times landed us both in more trouble than we needed. Of a sudden I wished that I had not asked him to join me that night, even though he was always begging me to be let out of our room.

Together we made towards the next shadowy *calle*, keeping our eyes on the ground, and following the many drops of blood. As we turned into the next street, I spotted a slight trail of smoke rising towards the faint light of a doorway, and I instantly knew it to be burning powder in the pan. I seized Maerten's collar and flung myself forward, our ears deafened by a pistol shot before we landed upon the ground in a heap. A loud cry of annoyance was heard, followed by the sound of Gabri making off again.

'Bastard's armed,' muttered Maerten.

I slowly pushed myself off him, with the filth from countless chamber pots dripping off us as we rose to our feet.

'What did you expect?' I snarled. 'We must be more careful. He is the shiftiest of the lot and cunning as a snake.'

'Certainly a wounded beast,' replied the youth, as he pointed at the large drops of blood before us.

'Make haste,' I said before we hurried on down the street.

In the flickering torchlight, we chased the fresh blood on the cobbles like hounds on a scent. When they ended, we sighted more of them to the street on our right, which led towards the western side of the city.

'Turned again,' gasped Maerten, rushing ahead of me.

With a low curse, I took a step forward and sprang at him, tripping him over with an outstretched hand before another shot smashed a window behind us.

'Bastard!' shouted Maerten, wiping the filth off his face.

'I told you not to run ahead!' I snapped. 'Now, swiftly, before he reloads.'

We were on our feet and running down the street again, just as the skulking figure of de Andrés vanished to the right.

'South?'

'Gradas,' I replied, having already guessed that our quarry was trying to shake us off before making back towards the offices he shared with Ramos and Salva.

These quarters had been provided to Ramos's gang by a shameless notary named Escobedo, who provided the stamp of law to their lucrative crimes for a cut of the profits. It was in Gradas that my former army sergeant and his henchmen hatched villainous schemes with both servants and enemies of the Crown of Spain.

The thought filled me with frustration, for I knew that if Gabri escaped us he would alert Ramos and Salva to Cristó's death. Such knowledge would have them double their guard, and overnight their killing would become twice as hard to achieve. As we kept to his trail, I also wondered whether de Andrés had yet recognised me.

'Can you see him?' I asked in the growing dimness.

A creak of wheels grew in the distance, revealing the horse-drawn carriage of a nobleman. As it drew towards us a tirade of blasphemy of the blackest pitch was heard further along the road. We then threw ourselves against the wall and shielded our faces with our arms, spattered by all manner of muck which was flung at us by both wheels and hooves.

'Christ's blood,' I growled, while Maerten wiped his face with his mantle and spat a mouthful of sludge into the drain that gurgled below us.

Further along down the road, I could again make out the slightest trail of telltale smoke rising in the light from a house.

'Down!'

I hauled Maerten to the ground again as I shouted my warning, with dust flying off the wall behind us as yet another pistol shot roared down the street. I was grudgingly impressed by the swift loading of my former comrade, despite his wounded arm. As we returned to our feet drops of filth fell away from us, with my Brabantian brother-in-law mouthing many curses as our chase was resumed.

'Left again,' I gasped as we hurried past a row of bawdy houses, with our boots scraping the cobbles.

The *Plaza de San Francisco* was soon reached, where some flicker of life endured after nightfall. We ran on past the odd passerby, having a care not to brush into any haughty Dons who might challenge us to a duel. Sham beggars lingered against doorways, with some cheering us on as we hurried after the elusive form of Gabri. His back was barely visible to us, so that I could tell that we were falling behind, as he made towards a crowd which had gathered before yet another inn. In moments, our man would be slipping among them and gone.

'Stop thief!' I yelled out as a last-ditch ruse, and at my cry de Andrés almost missed his step as he looked once over his shoulder.

'In the name of the king!' hollered Maerten in his best Spanish. 'Stop that cutpurse!'

Loud murmuring and exclamations could be heard among the patrons and tavern wenches ahead of us. They each turned their heads towards the beleaguered Gabri, whose gait slowed as he clutched at his bleeding arm.

''Tis a lie!' he screeched as he slowed to a standstill.

'Those men have slain my comrade and want me dead!'

'We'll be the judge of that,' declared a portly gentleman in a Genoese accent. The stranger approached the wounded musketeer with three other fellows, and their drawn swords glinted in the glow from the tavern.

My rifle was already loaded as I stopped running and pulled its stock to my shoulder, seeking to catch my fleeing quarry's head in its sights. Gabri was already hurrying towards the patrons who approached him, tucking his pistol into his belt, and holding his good arm in the air, while the left one dangled awkwardly to his side.

'Very well, good sirs,' he declared in as loud a tone as his hoarse voice would allow, 'as a gesture of my goodwill I hereby surrender myself to...'

My forefinger was already curled around the trigger, as I readied to plant a ball of steel in his head. Yet in that instant de Andrés ducked beneath the sword arm of the first do-gooder, then whipped a dagger from behind his back and slashed the man's knee in a sideways thrust. The Genoese swordsman collapsed into the sludge, howling with pain as he clutched his severed knee. At the sight of such expert savagery the crowd quickly dispersed, with the remaining swordsmen warily circling my former comrade.

'Bastard,' I said, losing sight of him amid the commotion. The rifle was slung back over my neck as we ran along the square, hoping to gain on him before he fled again, or before someone else stole our revenge.

'Get out of my way!' screamed Gabri at the remaining patrons. His back was arched like a cornered cat's as he whipped his pistol back out again and aimed it at them.

The men's mettle endured for a moment longer. Then the first took a step back, with the other two following his lead. The wounded musketeer raced past them in the very instant they drew away, astounding all present by his vindictiveness as he shot the closest swordsman in the knee. Maerten and I reached this second wounded patron moments later, as he howled from the ground with blood spurting from his leg. We barely afforded him a sidelong glance as we tore past the inn, even more resolved to get Gabri.

'Faster, Santi,' cried my former comrade ahead of us, his cruel laughter echoing in my ears. 'Is this the best you can do against your one-armed friend?'

'No friend of mine!' I yelled back, feeling further enraged by his mockery and by the fact that he had recognised me.

In desperation, my pace quickened despite my burning lungs, with the small of Gabri's back still visible until he quickly veered to the left. His movement made us slacken our pace as we approached the end of the street, fearing that he might have somehow already reloaded his pistol. I held my rifle up as we slowly moved forward, ready to shoot at any sign of danger. Meanwhile Maerten held his sword out before him, in the manner I had taught him during our journey to Seville.

As we neared the dreaded street corner, I feared that my heart might burst through my breast as I carefully crossed the *calle*, ready to fire at the first sight of my former comrade. In that moment I noticed the ornate facades and gratings of the buildings around us, so that I realised that we were already close to the cathedral, in the affluent Santa Maria quarter. A low bell toll from the Giralda bell tower confirmed this, and nearly had me jumping out of my skin.

'Whoreson,' I hissed at the sudden sound of his distant, hurried footsteps.

I slowly peeked round the corner, where I could only see the gay awnings and banners outside the archbishop's palace. Gabri had played us at every turn, then took advantage of our hesitation to leg it as fast as he could. The air was filled with hurried steps as Maerten and I rushed on down the next street, fearing that our quarry might resort to seeking sanctuary within the cathedral's walls.

In a last desperate effort, we hurried towards the cathedral courtyards of *Los Olmos and Los Naranjos*, which were the haunt of nocturnal delinquents. Bands of men in torn cloaks and wide-brimmed hats could already be seen, gathered round small fires where they played cards and dice, amid the odd laugh and jeer. As I lowered my rifle, I feared that we were too late.

'Where is he?' I muttered angrily. 'Where is he?'

Many a scowl was cast in our direction as we stepped through the countless tosspots and footpads, most of whom were distracted by the games at hand. I was about to approach one of them and risk asking the whereabouts of a wounded fugitive, when I glimpsed a man hurrying down the street ahead of us.

'It's him!'

At my cry we sprinted across the courtyard before we could draw any more attention. Upon reaching the next street corner I held my arm out to Maerten to slow his pace, then jerked my head past the wall. I pulled it back just as another shot rang out, with stone shards blinding me as they showered my face.

I angrily wiped the dust from my eyes and stepped into the street with my rifle held out before me, raising it towards the distant flicker of movement and jerking back the trigger. A loud thud of wood followed the roar of my shot, and when we ran through the gun smoke, we could see that I had struck a distant barricade which blocked the street.

'What's that din!' cried a man from a window above us, in a highborn accent.

His question went ignored as I reloaded my rifle, keeping my eyes on the street and feeling heartened by the sight of the distant city wall.

'This street leads nowhere,' I whispered to Maerten, hoping that our luck had suddenly changed for the better.

We slowly approached the barrier, which had been erected due to yet another outbreak of the plague. Two guards stared back at us askance, standing before carts loaded with piles of stripped corpses, which were circled by low fires that burned the clothes of the dead. Our skin crawled at the sight, as I realised that Gabri had risked the pox to flee us.

'Did he enter here?' I asked myself in disbelief, holding my gun before me as the guards drew their swords and stepped away from us.

They appeared reluctant to fight, having doubtlessly tired of the many scenes of death which they had already witnessed.

'If you are seeking the fugitive,' said one of them, 'you should know that he has already broken through us. He also took a lamp and is in the stables at the end of the street. Yet I warn you not to enter this place, for the plague has spared few.'

'I pray you to let us pass,' I replied, 'for that man is a thief and a murderer who must be brought to justice.'

'What did he rob?' asked one of them with slight interest.

'More than you could ever imagine,' was my reply, and I lowered my gun as I walked through the men unhindered, with Maerten close on my heels.

'Is it worth risking the pox to reach him?' asked Maerten.

'It is worth anything,' I replied, 'yet wait for me here, I beg you.'

'No chance of that,' he replied, as he hurried past me once more, leaving me to follow him with a low curse.

Together we slowly made down the street, which was full of the groans of the dying, and the protests of men who had been boarded up inside their houses. Large planks were nailed across all doors and balcony windows. At all times, my forefinger hovered over the trigger, as Maerten and I drew closer to a small glow which could be made out further along the street. As we approached it the stench of horse dung grew thicker, until the malodour was so strong that it even cut through the stink of excrement that lingered in the street.

'Slowly,' I whispered to Maerten behind me, as I wondered what devilry Gabri was up to.

We flinched when a loud crash was heard ahead of us. There was a flicker of light down the street, followed by the sound of a growing blaze. A highpitched whinny of horses could also be heard behind the stable doors. For a moment, I struggled to understand what had happened, then felt further confused when the first billow of smoke streamed out of the stable towards us.

'Does it lead to the other street?' I asked, quickly guessing Gabri's ploy.

I ran to the stable doors, abandoning all caution, then stood before them aghast. Horses kicked the air and issued highpitched shrieks, and through the flames around them I could make out the wicked features of Gabriel de Andrés. At his feet I could make out the remains of a broken oil lamp, with its flames spreading fast across the straw. It was a sight which made the hair rise on the back of my neck, and the musketeer grinned back at us in triumph, as he made to leave the stables which he had just set alight.

'Until our next meeting, Santi!' he laughed, then staggered away to the street, clutching his bloodstained sleeve.

With a cry of frustration, I held up my rifle, yet the bucking horses denied me a clear aim as they neighed and trashed the burning stables. Maerten tried to run in and rescue the beasts, yet I seized him by the shoulder and hauled him away from the growing blaze while he beheld me in outrage.

'Don't!' I snarled. 'They'll kick you to death if you set foot inside. In moments, the fumes will claim them, and they'll not know any pain.'

'I thought you said our revenge was worth anything!'

The glow from the fire revealed his fair features, reminding me of the woman I had lost. A huge outrage welled up in me at the memory, and I ignored the youth's protests as I studied the wall above us, where a barricaded balcony provided a way to get to a low roof. Yet reaching it would be another matter, for the only plank which offered a climber's grip was even beyond the height of two men.

Meanwhile the horses' screeching was heartrending as the roar of the fire grew louder. With a grimace I turned my head away from the doomed creatures, as the first of them passed out and sagged to its knees, slumping against the wall with its reins holding its head up.

'Hold your breath and help me,' I said.

'What?'

'Just do as I say!'

Maerten followed me as I ran across the alley towards a cart heaped with bodies, helping me to seize its wheels and push it before the smoking stables.

'Wait for me here,' I snapped, then held my breath again as I jumped onto the cartwheel and clambered over the dead bodies, my skin crawling as I hauled at legs, hair and arms until I was atop the pile and jumping towards the edge of the poorly nailed plank. For a few moments I hung from the side of the timber, my legs scraping against the other boards below until I managed to heave myself upon the roof tiles.

'Son of a flea-ridden whore,' I gasped, 'you'll not escape me that easily.'

In a flush of fury, I clambered towards the top of the edifice. The beauty of the starred summer sky went ignored as I reached it, until I found myself overlooking the street on the other side of the building. I could already make out the skulking figure of Gabri below me, who had been rendered by distance to about the size of a forearm.

My former comrade walked away with an almost cocksure spring to his step, as he headed towards the warehouses in the district of Gradas, many of which had been converted into offices. He was less than a musket shot's span away from me. I quivered with expectation as I unslung the rifle and pulled back the doghead again, knowing that the shot might pass clean through his head, which was firmly placed between the rifle's peep sights.

'Today the Lord shall deliver thee,' I began, 'and I shall smite...'

The threnody was broken by the sound of loud shouting from the street behind me, which rose above the raging fire in the stables.

'You, northerner!' cried a man. 'Surrender your arms in the name of the king!'

'*Hermandades*,' I groaned in disbelief, upon recognising those men of the Crown who were charged with patrolling the city and keeping the peace.

My finger twitched madly over the trigger, which had to only be jerked back once to send Gabri to the next world. For a moment I bristled with annoyance at the unexpected distraction of the yelling catchpole, for I yearned to plant a ball in the head of my wife's assassin. Almost as if he could read my thoughts, de Andrés looked back at the sound of the shouting behind us, then threw himself against a doorway.

'Christ's wounds,' I growled furiously, as I slid back down the side of the roof.

Below me Maerten could be seen backing away from the approaching peacekeepers, who closed in on him with drawn swords while holding kerchiefs close to their faces.

'You'll hang for your arson,' bellowed their leader, as he drew closer towards my brother-in-law, 'where is your gun?'

'Here!' I yelled from above, shooting the man's helmet off his head, and sending him and his catchpoles running back the way they came.

'Quickly, get up here!' I shouted as I jumped through the gun smoke onto the boarded balcony. The first tendrils of black smoke appeared at my feet, and beneath me I could hear the screams of the house's occupants.

I ignored the sounds and leant over the balcony, holding my rifle out towards Maerten. He had already climbed up the cart of bodies, then seized the rifle stock before I hauled him up over the balcony. Streams of black smoke from the stables engulfed us while we clambered over the roof ledge, coughing and spluttering when the first musket shot rang against it.

'Did you get him?' asked Elsien's brother, as he fell alongside me.

'No!' I snapped in annoyance.

'Now what?'

'Now,' I gasped, 'we run all over again.'

Together we dashed and climbed over the other rooftops, then lowered ourselves onto the balcony of the last building, where a window had been kept open because of the sweltering Maytime. The house's occupants stirred with a cry as we leapt over the railing and dropped into the street below, landing in a heap as we gasped for breath.

The cries of the *hermandades* could be heard all around us as I hauled myself to my feet and pulled Maerten up behind me. We swiftly made for the maze of backstreets we had scoured since our arrival in Seville, diving through doorways and flinging ourselves alongside beggars at the first sight of torches and running guards.

Within half an hour we had made our way back towards *El Arenal*, the Sevillian quarter which housed the worst of Spain's brigands and thieves. Upon reaching the Tavern of the Dog we refrained from knocking upon the main door, so as not to alert the innkeeper to our late return. Maerten instead climbed on my shoulders to reach the balcony to our room before he passed down bound bedsheets which I used to climb after him.

'That was too close,' he said between ragged gasps of breath.

I was far too weary to reply. I flung my weapons against the wall before stripping off my clothes, then pulled off my mud-spattered boots and toppled onto our bed.

'Sleep,' I muttered, as my eyelids fell.

IV

SEVILLE

22 May 1587

Rude cheers were heard outside, with orders being barked to the beat of a drum. Blinking at the light of the mid-morning sun, I slowly rose from my bed and crept stealthily towards the window. Fresh recruits could be seen in the street below me, being spurred towards the galleys while crowds of onlookers cheered them on.

'What is it now?' asked Maerten behind me.

'They've released more convicts to join the troops.'

The wretched hole we rented also held a fine view of the Guadalquivir, although not a glimmer of sunlight shone upon the mud-coloured river which curled through the city of Seville. On our side of the water, countless slaves bustled about like ants in the usual heat of May, bearing goods onto the galleys of the Grand Armada. I grimaced at the sight of the growing fleet, which was a distressing reminder of my army days.

'The troops!' exclaimed Maerten, with a loud huff. 'When will they set sail? I'm sick of hearing about them and the stupid Armada!'

He was interrupted by another cry from below, where haughty officers in an ox-cart waved their hats at the crowd. Some of them threw coins at the whooping mob that surrounded them.

'So it is true,' I whispered in disbelief, 'that the men have been paid.'

'Why the surprise?' replied Maerten. 'The king has forced loans upon everyone in Spain. The heretics are finished, their queen will be dead before the year is out.'

'It will not be easy,' I replied. 'I have myself fought the English. They are hard fighters.'

I spotted a pompous-looking sea captain below me on the passing ox-cart, sporting a waxed moustache. His olive-skinned features were pronounced by a forked goat beard, and he nodded and grinned at the people around him, with his chest puffed outwards and his gloved hands holding his sword belt.

'Captain de Cuéllar'!' called a bystander, and the officer met the cry with a flamboyant wave of his widebrimmed hat.

The sight of the captain's showmanship filled me with disgust, as I turned to collect my rifle and pulled its stock against my shoulder. It was raised against a cheek that had been bruised by over a thousand gunshots, and the cold steel of my weapon was a welcome change from the sticky air that filled the room. As the cart rattled past, I carefully centred the sea captain's head between the silver peep sights on my rifle.

'I could blow his brains out from here,' I whispered under my breath.

'You could,' agreed Maerten, 'from ten times that distance.'

I slowly lowered my rifle which contained neither powder nor ball, then moved away from the window. Any attention from others was undesired, for those days found me lying low in *El Arenal*. In recent weeks, I had only ventured outside the Tavern of the Dog at night, and then only to stalk the men I was after. Those same men who had caused me a pain that scorched my heart like an undying ember.

Sweat dripped off my naked body as I flung myself onto a stool and laid the gun across my knees. The stink of sewage outside slowly faded, as I drew in deep breaths of the musky incense that burned in a copper cassolette on the floor. The aroma had also helped reduce the thick smell of smoke from the clothes in our room. With a sigh I rubbed the gun's muzzle hard with a dry cloth, while thinking of the previous night's events, finding that I was overcome by a grim satisfaction when recalling the shooting of Cristó.

A woman had screamed at the sight, a drunken whore who had stumbled out of the inn the moment my pistol was drawn. I took no displeasure in recalling the episode, thinking that it was only fair that the people of Spain tasted a bit of the horror that was the daily bread of her far-flung soldiers. It seemed incredible to me that it had all happened the night before, and I gritted my teeth with frustration and worry upon recalling how Gabri had got away.

'That look on Cristó's face,' muttered Maerten, almost as if reading my thoughts.

My brother by marriage still rested upon our rickety old bed, with his arms outstretched like the wings of the Imperial Eagle. A ray of sunlight streamed through the window's torn curtains and played about the sandy linen beneath him, and his bared torso glistened with sweat. Above his head the discoloured wall was stained by the hands of previous tenants, who had thrust themselves against it during their trysts with ladies of fortune.

'Got him right through the eye,' he sighed contentedly. 'He would have been dead within minutes.'

Despite my own sense of vindication and years spent shooting people, the praise of others for my deathly work always left me feeling on edge.

'I take no joy in the memory,' I snapped, as I rose hotly to my feet, 'for our mission is one of justice! Not bloodshed, but justice!'

In truth it was a lie, yet I felt guilty at having enmeshed my late wife's brother in my perilous acts of retribution. Maerten rose from the bed as he gazed at me open mouthed, to find me pointing a scarred finger at him.

'And in coming days, justice will be ours.'

Elsien's brother trembled once at the severity of my gaze, before I walked over to the wooden bathing tub. Handfuls of warm water were splashed over my face and neck, when I caught my reflection in a piece of broken mirror which dangled from a nail in the wall. A man stared back at me with a face like a sun-dried water skin, with his moist hair of saltpetre falling around a beard of similar colour. Nicks and scars were pitted across his throat and chest, the constant reminders of years spent fighting in the service of Spain. Apart from his three gun spanners, two wedding rings and a lock of gold hair also hung from the chain around his neck, prized mementoes of a union which had been mercilessly torn apart.

The sight almost made me retch, for I resembled a man of sixty although I was at least two years short of forty. Hooded and bloodshot eyes blinked above a broken nose and calloused cheeks, while the fingernails resting upon my chin were ringed with black grit. These stains were a testimony to decades spent wielding firearms, with so many guns having left their indelible mark on me. In that instant, I realised that I had become like the barrel of a rifle, hard on the outside but hollow within.

In the mirror I could also make out Maerten sitting up on the bunched sackcloth which passed for a mattress, as he reached for a flagon of wine at his bedside. After a long swig, my Brabantian brother held the jug out to me. I tore my face away from my reflection, raising my hand to him and shaking my head.

'No, thank you.'

'Have you turned Mohammedan? Even the Turks drink wine!'

'No,' I said, with my hand still raised, 'I want my head to be clear for the rest of the day. And you should refrain from your drinking too, for we must soon be gone from here.'

'Where to?'

'The Triana quarter,' I replied, 'across the bridge.'

Maerten defiantly locked stares with me when I said this. Then he drained his entire cup and set it back on the table at his bedside. The stripling had grown in age and stature, and was each month more filled out and handsome. I sighed sadly upon thinking how proud Elsien would have been of him.

When the youth refilled his cup, I was of half a mind to tell him off, but turned my back on him instead, as I bent over to pick up my shirt from the floor. As Maerten slurped his wine aloud the blood rose briefly to my head, before I took deep breaths to keep calm. I reminded myself that he had not the discipline of a seasoned campaigner, and that much had been asked of him during our ride south.

In the months since we had left Willebroek, the loss that I had felt for my dead wife and child had been tempered by the brotherly bond which I shared with Maerten. Like me, the youth had lost everything to Spanish cruelty in the Netherlands, with our sole reason for living being revenge for the evils we had suffered. Yet I had also held to another purpose, which was to ensure that the youth's future was provided for by any means necessary, as well as that of his younger brother.

'I wonder what has become of Pieter,' said Maerten, as if reading my thoughts.

'He is probably far safer than we are right now,' I replied curtly, although a deep concern for Elsien's youngest brother had gnawed at my mind in recent months.

In a heat of blood, we had both abandoned him to the care of his aunt Margareta, without ever bidding him farewell. Our circumstances had required us to do so, yet a vendetta which I thought would be accomplished within the month had dragged on for almost two years. I often worried about him and Elsien's other relatives, wondering how they would have made ends meet without Reynier's help. Maerten had sought to relieve these fears, constantly reassuring me that his aunt Margareta had access to hidden silver, which his father had revealed only to her.

Yet even then I wondered how long the pieces would last her, what with the war in the Netherlands continually raising the cost of everything, and her husband a bullying drunk who would have squandered any wealth within weeks. Then there was the issue of the newly barracked Spaniards, who would have viewed Maerten's family with contempt and hostility after I had killed their ensign. Whichever way I looked at it, I could not imagine that Pieter had had a good time in our absence. I was distracted from my worries when Maerten's question reached my good ear, as I passed my arms through the sleeves of my shirt.

'Who knows when the Armada will finally set sail? It has been the talk of lie-parlours for months.'

It was also the question on the whole of Seville's lips, but none cared less for the answer than I did, for I only cared about achieving my vengeance. At midday, the poor of all nations would be gathering around the numerous convents in the city, and Maerten and I had to walk across the bridge to seek out new lodgings. At the thought of it I hurried towards a corner of the room, where I picked up the rifle's leather sheath from against the wall.

I slid the wheellock rifle back into it while Maerten watched me, shielding his eyes with his hand, to ward off the sunlight that flooded the room. My black hose was then pulled up to my waist, before my stockings were lifted over my knee. The sword belt proved more fiddlesome until it was secured, and when I turned to face Maerten my wide-brimmed hat and cape cast a deathly silhouette against the wall.

'Have you got everything?' he asked, in an amused tone of voice.

My reply was both brusque and dismissive, as I nodded at my belongings alongside the bed.

'Brass balls in the dogskin bag, priming flask in its usual place, right alongside it.'

I swiftly fastened the last of my shirt buttons, then approached the rickety bed, which had in recent days started to lean to the right. In one deft movement, my bandolier was snatched off the rusted bedpost, with the belt of charges slung over my head and shoulder. As it fell across my chest its twelve powder gourds struck one another, making a sound like rattling teeth. At this gesture Maerten swung over the bed, causing it to creak like a friction drum at Christmastide.

'That's the lot?' he asked.

'That it is, my brother,' I replied. 'In coming days, our kin shall be avenged, and we will then leave this city and ride back to the Netherlands. Once we recover your brother, we shall return with him to embark on the first ship bound for Puerto Rico. Together we shall make our fortune in the New World.'

My words rang hollow when I said them, for my plans to flee across the Atlantic had only been made with Maerten and his younger brother in mind. After all the youth was approaching the prime of his life, while I was fast approaching the twilight of an old soldier's years. Yet Elsien would have wished her brothers to be safe and prosperous, so I would have to do all in my power to secure their future. I could still remember my long talks with my late wife, late into the cold Brabantian nights, when we often spoke of sailing to the Americas.

'For what future awaits the God-fearing in this land?' she had often asked, as she sat back upon the bed.

As always, I observed her beguiling features and body in silence, thinking that I would follow her to the ends of the earth if it meant saving our union. It was a few moments before I could sidestep her memory and return my attentions to the matter of my vendetta. Maerten could be seen staring at the ground in silence, perhaps having wearied of my staring into space.

'Seize up your arms and let us make haste,' I said firmly, hoping to revive his spirits, 'for at midday the poor will block the streets as they gather around the convents.'

Yet the usually wilful Maerten seemed suddenly downcast, reluctant to meet my gaze as a heavy silence hung between us. Years spent watching my back in the Spanish army had earned me a keen insight into people's behaviour, so that I instantly feared that something was wrong.

'What is it Marti?'

He said nothing, as he fidgeted with his fingers and stared from side to side.

'Speak up lad,' I urged him, 'for 'tis almost midday I tell you, and we must away to the Arenal gate!'

He finally raised his eyes towards me.

'You know *La Lechera*, the mulatto trollop?'

The question was both sudden and unexpected, so that it was a few moments before I could respond.

'The vixen with the big jugs?'

'Yes, her.'

I thought of the striking whore, who we often spotted from our lodging towards dusk. Just before sunset, she could be seen walking along the bank of the river Guadalquivir, with her yellow half-mantle screaming her trade. We had often remarked on her appearance, for the sight of the shapely strumpet was as welcome as a rare summer breeze. At all times she bore herself with the haughtiness of a queen's lady-in-waiting, ignoring the whistles and catcalls from the wharves as she twirled a violet parasol over her shoulder.

'What of her?' I snapped, already fearing the worst.

At my tone Maerten looked troubled and fell quiet again. I had travelled and lived with him long enough to know that he was withholding something.

'Go on Maerten, you know you can trust me. Tell me what distresses you, I shan't be cross.'

'Yesterday afternoon I went to that tavern in the Triana quarter...'

'Yes...'

'She was there, she spoke to me.'

''Pon my oath,' I roared angrily, with drops of spittle flying everywhere, 'did I not tell you to avoid women of all kinds?!'

'It was she who approached me!' he protested meekly. 'Called me blondie and beckoned me to her side!'

'What? And you felt flattered just because you're blonde?! You think you're the first fair-headed northerner she's seen?!'

'She's just a whore, Abel.'

'Christ's blood!' I spat, slapping myself in the face with despair. 'Just a whore, he says. Don't you know that all whores are the eyes and ears of the underworld? Our fate may already be sealed!'

Maerten's cheeks went pale as his eyes fell to the ground once more.

'She showed me her garters, but I ignored her. But I think... I could almost swear... that she followed me...'

At his words I looked across our room in fear, when I thought I heard the slightest of squeaks on the staircase outside our door.

'Be on your guard!' I cried. 'Where are your weapons?!'

My hand fell to the sword at my side, which was already half drawn when the door burst open. A band of ruffians fell onto me, knocking the breath from my chest and pinning my wrists and ankles to the ground. As I gasped for breath, I realised that the men reeked of cheap wine, which was a stink often borne by common brigands who sought courage by turning to drink. Their wide-brimmed hats masked their faces from me, with the clumsy broadswords beneath their capes betraying little skill with the blade.

One of the ruffians was pushing my head down sideways, which forced my jaw into my collarbone and fixed my gaze on filthy toenails that peered through a torn boot. When I strained my eyes sideways a clammy hand appeared which was forced over my mouth. Its owner was a grey-haired man with sallow features, and a yellowed plait over one shoulder which resembled a weasel's tail. My heart sank as I recognised my tall, skinny assailant. For the man was none other than Corporal Salvador Ortiz. A hateful grin broke upon his twitching face, which doubled the wrinkles between his eyes and temples.

'Why if it isn't our long-lost brother,' he whispered, 'the deadly Lynx of Haarlem.'

A dark frown quickly replaced Salva's cheerful expression and sweat prickled my brow as I met his furious grimace. The corporal then cast his fellows a withering glare, baring a bottom row of small, black teeth.

'Which of you fools was pushing at the back?'

A fearful silence followed, in which none of his footpads dared reply. Salva then hissed at his men to disarm us, before releasing his hold from my face. I heaved a deep breath of fetid air, while counting the number of whoresons inside our apartment. In all there were six sons of bitches, and two of them held the bewildered Maerten against the wall behind me, with the points of their daggers pricking his throat.

'Don't you hurt him,' I shouted at them in sudden panic, 'or it will be your last miserable act!'

Salva's pale grey eyes narrowed at my words while a smirk grew across his twitching face. When he spoke, it was all I could do not to wince from the stench of stale onions on his breath.

'Do not make idle threats Santi. You'll both be fortunate to see out the day.'

'What do you want?' I asked angrily, only for the corporal to grin back at me knowingly.

'The Sergeant will soon answer all of your questions. He is on his way up as we speak. Until then, stay your tongue and make ready to accept your fate.'

His mention of Ramos made the hair rise on the back of my neck, as I tried to figure out a way to escape. Meanwhile the corporal bound my wrists with a length of twine, then rose from the ground with a grunt. He next issued a low whistle and strode across the room to inspect my gear.

Meanwhile three of his tosspots released their grip on me as they sprawled over my body and searched my clothes. The wretches cut the most ragged of sights in their torn sleeves and unstarched collars. They were some of the many miscreants who loitered around the docks, whose swords could be hired for a mere handful of coppers. As I lay upon the boards at their feet, I could not help feeling highly insulted by the low quality of men who had been sent to capture us.

The scrawniest of their number dropped to one knee and busied himself with searching the stitching in my doublet before reaching over for the sword pommel at my side. A sheepish smile played on his lips when the full length of Toledo steel was drawn from my scabbard to the sound of a reluctant scrape. 'To relieve you of a bit of weight,' he whispered in mocking apology, then rested my rapier across the palm of his other hand.

'Who are you?' I snarled. 'The runt of the litter?'

He ignored my question, as he held my blade up to the sunlight and gasped at the engraving upon it.

'Good Lord, a Sahagún? We had best keep that apart.'

While he said this, two of his fellows twisted their hands down each of my boots, pulling out hidden daggers that were longer than a Habsburg's jawline. Yet none of them had thought to search for my old throat slitter which was chained to my hip. Quick as lightning, I reached over sideways and whipped it out from behind me, slashing the grinning runt who had taken my sword. Blood spattered the floor and wall as the Sahagún blade fell from his hands. He fell over in a writhing lump, holding his face and howling in protest.

'My eye! My eye! Bastard got me in the eye!'

The tosspot to my right collapsed when I kicked him in the throat, with another thrust of my dagger missing another's head by a hair's breadth before its point was buried deep into his shoulder. A howl of pain left the cur's mouth, as he grabbed my wrists with the strength of a bull handler, leaving me unable to wrest them free.

'Holy host!' I cursed aloud, struggling to reclaim my blade.

Then Salva could be heard blaspheming loudly, before running up to us and slamming the toe of his boot between my legs. An almighty roar burst from my throat, as the corporal fell forward and buried his knees into my belly.

My grip was already released from my dagger, and specks fluttered about my eyes as the cry in my throat was muted by the sudden blow to my stomach, while the edge of Salva's blade was pressed against my cheek.

'Listen here whoreson,' he whispered in my good ear, with the stink of rotten onions filling my nostrils again, 'Ramos asked that we preferably capture you alive. He said *preferably*, you hear? So you pull another fast one and I'll drive a handspan of steel through your gut.'

In emphasis of his threat, he pushed the edge of his broadsword against my cheek until it drew blood, leaving me in no doubt that he meant business. Behind him, the room was filled by the groans of the three stricken men. Salva grimaced at me before turning to address his besmirched band, wiping his blade upon his tattered sleeve.

'Let that be a lesson to you, you fools. That this cur is a seasoned veteran of the war in Flanders. Keep two eyes on him at all times, and don't let your guard down again.'

Tears of anguish gathered upon my eyelids while I wheezed for breath, plagued by the throbbing agony between my legs as I bit my lower lip to keep from whimpering. The footpad who had been kicked in the throat coughed aloud as he returned to his feet. He was somewhat red in the face, and his fellow tosspot moaned when Salva pulled my dagger out of his shoulder, then ordered him to leave the room with the blinded runt to find a surgeon. The injured pair were not long gone, when heavy footfalls could be heard in the corridor, and Salva's voice was alert when he spoke again.

'We got them both, sergeant.'

'Not without some setback, I see.'

The deep voice caused the hair to rise upon the back of my neck, and the boards beneath us creaked as its owner entered the room. I turned my face towards a heavyset man with a long pout, whose eyes glinted with malice. Many months had passed since I had last seen him, but he was still one of the most hirsute men I had ever seen. Hair grew everywhere except on his bald pate, spreading like clumps of moss upon his hands, and running in tufts from his earlobes to the cricks of his fingernails.

'Fetch me lunch,' he said to Salva, with the corporal nodding but once before he made for the stairs.

In the two years in which I had tracked him from Willebroek, Ramos had come to assume the portly figure of some high born lord. My former sergeant from the Army of Flanders had once worn rags more wretched than those hanging off the backs of my captors, yet he now sported a gaudy doublet worn by hidalgos, those nobles who purchased their title from the Crown. His red-spotted cheeks sagged over his chin onto a white neck ruff the size of a cartwheel, and golden rings adorned his stubby fingers.

'Abelardo de Santiago. Now that's a sight for sore eyes.'

His words barely reached me before my hands formed fists that trembled with rage.

'You...'

A smile slowly spread across his face, almost as if he had just been reunited with a long-lost brother.

'Are you surprised by the sight of me, Abelito? You have spied on my whereabouts all over the city.'

My blood boiled at his use of the loathsome diminutive 'Abelito,' which had stuck to me like dog shit during my last years spent in the Army of Flanders.

The sergeant then fixed his attentions on Maerten, who was held against the wall.

'So, you sought the affections of a mulatto?' asked Ramos mockingly.

His words provoked a deep-throated laugh from the ruffians around me, which was soon interrupted by a cry from their Brabantian captive.

'That back-stabbing bitch!' shouted Maerten angrily, earning himself a smack in the mouth from one of the hired blades.

Ramos eyed him with flaring nostrils, as if he had just sniffed a whiff of offal.

'Gag him,' said the sergeant, waving a dismissive hand at Maerten as the two footpads proceeded to bind my brother-in-law hand and foot, after stuffing a piece of torn blanket into his mouth.

'You double-dyed scoundrel,' I growled from the ground, 'you have no right to do this to us.'

Ramos winced at my accusation before issuing a brief chuckle. His reply was delivered in a rasping voice which rose slowly, while he squinted at me like a judge sitting behind his court-room bench.

'Any more than you had the right to kill Cristó and wound Gabri. For shame, Abelito! Two good men who watched your back for years. Shot like common brigands in the street, without even the chance to draw steel in honourable combat!'

For a moment, his forked tongue cut me deeply, for I had long struggled with the choice of shooting my former comrades instead of facing them with a drawn sword. Yet I quickly recovered my composure, deciding to brush off his jibe rather than allow him to prod me with guilt.

'I would have gladly given them the chance to engage in honourable combat. Were they not a pair of low-born cut-throats without a shred of virtue between them, and I would shoot both bastards again if I had to!'

My fiery riposte left me gasping in outrage. For I was hardly in a position to provoke the sergeant, what with my wrists bound before me, and my captors' drawn blades resting upon my back and neck. One of them reached forward and prodded my earlobe with his dagger point, which left me shrugging my shoulder to push it away. When Ramos spoke again, his voice was softer, like that of a mother chiding her wayward son.

'But why did you do it, Abelito? Why try take the lives of your brothers-in-arms? For all those years we only had each other in that heretical inferno. A fellowship of brothers who shared everything. Defending one another to the hilt...'

His words brought the blood to my head again, which pounded my temples and left me staring into a red mist.

'Last I remember there was not much sharing. Although I was always tasked with watching your backs. Always the last to leave our skirmishes!'

A grunt of disgust resounded across the room when Ramos waved at me to keep silent. The sergeant's dismissive gesture only sparked another tirade from me, for the anger I felt at his betrayal had burned in my breast for months on end.

'Risked my neck in every scrap with the enemy! Not a fight went by that I did not blow the head off some whoreson creeping up behind you. And the one time I needed you, the only time I lost my footing on that cursed tree, I was left for dead by all four of you! Abandoned to the wood and all its creatures. And as if that were not bad enough, you returned to Willebroek and killed my wife and child!'

Muffled groans were heard behind my back. I turned to see Maerten thrashing upon the floor in a rage, his face as red as a Burgundian beetroot as he struggled to free himself from his bonds. At the sergeant's gesture, two of the footpads booted the Brabantian until he was a motionless heap, ignoring my cries of protest.

Ramos appeared ignorant to this violence as he rubbed his face with the palms of his hands and sat down on a corner of the bed. He then rested his elbows upon his knees and locked his chubby fingers into a furry ball.

'What am I to do with you, Abelito?' he sighed loudly.

I frowned back at him in astonishment, before blurting out the first thing which came to my mind, overwhelmed as I was by a deep and righteous anger.

'Release us and return our weapons!'

Ramos sighed.

'You are not a Don and cannot bear arms in this city.'

'Nor are your ruffians.'

Ramos fell silent at my curt reply, as the realisation slowly dawned on me that Maerten and I would have already been cold bodies in the gutter had the sergeant wanted us dead.

'What do you want from me?' I asked with a heightened cockiness.

At my question, Ramos cleared his throat slightly.

'The reason I have come here, Abelito, is to talk business.'

Shocked by his audacity, I stared back at him, trying to restrain a burst of incredulous laughter.

'What business would I discuss with a man I want dead?'

Ramos raised his hands before him, as if shielding off a quarrel over a petty game of cards.

'Now, now, Abelito. You are not the first to entertain such desires, nor will you be the last...'

With my rebuttal dismissed, he tapped his chin with his forefinger while he spoke, staring pensively in the direction of the balcony.

'Our business remains the same as it always was, Abelito. And that is plunder!'

He smacked his palm down hard on his thigh as he uttered the last word. His eyes shone as they always had when he referred to booty, which had been his daily obsession throughout our days in the army. The audacity of his suggestion left me dumbstruck for a few moments, and I gaped at him as though he had just uttered a stream of gibberish.

'What plunder?' I whispered at last.

Ramos grinned from ear to ear while his eyes twinkled with mischief, since he evidently thought that I was intrigued by his proposal.

'Plunder like we have never seen before, Abelito! It shall eclipse the sacking of Constantinople and Troy! For I speak not of the pillage of a single city, but of a whole kingdom.'

My old sergeant's design was instantly clear to me, that he yearned for the gains of battle once more, to be obtained through the Grand Armada bound for England.

'And this time,' he bellowed passionately, with his eyes almost bulging out of his head, 'the skirmishers will carry away the greatest part of the spoils! We'll stick our hands into every hidden treasure box, Abelito! Take all the riches that those heretics stole from the convents for ourselves! Their women and children can also be sold to slave traders, there'll be no end of merchants and villagers to tax. It shall be an absolute killing, Abelito! You know of what I speak. I have highborn courtiers backing my commission, men who have the ear of the king himself!'

'And how do I come into it?'

He paused for emphasis, fixing me with a keen stare which verged on the covetous.

'Marksmen with a steady hand do not grow on trees. You were always my lucky charm, Abelito. I shall forgive all your sins against me if you would serve me again. Sail with me for England.'

His eyes were still wide when his rant was over, which left me shaking my head in disbelief.

'Sail with you for England?'

'And why not? It is a holy cause! Besides, the English queen has stabbed us in the back for years. It is finally time for us to turn our attentions to her!'

I returned his gaze for a few moments, as my bunched fists began to tremble at his suggestion.

'You have some courage,' I hissed, 'I will do no such thing. My days spent killing innocents are over. I would rather be dead than serve a pig like you again!'

Ramos was speechless for a few moments as beheld me with a look of anguished confusion, then he jerked his head at Maerten with a loud sneer.

'Why of course you would not dare march with me again! You would much rather befriend these heretics and murder your own brothers in cold blood!'

I bristled at the sergeant's cheap branding of Elsien's brother as a Protestant.

'That man is of the faith, and well do you know it. As were his father and sister whom you put to the torch!'

Ramos met my accusations without batting an eyelid, for he was nothing if not possessed of the hide of an ox.

'So is that what all this is about? That wench of the miller's daughter? Is that really the cause of your reprisal against me? The reason why you shot two of our brothers in the street like dogs? We took you in when no one else would even look at you! When Alba left the Netherlands, you were but a reviled marksman, nobody's child!'

My eyes misted at his words, and for a few moments I could not bring myself to express my ire. Behind me were heard grunts and hisses of indignation which could only belong to Maerten, and a teardrop slid down my cheek when I traded a look with him over my shoulder. The Brabantian's eyes bulged in fury, with the boot of a tosspot planted firmly upon his neck while he struggled with his bonds. Meanwhile Ramos appeared impervious to our expressions of grief and outrage, with his final defence proving a shower of salt on a raw wound.

'You may blame me for her death, but it was never my intention to kill her. You should blame yourself and your own greed instead! No one forced you to form part of the skirmish. You volunteered, remember?'

He craned his neck forward and peered at me closely.

'We all lost loved ones abroad. Need I tell you that that is the nature of war? But I am giving you the chance to forget our quarrel, to join me and make a killing instead. Bring this heretic along too if you will, for God knows that there will be enough loot for all those who fight for the one true faith! Be shrewd Abelito, for you'll never receive a more profitable offer.'

A long silence fell across the room, and my eyelids closed as my cheeks dampened with boiling tears. The desperate efforts and sacrifices of the last two years had come to naught, with my dream of revenge vanishing like a wisp of smoke. All because of the carelessness of my accomplice, the very brother of the woman I sought to avenge. I drew a deep breath and met the expectant gaze of my sergeant.

'Curro Ramos, you are a swine. The very reason why the whole world hates the mention of our blessed mother Spain. Tosspots like you are a blight on our army, whose fame remains sullied by honourless filth like yourself. You are a murderer and a profiteer to your core, feeding off the misery of the weak and the unfortunate. I am proud that I came so close to killing you. I'll not hesitate to try again should the chance present itself.'

My bile was vented in a voice that was largely calm and un-faltering, and which only quavered when the most pointed of insults were uttered. I would have readily swallowed my tongue had I realised the fate which my words had just earned us, for death was far from the worst end which lay in store for me and my Brabantian brother.

A lengthy silence pervaded the room once more following the delivery of my insolent rebuttal, only broken by the odd sound from the street outside. It felt as though an unthinkable abomination had just been committed, the enormity of which could not be described in words. Maerten beheld me aghast from across the room, and his eyes were no longer bulging with rage but wide in amazement.

Meanwhile Curro still met my stare as he had throughout my tirade. His fingers began to tap the end of his right knee, and he took me in with an unmoved expression, which lingered on for almost a minute. The sergeant then stretched his neck awkwardly from left to right, blinked once and smiled.

'Are you finished?'

My legs buckled at the realisation of what I had just done, and it was no use trying to stop them. I was already reciting a Hail Mary in my heart, although I knew that even the intercession of the Virgin was unlikely to pull me out of the deep hole I had dug for myself. So I was almost grateful when a cheerful cry reached our ears, which had us nervously looking to the door.

'Ten-minute paella!'

Salva strode into the room, bearing a bowl that he handed to Ramos. The steam from the food drew a loud rumble from one of the ruffians' stomachs as I suddenly feared for Maerten's life.

'Spare the lad I beg you,' I blurted, 'he's just a whiskerless youth. He'll be on the next ship bound for the New World, I swear you'll not see him again.'

Ramos huffed aloud, as he dabbed his forehead lightly with a vellum sheet.

'The place for murderers is not on a ship bound for the Americas, Abelito. It is with the executioner.'

A taut silence hung in the air at his words, which was only disturbed by a low chuckle from Salva. I felt impaled by a piercing thrust of despair, knowing full well that if the army got its hands on me, I would swing from the noose. Meanwhile Curro eyed me carefully as his threat sank in, while I quietly prayed that his heart might hold that scintilla of mercy which was lacking in mine. As the smell of chicken, fish and saffron spread across the room, two more stomachs gurgled like drains before the sergeant raised a ringed fist to his mouth and coughed slightly.

'Readily would I give you up to the army,' he said, 'but that course bears nothing for me. Besides, that Flemish lad behind you has inherited his father's debts.'

I beheld him warily as I tried to guess the foul design which he had undoubtedly concocted for us. The sergeant leant forward and addressed me again.

'The king wants his admiral to get the galleys to Lisbon in all haste. To leave Seville before the Feast of Corpus Christi. The captains are desperate for more men, you would not believe the prices that rowers are fetching.'

At Ramos's words I felt the room swirl around me. Salva grinned wickedly at the sergeant's back, then chimed in himself.

'I have often wondered what it is like to pull the oar on a galley. It should not be much different from pulling the doghead, Abelito.'

With a laugh Ramos reached into his coat, and I cowered for fear that he might be about to draw a pistol. A loud rattle could instead be heard when two leg irons were banged down on the floor in front of him, causing his belly to quiver.

'It is time for some honest work, Abelito. I hear that you have recently gone by the name of Juan, and you should cling to that name if you value your life.'

I gritted my teeth in frustration, upon realising that he had seen through the name of Juan de los Hospitalarios which I had used ever since our arrival in Seville. It had been given to me by the Knights of Malta, when they had discovered me as an abandoned babe outside the door of one of their foundling homes.

The sergeant savoured the look on my face with a smirk. I felt only dread as I stared at the shackles before him.

'You are to sell us into slavery?'

The sergeant locked the fingers of both his hands and bent them backwards, issuing a loud crack.

'We must all contribute to the war effort, Abelito. Those of us who will not fight could at least row.'

'But we are free men!'

Ramos shrugged.

'Not in the eyes of the law. But ships' captains do not ask many questions, and the hangman will not miss two more outlaws.'

When he said this his eyes held the dull gleam of a blade, and when he spoke again, his voice was akin to the grim sound of a death knell.

'You shall fetch me a big pile of ducats.'

'Over a hundred if they are auctioned, Sergeant.'

Ramos waved away Salva's suggestion. He then got to his feet with a grunt and took his bowl from the top of the bed.

'No auctions: a deal has been struck with an overseer already. As for me, it is time to take my leave of this hole. After all, my paella must be stone cold already.'

V

SEVILLE TO LISBON

22 May 1587-16 April 1588

When Ramos left the room, Salva seated himself upon the edge of the bed and waited a few minutes for the midday toll from the cathedral's bell tower, before nodding to his remaining men.

'Now.'

His trio of ruffians quickly met their master's request, so that Maerten and I shared a savage beating. This hiding was as vicious as it was painful, with innumerable blows and kicks received from the hired swords. We were left to parry them with our hands bound at the wrists, and as yet another fist caught me in the jaw, Maerten dismayed me when he started to yell.

For a moment I hoped that the cries of Elsien's brother might alert others to our treatment. Yet Salva had thought of everything, for as soon as the large bell sounded from the distant Giralda tower, it was joined in the chiming Angelus by scores of other belfries. Maerten's cries were quickly drowned out by the tremendous din, which was matched by the midday cries of the poor in the street, who had gathered outside the countless convents for their free bowls of soup.

'*Sopa boba*!' was the strident cry of beggars outside, as a hefty boot landed heavily upon my shin.

'Bastard!' I howled in furious protest, only to receive a kick across the face which sent me rolling over the floorboards.

The torment was finally ended when the voices in the street subsided. Our clothes were in tatters, and my ribs screeched in agony when I turned over sideways. The miserable end of our failed mission was best symbolised by Maerten's swollen face, which was purple around the eyes and full of bloodstained teeth. Salva and his remaining scoundrels next hoisted us to our feet, laughing aloud at our trembling figures and our inability to speak.

As the corporal stepped towards me with a cruel smirk I glanced at him in fear, flinching slightly when he raised his hand towards me. In an instant he tore the silver bands from around my neck. His gesture enraged me as the blonde lock of hair and the three gun spanners fell at my feet, yet before I could react Salva pushed the rim of my hat down over my eyebrows. In vain did I try to feebly strike out at him, for his underlings were already dragging us from the room by the collar.

With a rumble of footfalls, we descended the stairs towards the ground floor, passing through the lengthy hall with a low-beamed ceiling. I looked across it for help, but the innkeeper was nowhere to be seen. Our captors' daggers prodded our backs as Maerten and I were next hauled outside our tavern and onto the street. One of the men grunted aloud when we reached it.

'Not even a bloody breeze.'

Salva and his men proceeded to shove their way through the sordid den of *El Arenal*. I cursed myself for having let myself be captured, just as I managed to snatch a glimpse of Maerten to my left. The battered youth appeared downcast as a grim footpad shadowed his every step.

After turning a corner, we ducked our heads beneath a nicked tankard, which hung outside the door of yet another alehouse. The gentle strumming of guitars could be heard from within the tavern, and I saw that many of its patrons were stooped over their cards and drink. These evil-looking men were served by a pair of well-endowed wenches, whose reputations were as loose as their unbuttoned bodices.

'After me,' snapped Salva, prompting his three ruffians to grab us by the shoulder and shove us in after him.

As we shuffled through the door, a skinny old soak lumbered towards us with a jug of wine in one hand. He waved an accusing finger, for in his drunkenness he had mistaken Salva and his men for *hermandades*.

'By the Virgin!' he bellowed, standing in the corporal's path. 'Leave these poor bastards alone!

They are innocent I tell you! Innocent!'

Salva's step never faltered as he snatched the drunk's face and shoved him aside. The wretch crashed headfirst into a table, causing a handful of patrons to spring to their feet. Their shouts of protest went ignored as we were led on to yet another bench where a man sat alone. He was a sallow-faced devil, blessed with shifty eyes and a sneer. His lip was curled in contempt when he saw us, slowly rising to his feet and drawing a coiled whip from his belt.

'Greetings Dimas,' said Salva, as he stepped aside to let the man inspect us.

'What happened to them?' exclaimed the other.

'They look like they've been to the wars!'

'They needed some breaking in, but they're none the worse for wear. Do you want them or not?'

Dimas scowled as he used his whip handle to prod Maerten's arm.

'Are these men or maids?' he said at last, in a sneering tone. 'Their arms are as thin as chicken legs, they shall bend like green saplings upon the oar.'

The slur was clearly aimed at reducing our price. Yet it was too hopeful an attempt, for each of us knew that the auction blocks in Seville were a seller's market, and that the Armada's captains were desperate for forced rowers.

'Very well then,' said Salva, 'I'll take them elsewhere.'

He turned on his heel and made to usher us away, when a snort of frustration was heard from Dimas.

'Wait!' he snarled, drawing a sack of coins from inside his leather jerkin. 'A man's got a right to bargain, hasn't he? Here's the four hundred ducats you asked for, with a little something else thrown in.'

The corporal made a great show of sighing wearily before turning to take the overseer's money.

'Nothing is ever straightforward with you Portuguese whoresons. Now I suppose you'll need us to escort you to your galley?'

'And also their papers,' said Dimas.

'First things first,' replied Salva, then seized me by the collar and hauled me back out towards the street.

The upset patrons had meanwhile gathered behind us with angry looks on their faces, yet the ring of the corporal's drawn sword sent them scattering from our path. The three other ruffians followed us out with Maerten held firmly in their clutches, with Dimas right behind them.

It was a slow slog along the wharves, and our captors formed a tight ring around us as they pushed and heaved their way through the market. Many Moriscos creaked past, shoving pushcarts that were full of dried fruit and vegetables. The general stench was quelled by the smells of roasted chestnuts and buttercakes from beyond the small shacks ahead of us, where fritter sellers swarmed about the Arenal gate like moths around a flame.

Across the water we could see the Triana quarter on the opposite bank, a withered den of vice that trembled in the shadow of the imposing *Castillo de San Jorge*. This loathed seat of the Spanish Inquisition soon vanished from view, as my captors pushed through the usual shouting matches of hawkers with outstretched arms and jabbing elbows, always keeping a good hold on us to ensure that we did not flee their clutches. At last, we stopped along the side of a huge galley, where Dimas stepped before us and issued a shrill whistle.

'Lower a gangplank!' he called out to the sailors on board the ship.

Seamen grumbled beneath their breath as they obeyed his command. I stared around me in a daze, briefly blinded by the sunlight as my eyes came to rest on Salva's furious face.

'Got off lightly, you cur,' he snarled in my good ear. 'Were it up to me your corpses would already be lying at the bottom of the river.'

I tried to insult him, but I was dumbstruck from the beating I had received at the hands of his men. The tall, lanky corporal spared me the effort, as he stepped forward and buried his fist into my stomach.

'*Adios* from *Cristó*.'

Maerten groaned aloud at my treatment, yet he went ignored as Salva whisked two scrolls with waxed seals from his jacket. They were both held out towards the Portuguese overseer.

'Signed and sealed by a notary. These criminals are convicted of murder and consigned to the rowing bench for ten years. My name appears nowhere, and we never met each other.'

Dimas snatched the forged papers without a word of thanks, as Salva and his men vanished into the crowd along the docks. Meanwhile a couple of our owner's slave wardens had already appeared at our side, seizing us by the collar and shoving us ahead of them. Together we crossed the wooden plank and found ourselves aboard the main deck of the large galley, where our new master ordered that our clothes be torn off our bodies.

'What's to become of us, Abel?' managed Maerten in the Brabantian dialect.

The buttons burst from his breast when a warden tore his shirt open, and I turned my head to protect my eyes.

'Stay close to me,' I hissed at him. 'Just do what I say and never show any fear. Never!'

'Silence slave!' snarled Dimas, crashing his whip handle into my broken lips. The blow left my jaw hanging open as fresh blood dripped onto the boards.

'Easy,' spoke a firm voice behind us, 'no use killing that slave before our voyage has even started.'

Dimas whirled around angrily and then engaged in a deep bow, while I raised a hand over my blinking eyes to shield them from the sun. The speaker was a slender specimen of a proud cast, who wore the severe black gown of a physician and a finely trimmed grey beard. The younger man alongside him sported the same attire, and both of them wore white neck ruffs and seemed possessed of a studious air.

'Your pardon Don Hurtado,' said Dimas hesitantly, with another low bow, 'your words are ever wise and true.'

I drew in my breath at the name uttered by the overseer. For the Hurtados were well known in circles of Spanish wealth, since they were at the heart of all New World enterprises, ranging from shipping loans to the African slave trade. Their skill in their professions was said to only be matched by their sharp minds for business, and it was widely rumoured that they were in truth Jewish converts who posed as devoted sons of the church.

'After all, a man cannot row if he is half dead,' reasoned the younger Hurtado, 'which is not to mention that our medical provisions are presently being brought on board, and we cannot yet attend to anyone's wounds.'

As he spoke, I observed about a dozen barber surgeons behind the two *prados*, bearing beakers and jars and countless other implements which I had previously seen in infirmaries. A hope stirred within me upon realising that our vessel was a hospital ship, that we would not be cast into the thick of any sea battles that the Armada might encounter.

'Your pardon, Don Blas,' said Dimas to the younger man, in a grovelling tone.

He bowed long enough for the two *prados* and their coterie to pass by and make their way down the stairs which led to the lower deck. Once they were gone, the overseer raised his head and squinted at me evilly. His forefinger prodded my cheek while he neared his face towards mine with bared teeth.

'You open your mouth again without permission, you Spanish whoreson, and I'll have your tongue cut out.'

The galley's sailors gathered on deck to watch as Dimas's men tore the rest of our clothes off. Maerten and I were left to stand naked while pails of muddied water were flung over us from the river. Pieces of black soap were then used to lather our bodies before a pair of barber surgeons set about us with drawn razors, shearing every single hair off our bodies.

'Don't move, fool,' snapped one of them, as I squirmed at the cold touch of his blade against my nether regions.

By the end of it I was as hairless as a newborn, with only a long lock of hair left hanging off the crown of my head, as a mark of my slave status.

'That should reduce the lice,' said one of the barber surgeons, before he made off with his pail and razors. Two sailors next appeared with more buckets of seawater, which were tossed at the scummy hairstrewn mess at our feet, sending it floating away towards the scuppers.

I secretly feared that they would next tattoo our cheeks, as was often the practice with outlaws condemned to the oar. Yet in their haste, the men instead passed us bundles of rags. At their order, we pulled on a sort of loincloth and a sleeveless tunic of sackcloth, which was open at the sides from shoulder to waist.

'That's a finely attired pair,' exclaimed Dimas mockingly, 'and now to see you off to your wonderful new living quarters.'

His wardens seized us by the arms and led us down the wooden steps. Upon reaching the middle deck we saw rows of beds and surgeons' equipment, with the older Hurtado seen inspecting a vial of yellow fluid. As we descended further into the ship it smelt more like an open sewer, so that our captors paused long enough to shove tobacco leaves up their nostrils before leading us on. Maerten and I observed their gesture in shock and were both coughing violently by the time we reached the rowing benches, where Dimas stopped to stretch his arm out towards the scores of slaves crammed upon them.

'Welcome, fair maidens, to the rowing deck of the Santa Maria de Visión. She is a hospital ship assigned to the Squadron of the Levant and will be your home for many years to come.'

A waft of rancid air plagued our nostrils, with Maerten coughing up phlegm from the evil stench.

'What's the matter, northerner?' exclaimed Dimas, sneering at Elsien's brother, 'are your new quarters not to your liking?'

His wardens grabbed us by the back of the neck and shoved us towards the benches further along, where the boards were stained black from human spew and excrement. My skin crawled as our feet squelched over the catwalk, while a sea of faces turned towards us, wearing expressions which were in turn dull and bereft of hope. Meanwhile my arm was planted across my nose and mouth, which were already filled with bile and sourness from the hellish malodour.

Behind me I could see Maerten's red eyes watering, with his nose fast leaking a bloodied snot. Our captors' gait ended halfway through the benches, and my heart sank when Dimas addressed a burly strokesman at the end of a port-side bench, who glared at us with the utmost contempt. This huge specimen wore a thick black moustache, with tattoos engraved on both his cheeks. His colour and profile hinted at Arab blood, and a pair of burly blackamoors sat alongside him with forlorn expressions.

'Let them through Esteban,' snapped Dimas in Sabir, the common tongue used in Mediterranean ports.

'Are you serious?' muttered the other in a heavy Berber accent.

'Do as I say!'

Glistening muscles rippled upon Esteban's bare chest when he moved his legs sideways, to allow us to reach the other end of his bench. My arm finally left my face as I seized Maerten's shoulder and shoved him ahead of me.

'What are you doing?'

'Be quiet,' I hissed at the youth, as I pushed him towards the other end of the bench. Upon reaching it we sat fourth and fifth from the catwalk, with Maerten closest to the slight breeze that fluttered through our oarhole. My brother-in-law was quick to realise the favour I had done him, as he quickly bent towards the opening to gasp the fresh air that blew through it.

'Sit up slave!' snarled Dimas, seizing the end of the oar and jerking it back hard so that the shaft hit Maerten's face.

A mocking laugh was next heard from Esteban as the slave wardens stepped over towards us to chain our ankles to the bench.

'Get a good rest, fair maidens,' called Dimas, as he made off with his snickering men, 'your training starts first thing tomorrow.'

Esteban was also chuckling as they walked away, as he took up from where Dimas had left off. He first taunted and harassed us, then shouted at Maerten to sit up straight. When I told him to mind his own affairs, the towering strokesman sprang from his seat and dealt me a crunching punch in the nose.

'From this moment on there are no affairs of our own!' he roared, shaking his fist in my face. 'My every last order must be obeyed. We row as one and sink as one, and you do not dare even draw breath without my say-so.'

In the days that followed he was as good as his word, fast becoming the scourge of our existence. We learned that he was formerly a pirate from Algiers, who had been taken captive during a surprise attack on his vessel by a Spanish galley. He was tall in stature and as strong as a Turk, having been a slave on our galley for over five years. During that time, he had converted to Christianity and been rebaptised, in the hope that it might reduce his years at the oar.

None dared to ask him his real name, but some of the slaves behind us sometimes called out 'Ali', then mimicked the call of a muezzin amid cruel cackles of laughter. Whenever this happened, the Algerian would shoot to his feet and turn towards them, baring his teeth and shaking his fist, while also making the gesture of slitting his throat with his thumb. I dared not think what fate would have befallen his mockers had he not been restrained by his leg iron.

The whoreson was misery and malevolence combined, and always quick to report our slightest misdeeds. Yet despite his odd bouts of violent rage, the strokesman was not half as cruel as Dimas. Our Portuguese master soon proved himself to be a born sadist who ruled by fear. He lavished particular attention upon his Spanish charges, having us whipped and beaten for the slightest of perceived misdeeds.

Dusk brought a respite from both their attentions that was all too welcome, as Maerten and I slumped against each other upon the rowing bench, drained from toil and incessant worry. At dawn we were rewarded with the same stench of sweat and filth, as we relentlessly scratched ourselves due to the burning itch of lice. Some of the more fortunate souls among us could reach the nearest loophole through which they relieved themselves, while others had to do so where they sat.

This meant that our morning bread ration was always served to the stench of fresh excrement, after which Dimas appeared with his whip and whistle to start our training. Hours were spent bringing us to move as one, rowing the ship downriver and turning it before returning the galley to its mooring. Throughout our exercises the whips of our overseers cracked endlessly, with a drumbeat guiding our movements. It was back-breaking work, which was made even harder by the fact that Maerten and I were both novices.

Our ungainly movements often meant that the oars behind us crashed into the back of our heads, leaving us bruised and dizzy. The first session was said to have lasted an hour, and by the end of it we were left slumped over the oar handle, breathing deep gasps of foul air with Esteban cursing us in Sabir from the end of our bench.

'What is he saying?' asked Maerten between gasps, for the youth did not understand the common tongue of the ports.

'He curses us for our lack of skill with the oar,' I replied, resting my shaking, bleeding palms upon my knees, 'and he also mentioned our mothers.'

'Are we meant to do this every day?'

'Most days,' I sighed, trying to ignore the fevered trembling of his arms.

'Christ's blood, Abel,' he said, 'they may as well hang us now and be done with it.'

'Keep silent,' I snapped, as Dimas appeared farther on down the catwalk, 'or do you want another hiding?'

'But how can we do this for ten years?'

'It will get better,' I lied after a few moments, then held my face in my hands.

Our training was to last another month, in which time we rowed for three shifts a day. At night we collapsed upon each other along the bench, doing our best to avoid touching the blackened sticky floor at our feet. My back was often raw from Dimas's lashings, yet sleep always claimed me due to sheer exhaustion. It was an inhumane toil that we exerted in the hottest months of summer, so that our bodies constantly dripped with sweat.

Never did time pass as slowly as it did for galley slaves. In our desperate plight, we craved for rumours that trickled below decks, in the hope of some unlikely tidings which might ease our desperate condition. These snatches of gossip might as well have been our eyes and ears. For aside from the fleeting glimpses of the ocean through the oarholes, the only thing we saw all day was the huge bulwark in front of the rowing benches, which separated our compartment from the other cargo spaces on our deck.

As the days wore on, our main bearer of hearsay was Costa the enslaved cook, who also brought us our meals. He was a wretched creature who also wore sackcloth, and constantly crouched as if expecting a blow from someone. The slave was short of an ear, which had once been cut from his head as a punishment for stealing food. He had put his remaining one to good use, however, feeding us scraps of information from the upper decks which ran along the benches like wildfire. It was from him that we learned of our impending voyage to Lisbon, which would free us from the hateful training sessions in the baking swelter of Seville.

'When Costa? When?' we often called out to him, as he passed us our dried-bean soup.

'Any day now, brothers,' was his usual reply, 'do not lose heart.'

Before the week was ended, large crowds of Sevillians were seen gathering upon the banks of the river. The voice of the city's mayor could be heard rising above several priests of all denominations, delivering a solemn speech to the crews of the three galleys which were moored in the Guadalquivir.

'From here do you depart,' he declared in a booming voice, 'sailing north with all of the prayers and blessings of Seville. Upon joining the invincible and most fortunate Armada of our king, may you swiftly deliver God's justice to the English Jezebel and her wicked cohorts!'

No sooner was the rest of this address delivered than a salvo was fired from the ships. Our Venetian captain, Vincenzo De Bartulo, then ordered that the Santa Maria cast off and follow the other two warships, which were already making their way along the river. Loud cheers were heard along the wharves as we strained at the oar, steering our six-hundredtonne ship after the other galleys. Yet a few of the bystanders also shook their fists at us and cursed aloud, for endless fights had broken out in previous days between the galleys' sailors and the city's guards, with the latter often having the worst of them.

After weeks of training our hands were calloused and our arms bulged with muscles. To a man we rose from our benches, taking one step onto the footrest before us, and dropping back with our arms outstretched as the oar blades struck the water. This rowing movement had been repeated constantly during training until we executed it to perfection, so that the oars never once hit each other. Through the oarholes we glimpsed groups of grimy-faced urchins who ran along the wharves. They shouted and waved to us all the way to the tower of gold, where we made our way through the city walls.

Despite the brisk wind which had picked up that morning, the captains of the galleys chose to keep their rowers at it for another hour, to serve as additional training. Afterwards we slumped onto our benches with our limbs aflame, gasping for breath as the sails were raised, and turning our faces towards the wind that blew through the oarholes. When the ocean was reached, the gales were still strong enough to hurry us along to our end, allowing me to slumber for many hours in the days that followed, until I was rudely woken one morning by the jabs of Maerten's elbow in my side.

'Look!' he exclaimed, pointing through the oarhole.

'They say it is the São Jorge Castle!'

The sun's glare barely allowed me to make out the distant promontory; then I nodded back at Elsien's brother before he asked the very question I was thinking.

'I wonder how long we'll be here for.'

Esteban snored aloud from the other end of our bench, and we took advantage of the respite to stand up and take a closer glimpse at the growing sight of Lisbon outside. As we drifted through the ships in port the men above us could be heard asking where to drop anchor, and a pinnace could be seen approaching us. At the prow of the small boat stood an aged man in a flowing white beard, and I gasped aloud at the sight, for I had seen him before.

'It is Santa Cruz,' I whispered, 'the hero of Lepanto.'

'Get your slaves to work and follow us,' bellowed the famous admiral, wagging his finger at our crew.

'You can't just leave your ship there!'

He had hardly spoken when a shrill burst from a whistle had us turning in fear towards Dimas, whose eyes bulged madly above the tobacco leaves stuffed into his nostrils and the raised whip in his hand. Esteban was already barking at us to seize the oar, with the slaves to starboard pushing their handles while those to port pulled theirs, causing the galley to turn around. It was a manoeuvre which demanded a huge effort from us, so that tears of exertion ran down our cheeks when it was accomplished, before we rowed as one to a slow drumbeat, following the admiral's pinnace into port.

When we anchored, Dimas vanished up the steps, and we marvelled at the sheer number of galleys which were already gathered at Lisbon. It was a vast and colourful fleet, which also included converted merchantmen and enormous hulks of a size that left our jaws hanging.

'They call them urcas,' said a voice behind us, and we turned to see Costa handing out bowls of soup. 'They say they come all the way from the German port of Rostock.'

I observed the giant ships in awed silence, then swallowed hard as many more ships came into view, with the enormity of the whole enterprise slowly sinking in.

'Incredible,' I muttered, as Maerten pulled a piece of dried bread out of his garments, which was dipped into his soup.

When we had eaten, I briefly raised my raw buttocks and stood onto our bench, then stepped past my Brabantian brother to relieve myself through the oarhole. A deep concern had slowly overtaken me, as I realised that we might be left to rot on the rowers' benches for weeks until the entire fleet was assembled. Yet in the event my fears proved unfounded, for there was plenty of work to be done on shore.

'Get yourselves a good rest,' warned Costa towards sundown. 'They say that a day of hard labour awaits you tomorrow.'

His warning rang true at first dawn, when we were roused to shrill bursts from Dimas's whistle. After the anchor was raised, we were made to row the galley towards port, where it was moored, before we were released from the benches and chained together. Our next orders were to climb the steps up to the infirmary and then the ship's waist, under the watchful eye of Dimas and his slave wardens. Upon reaching it the scents and stenches were like fresh mountain air when compared to the hell we had just abandoned, as our masters led us bewildered and blinking into the enormous shipyards in the sprawling port of Lisbon, where we were made to carry all manner of goods and weapons onto other galleys.

'So many fine ships,' whispered Maerten in awe.

Yet we soon came to hate the sight of them, and of each distant speck along the horizon which announced the approach of yet another galley. We were utterly dismayed by each new arrival, which meant yet another day spent toiling like Basques, with our hides licked by the unforgiving sun and the end of Dimas's lash. During these days of hard labour, we often caught sight of the lord admiral himself, the Marquis of Santa Cruz. The years had not been kind to the revered Spanish hero, who wore a constant frown on his heavily lined face.

'He looks worse each time,' muttered Maerten one day, as we strained to lift a heavy barrel of shot from the ground in the hour before dusk.

'Hold your tongue,' I snapped, for fear of our master, although I could see that the youth spoke truth.

When he passed by us the old commander cut a haggard, desperate figure, while he observed preparations. Meanwhile Maerten and I panted like dogs from the day's toil, with another fifty slaves who had been picked off the benches. Our efforts were closely watched by Dimas and his wardens, the foremost of whom was Georg. He was a portly German from Mainz who was not inclined towards cruelty, although he could serve it out when required. In one hand he held his *bastinado* rod, which he had often used to whip our backs, as well as the soles of our feet.

'That Santa Cruz worries me,' he said, then tutted aloud. 'He looks like a walking corpse.'

Dimas snorted, then jerked his head at the stables which stood next to the long row of warehouses behind us. A newly arrived horseman could be seen walking towards them, leading a sweat-streaked stallion behind him and holding several letters in his free hand.

'One of many messengers from Madrid,' said the Portuguese overseer. 'Every day they bring new letters written by the king's own hand, urging the admiral to set sail for England in all haste.'

'That is most curious,' observed Georg drily, 'for is Philip not called the prudent king? Always slow to make decisions?'

'How would I know?' snarled Dimas, squinting mercilessly at a passing slave. 'He's not my king but my conqueror. He certainly wasn't slow to seize the crown of Portugal eight years ago, the greedy Habsburg pig!'

He spat on the ground when he said this, leaving us in no doubt as to his feelings towards his recent Spanish rulers.

'Not so loud,' hissed Georg, as he threw a nervous look over his shoulder, 'these Spaniards take God and king seriously.'

He had hardly spoken when Admiral Santa Cruz could be seen walking back towards us, surrounded by a coterie of naval officers which had almost doubled in number. Armed retainers also came into view, surrounding the lord admiral who was flanked another highborn dignitary we had not seen before. This personage was a slender youth who could not have been far beyond twenty years of age. He had a high forehead and was of average stature, wearing a neatly trimmed brown beard around a pale face tinged with roseate cheeks.

The young lord wore a suit of the finest white satin, his doublet and breeches cut in the Spanish fashion, with russet silk stockings raised over both knees. Yet the thing which struck me most about him were the gems on his fingers. They sparkled in the sunlight as he gestured foppishly, all the while addressing the weary-looking Santa Cruz. Chief among the fop's trinkets was a sizeable emerald on the fourth finger of his right hand, which dwarfed the other baubles in both size and beauty. A long silence lingered after the group had passed, until Dimas and Georg exchanged low whistles.

'Must be that whoreson prince,' remarked the Portuguese overseer.

A thoughtful pout appeared on his face, as he stretched a coil of his whip with both hands.

'Did you see the size of the emerald?' remarked Georg. 'It must be worth a king's ransom!'

'Two kings' ransoms!' replied Dimas, shaking his head in disbelief.

'Who on God's earth is that foppish whoreson?'

Dimas raised a hand at Georg, with it being his turn to look around him nervously.

'Don't shout, fool, do you want us both killed? That's the bleeding Prince of Ascoli you're calling a whoreson!'

The German slave warden's face became violet, and for a few moments he said nothing until Dimas spoke to him again.

'It's amazing the riches to be found in the Americas. When I am done with this Armada caper, I'll seek my fortune there next.'

'We'll be fortunate to see the end of this caper before the year is out,' replied Georg, as he calmly raised his rod to beat a slave who had stumbled to the ground in front of him. 'There are too many preparations still to be undertaken. And they say there are many other ships yet to arrive in port.'

Maerten produced a low groan upon hearing this, and for a moment I feared that Dimas might have heard him.

'So long as I get my share of the booty,' said the Portuguese overseer with a loud snort, 'I could not care less when we set sail.'

'Still,' said Georg, drawing his clanking keys from the thick belt around his stout belly, 'one has to wonder about the prophecy.'

'What prophecy?' asked Dimas, as we were rounded up and led back towards the hospital ship. 'The Regiomontanus one?'

'What else?' replied the German.

The overseer pulled a face.

'Just the stupid predictions of a long-dead astrologer! As if we hadn't enough gloomy Germans around as it is!'

Georg winced at the jibe as we made our way towards the pier.

'Astrologers from other nations have confirmed it too...'

Dimas ignored the remark and did not speak to Georg again until we were all chained back to our benches. When the overseer and his slave wardens were gone, Maerten turned towards me with a look of concern.

'What prophecy do they speak of?'

I was lost in my thoughts, pondering over the huge emerald ring we had seen earlier.

'A king's ransom,' I whispered beneath my breath, as I lay back on Maerten's chest, who in turn rested against the ship's timbers.

Then a loud grunt from Esteban silenced us for the rest of the evening, and Maerten had long drifted off to sleep as I kept thinking about the sheen from the lustrous emerald. The thought of it brought back dreams of the Americas, dreams which I had so often shared with Elsien. As the sea lapped against the side of the galley I quietly sobbed at her memory, feeling both dismayed and furious that I had not yet avenged her passing.

While I lay upon the foul-smelling rowing benches of the hospital ship, it hardly seemed possible that only two years had passed since I had been a soldier of some repute in the king's army, married to a woman of prized wit and beauty. The memory of her face haunted me late into the night, a memory which had been sparked off by the sight of the prince's gemstone.

As the summer months drew to an end, Costa bore us yet more gossip during the day and at dusk, telling us of the prophecy of Regiomontanus. The grim foretelling had long been the talk of taverns and inns across Christian Europe.

'It is said that a terrible disaster shall strike next year. Men fear that it is an evil portent which will seal the doom of the Grand Armada.'

'But it is already September,' lamented a strokesman ahead of us, 'and the sailing season is practically over. Which leaves us with no choice but to put to sea next year! What is to become of us?!'

'That I know not,' frowned the enslaved cook, as his face became clouded with despair, 'yet so many are said to be on the point of deserting the fleet that we may not ever set sail at all.'

'Would that I could join them,' howled another slave behind me.

'Were it not for this cursed chain on my ankle!'

As the months wore on, word often reached us of yet more sailors and soldiers who had deserted the gathering fleet. Autumn turned to winter and we had not yet set sail, and I watched each sundown through the oarhole with feelings of deep unease. On the one hand I feared that we might not set sail until the coming year, while also dreading the prospect of yet more days spent loading supplies and ordnance onto the galleys.

Despite the months of slavery, we had not yet become used to our rancid quarters, living with a constant acrid sourness in our mouth and nose. Each day we flinched at the sticky parts of the hold that touched our flesh, which often bled from our endless scratching at the infernal lice. At the turn of the year our delayed voyage meant that the festivities along the quay-side were muted. Yet the local Portuguese, ever keen to wallow in the misfortune of their Spanish masters, could be heard cat-calling and cheering throughout the city.

Rumour soon reached us that Santa Cruz had become an ever more desperate and lonelier figure, caught between hundreds of men abandoning his fleet and a king in Madrid who accused him of failure. Despite my miserable plight I almost pitied the aged hero of Lepanto, who was enduring the same unjust mistreatment that many other commanders who were loyal to the Crown had also suffered. In January, the old admiral ordered that men be pressed into service from nearby prisons and hospitals, also forcing enlistment upon crew members on merchant ships and the peasants in the fields around Lisbon.

When this was accomplished, the exhausted Santa Cruz ordered that the fleet set sail in early February. A few days later shocking news reached us, which brought all harbourside preparations to an abrupt end.

'Dead? What do you mean, dead?'

Dimas slapped his head and held his hands in his face.

'And I went and put all my savings into this fool's venture!'

Word had only just reached him that the lord admiral had been found dead in his bed. The first reports were that Santa Cruz had perished from exhaustion.

'They say the king had already ordered that he be relieved of his post,' said Costa, two days later, 'so at least he did not die heartbroken.'

'That's what you get for loyalty,' snarled a slave to our right, and I could not help but nod my head once in agreement.

All hell broke loose among the leaderless fleet in subsequent weeks, and we spent many a day huddled below decks in the rancid filth, shivering from cold and fear as brawls and scuffles raged along the docks.

The more powerful squadron commanders raided the ships of the less mighty ones for arms and provisions. Our own galley was also not spared from this mad plundering which ensued, with an armed band of Recalde's men forcefully boarding our own galley one night and taking all our cannons. Yet worse news was to follow the unexpected death of the lord admiral, when we learned the identity of his replacement.

'Who?' snarled Dimas, as Costa handed us the evening rations.

'Alonso Pérez de Guzmán y Sotomayor, 7th Duke of Medina Sidonia.'

'Never heard of him.'

'They say he was a childhood neighbour of the king,' said the German slave warden, 'and that he begged Philip to reconsider his appointment.'

'What a disaster,' sighed Dimas, and Georg raised an eyebrow at him, as if to remind him of the Regiomontanus prophecy.

The new lord admiral arrived in port a few weeks later, to be met by an absolute mess, what with some ships overly laden with guns, while others did not hold a single demi-culverin. It took three long months of meetings and inspections for the duke to sort out the whole mess, which also meant more back-breaking work for those of us below decks. Once again, we were led away from our benches, to carry the guns from some ships onto others. It also meant further delay to our voyage.

Despite being an inexperienced commander, the new admiral proved himself a leader of little hesitation. As we pushed and shoved the cannons up and down the wharves, we often sighted him in his black doublet and hose, studying the many ships in port with a group of high-ranking seamen around him.

'When will it end?' croaked Maerten, as we hauled yet another bronze cannon across the boards of the Santa Maria's main deck.

Little did we know that the worst of our labours had only just begun. It was only a few weeks after the new admiral's arrival that Dimas descended with a face like a thundercloud, holding his whip at the ready as his wardens unchained us from the benches to lead us back on land.

'What now?' asked Esteban, as he reluctantly got to his feet and followed Georg.

'Admiral's orders,' grunted the German, as we made our way out after him, 'he wants all of the ships careened and tallowed.'

'All of them?' exclaimed Esteban in fright, as he almost lost his footing upon the steps.

'All of them,' sighed Georg.

Some of the worst days of toil awaited us as the slaves of the Santa Maria de Visión were made to haul the galley sideways, by pulling ropes which were attached to the top of its masts. In this way, half of the bottom of its huge hull was exposed, with our next task being to clean it of all grasses, seaweed, worms, mould and barnacles. It was thankless, harsh work, with many slaves suffering cuts and grazes until we were then made to clean the other half of the hull.

At dusk we were led to the large row of warehouses we had previously seen near the stables. Once inside we were chained to the damp, flaking walls of our temporary quarters to succumb out of sheer exhaustion to a dreamless sleep. At dawn we were served our breakfast, before returning to the yards to clean our galley's hull. When this was accomplished, we were put to filling cauldrons with water and carrying them back to our careened ship, so that pitch could be melted and used to caulk the galley's seams before a coat of tallow was also applied.

Worse humiliation was to follow one morning in March, when Dimas and his wardens led us in chains towards our careened galley. We carried huge cauldrons in pairs, filled with seawater we had drawn from the quay. Along the way we passed a stall which served refreshments to the many sailors and troops who idled on land. My hair stood on end when a familiar voice was heard from it.

'There goes the Lynx of Haarlem, doing his bit for God and king!'

The cauldron's handle fell from my hands as I whirled about in a mad rage. Barely a few feet away from me, tankards in hand, stood Ramos. He was decked in fine livery and grinning foolishly as he raised one of the mugs towards me. Alongside him stood his henchmen Salva and Gabri, who also held mugs of wine. It was a most familiar scene I had seen all too often in the Netherlands, except that the murdered Cristó was missing, and de Andrés wore a wooden limb to replace the arm which I had destroyed for him in Seville, which curled at its end like a withered branch. The deadly threesome was surrounded by many ladies of fortune who each wore whimsical pouts as they waited upon the pleasure of their latest hirers.

'This drop of claret is just divine, Abelito,' exclaimed my old sergeant, as he mockingly held his cup up to me in a beringed hand. 'What a shame that you cannot also drink from it.'

At his words, a peal of raucous, forced laughter was heard from his two henchmen. It was quickly echoed aloud by the whores to please their clients, although they clearly had no idea what the merriment was all about.

'Why you sodomised, pig-humping bastards!' I snarled, stepping out of the slave line, and shaking my fist at them. 'Come here and mock me to my face if you have the courage!'

'In line you dog!' shouted Dimas behind me, then unfurled his whip and cracked it before me. 'What in Christ's name do you think you're doing?'

'Come back here, Abel,' hissed Maerten at my back, still holding the cauldron's handle as he beheld me in fear.

'Keep a rein on that ass!' howled Salva, with his face stretching unnaturally in different directions due to his spasm and his barely restrained giggling.

Ramos slapped the corporal on the back as they both shook with overly forced laughter. The sound of it had my bunched fists throbbing in hatred as I bit my lower lip until it bled. On his part, Gabri smiled at my torment with his mug held to his lips, until he lowered it and glowered at me with unmasked hatred.

'What are you glaring at?' I snapped, returning a grimace of my own. 'You can't even pull your hose on without the help of those two tosspots.'

A small vein throbbed at the side of Gabri's forehead as he took in my insult, before a lashing from my overseer seared my back with agony.

'Get back into line!'

The laughter from Ramos's party grew with each blow of Dimas's whip, leaving me to shield my face with outstretched arms as I hobbled towards Maerten to bear the cauldron once more.

'You might have cost me an arm, Santi,' called Gabri, 'but you'll pay for it dearly in coming days. One of those famous eyes perhaps, maybe your ears too. Our company has been charged with guarding this quayside, so I promise that we'll come pay you a nightly visit soon.'

'Come on then,' I shouted back at him, 'and do your worst! For there's nothing I hate more than idle threats.'

'All in good time,' he replied, resting his tankard on a bench and sliding his remaining hand behind the back of a red-headed strumpet. 'You'll understand that I first have some long-overdue priorities to attend to.'

'So long as she goes on top!'

Another crack of Dimas's whip silenced my baiting as I returned to the line. I scowled with rage as I lifted the cauldron once again, following the other slaves as we made our way towards the overturned galley of the Santa Maria de Visión. Throughout the day I bristled with a murderous fury, throwing myself at my tasks with renewed vigour as I sought to vent my hatred upon the wretched barnacles.

At night, we returned to the warehouse entirely worn out, yet there appeared to be no relief close at hand. For word soon reached us of the lord admiral's next order, which was to chop wood down from the trees around Lisbon to build tower castles for the fighting galleys. In the event we were not spared, despite us being the rowers of a hospital ship. Each morning we were led through the bustling streets of Lisbon towards the forests outside the city walls, where we cut down trees and sawed the ends off the fallen trunks.

We were worked hard during days that left us shuddering from toil, after which we staggered back to our crude lodgings at dusk, streaked with sweat and flecked with wood chips. After a time, I could not take the back-breaking work any longer, and Gabri's recent threat had also come to weigh heavily on my mind. One evening, after our ankles had been chained to the wall, Maerten and I traded low whispers.

'Could there be an existence more wretched?'

'No,' I replied as the other slaves snored heavily around us, amid the odd breaking of wind, 'but at least we are breathing some fresh air again.'

'Much good it will do us,' responded my brotherin-law, 'for we have another whole day in which to break our backs to-morrow.'

'True,' I replied wearily, as I fidgeted with the end of my blanket, 'unless we attempt escape.'

'Escape?' said Maerten, cocking a suspicious eyebrow and shaking his foot to rattle his ankle chain. 'Aren't you forgetting something?'

'We all wear chains in this life,' I replied. 'It doesn't mean that we shouldn't seek to break them.'

'So what are you thinking of doing Abel?' asked Maerten nervously. 'We are in enough trouble as it is, and the odds are hardly in our favour.'

I sighed aloud at his words, absently picking a small splinter out of my hand while I answered him.

'You of all people should know, Marti, that when I served in the Army of Flanders, the odds were nearly always against us. It is nothing new to me. Imagine being ordered to march for days through freezing rivers and dykes, with water up to your neck and not a scrap of food in your belly, to then besiege and take a town full of native defenders, armed to the teeth. Yet that was a venture that was all too common for us.'

I raised myself upon one arm and stared at him intently.

'You know how they say that a man who defends his home is worth ten invaders? Well, time and again we made light of that saying, both during sieges and on the field.'

Maerten appeared worried by my words, for he had not heard me talk at such length for months.

'And how does that help us now, Abel? What are you trying to say?'

'I am saying that the Spanish tercios are the best trained, most highly feared soldiers in the world. Some say the best troops the world has ever known. We are also renowned for our precision, for every last detail of the terrain is studied before any of our missions or engagements. I am not merely a galley slave but also a former soldier, and I have observed our surrounds for many days now. I have also formed a plan.'

The Brabantian's jaw hung open as I started to cough as loudly and as raggedly as I possibly could, until some of the slaves started to complain of the din. Which was, of course, the desired effect, so that I redoubled my efforts.

'Santi,' hissed Maerten worriedly, 'Santi, what is wrong with you? If this is an act...'

'Water!' I rasped, ignoring him as I continued to cough and produce as much foam as I could on my lips.

The stir around us only increased as some of the slaves shouted at me to keep silent, while others showed signs of genuine concern. Throughout I hawked up spittle like a fiend, now and again kicking my blanket for dramatic effect.

'Water,' I hissed, jerking my eyes back as Maerten held my face in his hands. 'Water!'

'What the devil is astir?' cried one of the wardens, entering the warehouse.

I could tell from his voice that it was the burly German, Georg, who entered our building, with a pair of other wardens at his back. My eyes began to roll as I shifted animatedly from side to side, and although I lost sight of him, I knew that he would be carrying a cudgel and his dreaded *bastinado* rod. Slaves drew away from it as he walked past, having found themselves at the end of it all too often. The hefty slave warden stopped a few feet from us, observing my movement with a concerned frown as he held his chin in one hand.

'Water,' I rasped, fearing that he might hesitate long enough to see through my act. 'Water!'

'Have you not heard him?' shouted Maerten. 'He wants water!'

'Fetch a skin,' said the German to one of his men, 'and the physician, Hurtado. Make haste.'

The warden ran off to do his bidding, as Georg took a step towards us.

'Don't get too close,' said his remaining man behind him, taking a step forward and seizing the German by the shoulder.

Georg shrugged off the warden's hand away, and his stride never faltered.

'This one cost us two hundred ducats,' he said. 'If something happens to him the master will have my head.'

He next pushed Maerten away after he knelt beside me, leaning his rod against the wall. The other warden slowly stepped behind him as he looked from side to side, nervously raising his cudgel and ready to strike out at the least suspicious movement. Meanwhile I continued to twist and turn beneath my flapping blanket, still coughing aloud and jerking my head up and down. The German seized my forelock and bent over towards me.

'Santiago?' he growled. 'Are you causing trouble again? If this is some kind of prank...'

I pounced at him, jabbing his eyes with two fingers. Georg threw his head back and clutched his face with a howl, which was just the moment I needed to smash my fist into his throat, grab the rod from the wall and spring to my feet. I quickly side-stepped a swing of the second warden's club and brought the birch down hard on his head. While he collapsed before me, I dropped to one knee and snatched up Georg's cudgel, then whacked it across the rasping German's face.

A tooth bounced at my feet as he fell over alongside the other dazed warden, so that both were lying at my feet in a daze. I did not spare them a second thought as I quickly un-did Georg's belt and yanked the keys off it. Each night I had counted the ones used to lock our chains to the walls, so that I already knew to use the seventh from the left. I shoved it into the hefty padlock which bound my foot iron, giving it a turn to unlock it and holding the eighth key on the bunch out to Maerten.

'Make haste if you're joining me.'

Around us the other slaves were already cheering aloud and rattling their chains, and as soon as Maerten unlocked his irons I cast the heavy bunch of keys to the outstretched hands ahead of us. I then turned to run towards the window at the other end of the warehouse.

'Guards!' roared an all-too-familiar voice to my left, and I saw Esteban shaking his fist at us before he resumed his cry to alert the soldiers outside.

'Where do we go?' said Maerten.

'Follow me,' I replied, 'and keep close.'

Moments later another warden's cry was heard behind us, but we were already through the window and making towards the stables across the docks, where distant clusters of seamen and soldiers could be seen gathered around low fires. It was the hour when they cooked their dinner in the dimming light of dusk, with the Portuguese locals casting dirty looks in their direction.

'After me,' I hissed, as we quickly came upon the stables.

A look through the doorway revealed that there was no one inside, and I led Maerten towards the horses, which I swiftly unhitched and saddled.

'We make for the open country,' I said, as we climbed upon the mounts and kicked our heels into their flanks. 'Keep to my tail, and do not stop until I say so.'

The horses made towards the quay at a canter, which became brisker as we spurred them on. The imposing Ribeira palace was put to our backs as we made for the western docks, with the shouting from slaves and wardens growing behind us. My heart leapt as our steeds gathered pace, and a low cheer was heard from Maerten as we made away from the warehouse where we had been kept captive. Suddenly a shadow appeared to our left, striking the front legs of Maerten's steed with the flat of a sword and sending the Brabantian flying from his saddle.

'Leaving so soon? We were just about to pay you a visit.'

My backward glance revealed the grinning presence of Gabriel de Andrés, with his curled wooden arm casting an eerie shadow across the warehouse wall. As he approached my fallen brotherin-law, I could also make out Ramos and Salva behind him, from the red sashes worn across their breastplates. Both men were yelling at the tops of their lungs, loud enough to alert every soldier along the quay.

'Flee!' cried Maerten from the ground, leaving me relieved to see that he had survived his fall. 'Just go!'

I whirled the horse around with a gasp of desperation, slamming my heels against its flanks again as I rode off towards the wharves. Yet it was all for nothing, since groups of soldiers had already gathered to block off my escape. With a low growl I resolved to at least go down fighting, and I rode upon a group of musketeers who were already ramming their balls down their guns, to fire at me if I broke through their ranks.

Their stern faces turned pallid as I thundered towards them, then flung myself upon the man closest to me. To the amazement of his comrades, I beat the musketeer senseless as my horse bolted, then snatched the glowing match-cord off his wrist and picked his gun off the ground. The men drew away from me as I blew hard upon the cord and wedged its end through the jaws of the serpentine. I then swivelled upon my heel and made out the distant figure of Gabri, who was shaking Maerten by the forelock as he kicked the Brabantian's side.

'Stop him!' shouted a guard, as a rumble of footsteps could be heard behind me.

'What's he aiming at?' asked another, since he could not believe the distance from which I was attempting the shot.

The entire quayside was already astir because of our escape, and my view of de Andrés would soon be obscured by the men who rushed towards him. I quickly raised my thumb in his direction to size up his form, then tilted the gun slightly forwards and jerked back the trigger. A slight plume of gun smoke arose from the pan before the shot was fired, which all but knocked me off my feet as I was covered in a billow of foul smoke.

When it cleared, I was elated to see Gabri upon his back, with Ramos and Salva running towards him. It was a joy that met with an abrupt end, when a musket butt crashed into the left side of my face. Strong arms then curled beneath my armpits after my tumble, with the moored galleys ahead of me spinning about as I was dragged back towards the warehouse. As my forehead scraped the ground, I could barely lift my head, nor cared to do so since I could not face what lay in store for me.

'And now for some real punishment,' I whispered to myself, then barely restrained a shudder as I spat out some blood.

VI

LISBON TO CORUNNA

16 April-20 June 1588

'How dare you!' roared Dimas, with his eyes about to burst out of his head. 'I'll skin you alive for this!'

Guards milled around us as the overseer screamed in my face, and my head dropped again for I had not the strength or spirit left to face him.

'Look at me when I talk to you!' he shrieked, seizing my forelock and raising my head. 'Tonight you'll wish you had never been born.'

I flinched slightly at his tirade, then thought to ask a question which nagged at me.

'Did I kill him?'

Dimas took a step away from me, seemingly aghast at my boldness.

'The man is mad,' he whispered, unable to resist a chuckle. 'I'll clean all the barnacles off the Santa Maria's hull with his back.'

'He is also a dead shot!' said one of the men holding me. 'I've never seen such a clean shot with a musket from that distance.'

'It matters not,' replied the overseer, 'he'll still clean the hull.'

'Move aside,' called a voice through the crowd, 'let the captain pass!'

Men scattered before the officer, who strode through the soldiers and guards that were pressed against us. I never stirred until his boots were in front of me, and when my forelock was pulled up again, I found myself face to face with a man I had not seen in almost three years, and who stared back at me in horror.

'Santiago?'

'Captain Fernández,' I uttered hoarsely.

'You're alive? Ramos said you were either captured or dead.'

'Never one to twist the truth,' I managed, as the captain frowned at my words.

'What happened to you?' he said, then released my forelock as my head fell forwards again.

'I will tell all,' I replied, 'given the opportunity.'

Fernández considered my reply for a few moments, then shouted at the men around him to move away, as the musketeers dropped me to the ground.

'Back to your posts!' he cried. 'The slaves have been recaptured. Back to your posts or you'll face charges!'

He then beckoned to his men to seize me and Maerten, and to lead us back to his quarters.

'But they are my property!' howled Dimas in disbelief, as his face became red in the growing dusk.

'It matters not,' replied the captain, 'I am tasked with the protection of this quayside, and I must make my own investigations.'

'What investigations, you Spanish oaf?' yelled the overseer. 'Have you never heard of two slaves attempting an escape before?'

Fernández drew himself to full height, looking impressive in his feathered helmet and the shining breastplate which was emblazoned with a red saltire. He then leant towards Dimas until their noses were almost touching.

'A Portuguese subject shall not teach me my business. Now begone before I have you arrested for contempt of a king's officer. And leave that Fleming behind you too.'

Dimas visibly glowered with rage, yet I was too dazed to smirk back at him before he turned around and trudged off to the warehouse, with his slave wardens behind him. The captain then returned his attentions to us, removing his mantle and hurling it over my shoulders. He also demanded that Maerten be wrapped in a cloak.

'It gets cold at this time of day,' he said, seizing me by the arm and walking towards another row of small warehouses further along the shipyards.

Ten of his men followed us, with two of them holding Maerten in a tight grasp. We were halfway towards his lodgings and walking beneath a starlit sky. I stared around me in the deepening dusk, marvelling at my narrow escape from Dimas's ire.

'Hey Captain!' shouted a familiar voice behind us, which left me trembling in Fernández's grasp.

We all turned to find Ramos approaching us, as he kept the pale-faced Gabri upon his feet with the help of Salva. The one-armed musketeer was holding his side, and I was dismayed to see that he wore a shirt of chain mail beneath his cloak, which had spared him a fatal injury.

'Captain!' yelled my former sergeant, with a look of outrage. 'That slave's gunshot broke Gabri's ribs! He must pay for this, Captain!'

Fernández beheld the three of them with a look that verged upon disgust, before he finally spoke.

'He's got a very good aim for a slave. Do you not recognise him?'

Ramos feigned surprise at his officer's words, then blinked at me for a few moments as a smile of incredulity was forced onto his face.

'Abelito?' he asked. 'Whatever happened to you?'

'You lying bastard,' said Maerten, still holding his side from the kicking he had received from Gabri.

The sergeant seemed taken aback by my brother-in-law's words, feigning indignation as he glared at the youth.

'You are one to hurl insults at me, heretic,' he growled, 'you who aided this murderer to rid me of one of my men!'

'And well rid of the vicious brute, too!' shouted Elsien's brother.

'Enough!' roared the captain, annoyed by the exchange. 'Get de Andrés onto the hospital ship while there is still some light left. Tell them I sent you.'

'Yes, Captain,' said Ramos reluctantly, then tottered off with his men towards the Santa Maria de Visión. As we walked to

Fernández's quarters, I could feel the sergeant's eyes on our backs every step of the way.

Upon reaching the other warehouses across the quay I could see that they had been converted into barracks for my old company. Some familiar faces loitered outside, playing cards and dice, and a few of the men saluted the captain as he wordlessly walked past them. Many stared at me and Maerten in curiosity, yet none seemed to recognise us although a fair few of them were known to me. We entered the leftmost part of the warehouse, which had been sectioned off for Fernández and some of the company's other officers. He briefly left us to fetch a carafe of wine, then asked us to follow him to one of the smaller campfires, where a few of the other officers were gathered.

An awkward silence hung over us as we sat crosslegged around the flames, sharing the wine after his guards had left us, save for the sergeant with drooping cheeks who I recognised as *El Perro*. At no point did Fernández request that we be bound or restrained, and on my part, I refrained from attempting any escape, due to the captain's trust in me and my respect for him. In any event I was still lightheaded and made drowsier by the wine, with my head throbbing from the musket blow I had received. Meanwhile the captain's features shone with decency in the glow of the fire, and I was awed by his presence until he finally addressed me.

'Tell me everything that happened Santi,' he said, 'without delay. From the day of the De Groote ambush near Willebroek. Leave nothing out.'

I took another long swig of wine, then took a deep breath and did as I was bidden. At one point during my account, I hesitated to speak, with Maerten sobbing softly while he recounted what had happened to his sister and father, following the imposition of the fire-tax by Ramos and his men.

'I am sorry to hear of her passing,' said the captain after a few moments, as he stared at the ground. 'She was a good woman. I tried to stop the men from burning the houses, even insisting that it not be done with people inside them. And I am ashamed to say that it all went unpunished by the sergeant-major. For the men were in a mutinous mood upon learning about the fall of Antwerp. It would not have happened under the Iron Duke's command.'

'The Iron Duke is long gone,' I said, then proceeded to tell him the rest of our tale.

At the end of my account there lingered an even longer silence, until at last Fernández spoke again.

'Then the rumours about the ensign were true. But what of Cristó? He was your comrade.'

'And do you think that I would kill someone without good reason?'

'No,' he said, looking at me once and then looking away again, 'no you would not. You are an honourable man, and I owe you my life twenty times over.'

He buried his face in his hands, seeming to grapple with a difficult decision until he spoke again.

'Tell me, which ship are you on?'

'The Santa Maria de Visión.'

'Ah, De Bartulo's ship.'

He went quiet once more, thinking to himself. Then his eyes slightly widened as he rose to his feet.

'I'll do what I can for you, Santi, although the Lord knows that you have not made things easier for yourself. The slaying of an ensign and a fellow soldier cannot be easily overlooked. You must stay here with your brother-in-law until I summon you again.'

He next beckoned to *El Perro*.

'Place a watch on these men,' said Fernández, 'until I send for them. No one is to approach them without my express order.'

The captain then bade us goodnight and walked back to his quarters. Meanwhile *El Perro* did what had been instructed of him, but not before he shared a few words with me.

'Santi,' he said, raising an eyebrow, 'we thought we had lost you. Ran afoul of that whoreson of Ramos, did you?'

He then sniggered to himself and left us to sleep beside the fire. We passed out from exhaustion, being merely grateful for having been spared a hiding, and for the chance to sleep in the open air beneath a starlit sky. At mid-morning the next day *El Perro* reappeared to rouse us from our slumber, then ordered that we follow him back to the ship.

'What's to become of us?' I asked, dreading our return to the galley.

'You will soon find out,' said the sergeant, as he led us onto the hospital ship and straight to De Bartulo's cabin.

After a half-hour spent waiting outside it, Fernández appeared through its opening door.

'I have done what I can for you,' he told us. 'A compromise of sorts has been reached, although you will not thank me for it. But I've at least spared you the rower's bench and earned you both a respite from the clutches of your enemies. It also buys me time to further intervene on your behalf. Until then, good luck, and try to keep out of trouble.'

He eyed me warily when he said this, and I didn't blink once as we tightly clasped each other's forearms.

'I will, Captain.'

He then made off with *El Perro* and the rest of his men, as two sailors took over from them and led us into the quarters of Vincenzo De Bartulo. The sea captain of the Santa Maria de Visión was seated behind his oaken desk. He was busy scrawling upon a piece of parchment and ignored us for a fair while until he finally raised his head.

'Ah, the famous fugitives,' he observed drily, in good Spanish.

We stood in silence, waiting for him to invite us to be seated on the stools before us. Yet the offer was never made, and he only beckoned us to take a step closer towards him. De Bartulo had a long, sallow face, which nested two cruel blue eyes, which stared like a wolf's at its helpless prey. A wisp of thinning black hair was combed back over his balding head, which gleamed with oil. Like the Armada's admiral, he was also dressed in an austere black doublet which rendered him even more intimidating.

'I don't want you on this ship,' he said, in a voice both curt and decisive.

A few moments of silence passed in which he seemed to be expecting an answer.

'Why?' I asked cautiously, uncertain where the discussion might go.

Captain De Bartulo sat back in his chair and crossed his legs. We stared at him across his desk, hoping that we had not landed ourselves in further trouble, and little suspecting the fate that awaited us.

'Where do I hail from, Santiago?' he asked.

'From Venice.'

'Correct, Santiago. And what is the Most Serene Republic famous for?'

'Glass?' offered Maerten, earning himself a swift glance of disdain.

'Canals?' I said, hoping to fare better.

De Bartulo sighed aloud, then raised a hand in front of him, as a signal for us to refrain from any more guesses.

'Espionage.' he said. 'Surely even a pair of wretches like yourselves know that Venice is famous for espionage? I need not remind you that all the powers in this world have excellent spies, but none match the ones in the pay of Venice. Yet we have come to be rivalled in this field by another plucky power, which like Venice is also threatened by much larger, more powerful enemies. For just like Venice, the kingdom of England's very existence hinges on learning things first. Hence the fame of the English queen's spymaster, Francis Walsingham.'

'What do you mean?' I said nervously.

The captain's chair creaked aloud as he sat back in it, locking his fingers as a frown appeared on his face.

'By now, English spies would have learned the cause of the commotion on the quayside last night. They would know that the Lynx of Haarlem, a man reviled by all heretics, is a galley slave upon the Santa Maria de Visión.'

'So you'll give us a little rowboat and set us free?'

Maerten and I shuddered as De Bartulo banged his desk with his fist, upsetting the maps and charts he had laid upon it. A high-pitched shriek was next heard from him, and he was doubled over with laughter for long moments, until he had recovered enough to speak.

'How can you be Spanish, Santiago? You have wonderful wit.'

'Well,' I said after a moment's hesitation, 'I was born and raised upon the island of Malta. Although that would not quite explain it.'

'Urgh, do not mention that place,' he said, pulling a face. 'with its pirating knights who prey on the Most Serene Republic. But, tell me, did you not also serve in Italy?'

'All Spanish soldiers serve their first two years in Italy,' I replied. 'At least they used to even after the army went to the dogs.'

'Ah, perhaps that explains it,' he said, 'but I think we digress. You know I cannot set you free. My overseer has shown me his documents of title, as well as the sentences condemning you both for murder.'

'False documents,' I replied, 'for I swear to you by the Madonna of Ontanar, that we never faced trial.'

De Bartulo tilted his head sideways and blinked slowly.

'Be that as it may, Santiago. I have not the time nor the will to review your claims of injustice. In fact, if I were you, I would stay your tongue and not breathe another word unless questioned. Unless, of course, you would rather return to the rowing bench...'

No sooner did he utter the threat than our backs went bolt upright and we became still as statues, giving him our full attention. A small smile grew upon the sea captain's face at our stiffening, before he spoke again in a severe tone.

'What do all sea captains fear most, Santiago?'

'Shareholders,' I replied.

'Correct,' he snapped, banging the desk again as his eyes widened, 'shareholders! As I said, I am Venetian, and like all good Venetians I hate Spain. Believe me when I tell you that I could not care less if every last Spanish whoreson in this fleet is killed on this expedition. But this ship must return home whole, or it will be my neck.'

I nodded my understanding despite the harshness of his words, still uncertain whether he was going anywhere with his talk, or if he was simply delighting in jerking my chain.

'Your old Captain Fernández has assured me that he has never met a man blessed with better eyesight than yours. Which is not hard to believe, for fame of your exploits has also reached Venice.'

'He is too kind,' I replied.

'Be that as it may,' cut in De Bartulo sharply, clearly not intending to make friends or exchange pleasantries, 'the fact remains that this ship's hull has twice been scraped since we have been loitering in Lisbon, and both times for naught, in my view. For my lookouts fled port during Christmas last year, their heads full of the cursed prophecies of Regiomontanus. Their replacements are said to be the best-sighted men among the crew, which must mean that the rest of us are as blind as bats.'

'You want me to be your lookout,' I said abruptly.

'Yes,' he said after a while, during which time he stared at me half suspiciously and half expectantly. 'I need a man who can watch the sea, and I could do worse than give you a try.'

His dire need was laid bare before me then, and since he was a Venetian I knew that he was not relieving me from the bench out of the kindness of his own heart. Yet the crow's nest was a place that was hated by everyone on board. It was commonly known that the role of a ship's lookout was only better than that of a galley slave.

'The crow's nest is hardly an improvement in fortunes,' I said aloud, thinking of the platform secured to the highest cross-beam on the main mast, where the ship's slightest movement left one feeling like he was being tossed in a tempest.

'You'll be spared the lash...' said De Bartulo, half hopefully.

His unexpected coyness left me feeling confident that I had half a chance, albeit quite small, to bargain.

'I accept,' I said, as his face lit up with hope, 'but on one condition.'

'You are hardly in a position to make demands...' he said.

'My brother-in-law must join me. I'll not abandon him to the mercy of Dimas.'

De Bartulo pulled a face.

'I can relieve the overseer of one slave, but two... it is simply not possible.'

'I need a man I can trust!' I exclaimed, seizing the end of his desk and shaking it hard. 'Am I never to sleep at all?'

The Venetian sea captain observed me in shock, then gestured to the sailors who seized us to relinquish their hold.

'Look Santiago,' he said at last, 'you cannot tell me that another man cannot keep watch as well as him.'

'With respect, Captain,' I replied, as the heavy hands of the sailors fell away from Maerten and me, 'you should hardly waste a good sailor up there, when an idle galley slave could do the job. The winds are slowly picking up and shall hardly abate any day soon.'

The sea captain twisted awkwardly in his seat and pursed his lips, then stared into space for a while before he finally replied to me.

'Tell me Santiago,' he said at last, 'are you truly famous for your shooting? Or did you cajole everyone into believing it?'

For the first time since Elsien's passing, a grin appeared on my face at his words, until my cheeks ached.

'Then we have a deal?'

'Yes,' he said with a sigh, resting his elbows on the desk in front of him and rubbing his face with his hands, 'but you can forget the rowboat.'

Maerten stared at me expectantly as the sailors led us away, hardly believing the miracle which had somehow spared us the murderous rage of Dimas and Esteban. While I also felt swept up by a flood of relief, a last call was heard behind us, causing our captors to pause in the doorway of the captain's cabin.

'Oh, and Santiago?'

I turned my head towards De Bartulo, who glared at me like Lucifer upon his throne, with his hands clasped tightly together.

'Surely even you know not to try and cross a Venetian. If you attempt escape you shall not find me merciful.'

With the stark warning delivered, his men shoved us out of the cabin, then ordered us up the rigging of the mainmast. One of the sailors followed us as we began our ascent towards the distant platform. We were already feeling sick before it was reached, hardly daring to look down for long at the quayside beneath us where the men had shrunk to the size of ants. No sooner had we climbed over the waist-high rails surrounding the wooden platform than we found it empty, save for a couple of blankets. There was also a stinking pisspot which was half full, and a small food basket which was bound to the Crow's Nest by a slender cord.

'Hold still,' snapped the sailor, as he climbed over beside us.

He then fell to one knee and drew a long chain from the knapsack upon his back, proceeding to pass it through two of the highest rails around us, and then binding its ends to our ankles using two padlocks. We stared on at the man in silence, while I resisted the temptation to seize him by the shirt and fling him towards the deck far below us. For five burly sailors could be seen staring up at us from the base of the mainmast, and there was no escape path open to us.

'There,' he exclaimed at last, as Maerten's ankle was also locked, 'you shouldn't get far with these! Now remember to yell 'stand clear' before you fling that pot's contents over, and the cook will call out twice daily to fill your food basket.'

So saying, the burly sailor climbed back over the rail, then made his way back down the rigging with his knapsack swinging against his shoulders, all the while whistling happily to himself.

'Stand clear,' I yelled when he was not yet halfway down, so that I caught the sudden look of dread on his upturned face.

I then emptied the pot's stale contents right over his head, so that they could not fail to spatter him. Peals of laughter could already be heard from the other sailors below who had already scattered, which also confirmed that my aim had been true.

'I can't believe it,' said Maerten as I flung the pot away and leant over the rail. 'We are finally spared that infernal stench.'

'Get some rest,' I said, as the sailor below us howled abuse at me and shook his fist, 'I'll take the first watch.'

Maerten gratefully took up the offer, curling up on the wooden platform and laying his head on his arms. Before long he was snoring lightly, jerking the chain at my feet as he tossed about. Its clank went ignored as I diverted my attentions from the bustling quayside ahead of me to the grand buildings upon the hills. I next turned to look past the ships behind us, towards the distant horizon which ran across the grey ocean.

It was a sweeping vista, and I knew that the New World lay beyond it. The thought reminded me of the prince's emerald ring we had seen on the quay, and also of Elsien's killing. My knuckles whitened as I clenched the edge of the rail, with a great rage growing inside me as ripples from the smallest of fishing boats caused us to rock wildly from side to side. I then reached in vain for the two wedding bands and the lock of blonde hair which had once hung from my neck.

'Curse you Ramos,' I muttered beneath my breath, 'I'll yet kill you, Salva and that skulking street cat Gabri. Not to mention that spying harlot of *La Lechera*.'

My hatred for them burned in my breast like a slow match, and I could hardly believe that de Andrés was receiving treatment on our very same galley. I looked down at the chain which bound me to Maerten, trying to think of a way in which I might release my bonds to go and seek out the devil below decks. Then the thought was slowly abandoned, as I was finally overcome by my first bout of sickness and quickly seized up the pisspot.

In the days that followed, our relief at having been spared the oar was soon replaced by despair at our new posting. For our sufferings from the whip were soon replaced by constant bouts of seasickness and frequent vomiting, even though our bellies were hardly ever full. At times we were so green in the face that we hesitated to lower the food basket, despite Costa's calls for it.

There were many long hours of tedious waiting, sitting in wretched isolation while the grand port city of Lisbon buzzed with the daily inflow of new imports and the Armada's ships behind us steadily grew in number. Sometimes our boredom was eased by the curious goings-on below us, like the time we saw a wealthy Florentine merchant descend from his brand-new brigantine, which was newly arrived in port. With his chest puffed out he showed off his craft to the Armada's commanders, only to howl in protest when they informed him that his craft had been impounded and would be joining the great fleet on its voyage to England.

On other days we sometimes found ourselves the objects of ridicule and abuse. Dimas would often point at us from below and howl insults along with the slave warden Georg, whose head was still bandaged from the trashing I had dealt him. The summer afternoons were long and stiflingly hot, leaving us with no choice but to sweat for long periods, as we shielded our heads and shoulders from the sun with our blankets.

It was a grim and lonely time. Maerten and I scarcely traded a word as we sat up in the cock, with only the winds and the birds for company. Eventually we found ourselves too tired to bother about men who jeered at us from below, where once we would have shouted abuse back at them. In time, we grew more used to the constant rocking of the galley, while the other galley slaves laboured in the yards before us. Brighter times were to follow when cries ran along the quay like wildfire, with men cheering and punching the air with joy when it was announced that the Armada's departure was imminent.

On April the twenty-fifth we could see the lord admiral carrying the blessed standard of the expedition across the *Plaza Mayor*. Medina-Sidonia took it to the Dominican convent, where it was said that he laid it on the altar as a token of his personal dedication. The banner was then passed among long lines of kneeling soldiers and sailors, who handed it to one another while the gathered friars read the Pope's absolution, which forgave the sins of all those who sailed on the most holy crusade. My blood boiled as the Latin words reached my ears.

'I can just imagine...' I growled as I grasped the railing tightly, 'I can just imagine those two hypocrites of Ramos and Salva kneeling there right now, feigning all piety and holy intentions to impress Captain Fernández.'

'Indeed,' replied Maerten between gritted teeth, 'that pair would almost leave you sympathising with the likes of Calvin and Luther.'

I could not bring myself to scold him for his words, and we stared on in silence as the hundreds of men rose to their feet, each waiting to give their confession to the priests who had gathered to offer the sacrament. While they waited, they received an address from the Archbishop of Lisbon, who warned them against blasphemous swearing and all other sins that were typical of soldiers and sailors. Above them flapped the banner of the blessed standard, with one side bearing the image of Christ crucified, and the other that of the Holy Virgin. Beneath it hung a scroll which bore the words of the psalmist:

Arise O Lord and vindicate thy cause.

On the ninth of May, we could make out soldiers searching the hold for any hidden women. It was always the last endeavour before ships left port.

'I can't believe it,' cried Maerten as we stared at them in disbelief, 'we are finally off to sea again!'

I nodded my head in muted understanding, staring below us as sailors made ready to cast off from the pier. Throughout I observed the movement of other ships in port, shouting their whereabouts to our crew. Before long a procession of priests made its way down to the wharves, with huge crowds gathered around them as some dignitary addressed those on board as the Armada readied to cast off. Great cheers and a salvo of cannon fire could be heard as the 130 ships made away from Lisbon.

'Get some sleep Abel,' said Maerten, tapping me on the shoulder, 'I'll rouse you at dusk.'

His offer was gratefully accepted, and I dropped to my knees and pulled my blankets over me. At first, I tossed and turned on the rough boards, for I could not help thinking of Ramos and Salva who had sold us into slavery. They were no doubt standing above decks somewhere, the wind filling their hair as they rubbed their hands at the thought of the rich booty they would soon secure upon invading England. My anger at these thoughts kept me tossing about in my sleep all the way to the Belém Tower.

'Northerly grows stronger!' cried Maerten to the sailors below.

I rose to one knee in bafflement, sighting the first white crests upon the growing waves ahead of us, which slowly grew with the gales as they rushed towards us, blocking our advance.

'Winter winds in spring?' I asked, then snatched the rail as the galley started to sway madly.

The oars of the many ships around us could be seen rising and falling, as the slaves were put to work to spur the Armada's progress. Yet in vain did the rowers labour, for hours later the galleys remained blown to a standstill, and I dared not think how much blood Dimas had squeezed from his whip far beneath us.

A sudden splash against my back had me turn around in fright, to find that Maerten had vomit sliding down his chin. It also dripped through the planks at our feet, before falling towards the ship's waist below. Cries of outrage were heard from a few of the sailors, whose misery at our stalled progress was further compounded by my brother-in-law's spew. Yet both Maerten and I had it worse than them, for the stink from his retching was to last well beyond the three weeks in which the cursed winds kept us stuck in the Tagus.

Meanwhile our time at the cross-beam appeared without end as we were forced back towards land. Often did I drift off from our hellish post, falling into a trance-like state in which I dreamt of my time spent among the van der Molens, gathered beside their hearth as Elsien's Aunt Margareta, a woman of fine bearing who always dressed in a fetching style, stood at her brother's shoulder as we sat around her. Her voice rose and fell like the ocean that surrounded us as she read the latest book Reynier had managed to obtain from his contacts to the south.

In our hopeless plight, the memories of Willebroek were a refuge for the mind, and I sometimes spoke of them to Maerten as we lay huddled alongside each other. In truth, galley life had been harder on him than it was on me, since my years as a soldier had seen me occupy worse quarters for longer periods. Yet months at the oar and in the crow's nest had dented Maerten's indomitable spirit, and he seemed overcome by a terrible dejection. Like me, he was reduced to a gaunt figure trussed in rower rags, with his blonde forelock hanging over his shoulder as he seemed to gaze into nothing.

'What is the matter, Marti?' I asked him one day. 'You are not yourself.'

His eyes seemed like blank holes of nothing, with his face ashen and cheeks sunken. My outspoken brother-in-law's lips seemed not to move when he replied with the faintest of whispers.

'I cannot go on like this, Abel. I cannot. Would that they had thrown me overboard, for I am spent.'

'Don't be a fool,' I growled. 'What of our revenge?'

'Revenge,' he uttered almost absently, then returned to staring at his feet, which were brown and stank of urine.

'Take heart,' I hissed, grabbing him by the shoulders and shaking him hard, 'do you think you're the first man to find yourself in this plight? Wherever it is you find yourself, you must fight every day that God gives!'

'Forgive me, Abel,' he said at last, with a hint of hope returning to his voice, 'yet it is hard to resist despair...'

'I know,' I replied, 'things cannot be much worse for us. Yet remember that we are at least free of the benches and the blackened flea-ridden sheepskins. Not to mention the muck underfoot.'

'True.'

'Then just do as I say,' I replied, 'and I'll do all I can to set us free again.'

'If only our fortunes would turn like the weather,' he said, and for once I welcomed his sarcasm, which hinted at his old self.

His words were also a portent of what was to come, and in the next hour the wind fully subsided.

'The gales are ended,' he said in disbelief, then laughed hysterically as he rose to his feet and cried out over the rail. 'The gales are ended! The gales are gone!'

'There see, brother,' I cried, slapping him on the back as cheers rose from below, 'you never know what the next hour might bring!'

Maerten nodded back at me with a faint smile. Meanwhile the galleys sailed on past the Rock of Lisbon in a two-line formation, making for Corunna. This journey towards the Spanish port met with little to no wind at all, although our progress was hellishly slow, to allow the huge Urcas to keep within sight of us. It was a fourteen-day slog along the coast of death, until Cape Finisterre was finally reached. To our shock this leg of our journey was again hindered by sudden tempests, which were as savage as they were unexpected. Yet further setback was encountered at Finisterre, where we were dismayed to receive only a half ration of water.

'What's this?' I yelled down at Costa, through a hoarse throat as dry as parchment.

We had been waiting to drink for nearly a whole day, and Maerten looked crushed by disappointment. Elsien's brother frowned as I took only a half sip of water from the bowl, then pushed it towards his charred lips so that he could have most of my ration. To his credit the youth tried to refuse it, only for me to remind him that I had grown up on the sun-blasted rock of Malta and was used to longer spells without water than a fair-skinned northerner like him.

'Admiral's orders,' shouted back Costa. 'It's been discovered that the fleet's water casks are defective.'

'What do you mean, defective?'

'I've seen it myself,' called the cook. 'Stinking green slime floating upon the surface.'

'Dishonest contractors,' I rasped with a shake of my head, being all too familiar with merchants who took advantage of the king's purse. 'That's what happens when things are done in haste.'

Word soon reached us that the lord admiral planned to obtain new water stores at Corunna. All of which made the port town a welcome sight as the Santa Maria dropped anchor under the stars. After we had eaten our dinner, I lay back against the rails and pulled my blanket up against me.

'Get some sleep,' said Maerten, who had rested for most of the afternoon and was ready for the night watch.

As I drifted off, my dreams were unexpectedly visited by Elsien. She wore her tight-fitting olive kirtle, which revealed the slight swelling at her belly. Alongside her stood Maerten, with his face filled with the flush of youth, and the quiet and timid Pieter. The three of them beheld me in awe, as they had always done, and I reached my hand out to them, only to find that it was suddenly only Elsien who stood before me. Her presence lingered with me like an uplifting radiance, her breath on my face as I found myself resting against the Empress tree in the nearby wood, with her leaning in closely towards me.

'We have each other Abel,' she whispered, 'for better or worse.'

'And what does that even mean,' I replied, 'in this cruel world?'

'It means no more than that,' she said, 'that we have each other.'

Her breath on my face seemed to grow stronger and stronger, and I stirred from the boards beneath me, waking to the sight of Maerten's flailing arms and the howls of men below.

'Not again!' I cried in disbelief, as Maerten tumbled towards me.

We were violently shoved towards the railings in front of us, missing them by a hair's breadth as our chain stiffened just in time.

'A terrible squall,' he cried as he landed against me, accidentally jabbing me with his elbow as he tried to seize the railing behind us, 'unleashed at midnight!'

I could see the waves rising and falling across the ocean, as we were flung from side to side like a puppeteer's dolls. All the while our hospital ship tossed herself at the open sea like a chained hound, while a screech rose above the din and the fracas beneath us.

'Man overboard!'

Amid the stricken howls across the galley, I gathered my wits as best I could, before I was hurled against the mainmast and left winded from the ensuing blow to the stomach. There followed a roar of my own when the chain at my ankle was pulled hard, with my side opened as it was scraped against jagged wood. I then caught sight of my brother-in-law, who lay limp and lifeless beside me.

'Marti!' I cried, as the galley threw us both backwards once more.

The blazing pain in my belly and side went ignored as I somehow seized the youth by his shoulder and dragged him towards me, then curled my other arm around a wooden railing which was as harsh as shark skin. Bodies could be seen flying about the decks below, thudding into one another as the other galleys also bobbed about recklessly. Blood warmed my cheek from Maerten's forehead as the whole world seemed to spring away from the harbour, only to do so again and again. My side throbbed in agony from it being torn open against the mainmast, with blood from my stomach wound warming my thigh as my forearm was rubbed raw against the rail, while I still clung to Maerten.

'The anchor! The anchor!' cried another below.

A cold dread seized me as our ship's lunges grew stronger. The cable to the galley's anchor had snapped, and our tossing and jolting increased as the ship was hurled about by the waves like a piece of driftwood. We were flung like hooked bait until mid-morning, and at the end of the storm I raised my head to peer around me in disbelief. I then threw my head sideways, as a fresh burst of spew flew over the edge of the platform.

'Aaaaaaaaaaaarggggh!' cried someone far below, yet I was too worn out to care.

When the discomfort in my stomach finally eased, I immediately turned my attentions to Maerten.

'Marti!' I gasped at the lifeless form in my arms, wiping the orange vomit off his face which was half blackened with dried blood from the gash in his head. 'Answer me, Marti!'

His eyelids fluttered but once before they fell shut again, but I could feel the warmth of his breath on my shoulder.

'Help!' I cried, looking around me in fear. 'Help! Help!'

Yet my cry had already been taken up by others along the deck, since countless sailors also required treatment or had comrades who had suffered grievous wounds. It was half a day until anyone paid us any heed, when the ship's bosun called up to us from below.

'Hey you up there! Can you see land?'

'Free us of this chain!' I called back. 'My companion is wounded!'

'All in good time,' he shouted, 'first tell us what you see.'

We argued back and forth until at last De Bartulo himself appeared, quickly ordering two souls to release us. The first splash of corpses could subsequently be heard, as dead slaves were brought up from the hold and flung into the sea by their wrists and ankles. At the sight of this I grabbed Maerten by the shoulders and shook him hard, as the two sailors slowly climbed up the rigging towards us.

VII

Vivero to Gravelines

20 June-12 August 1588

'Marti!' I hissed, slapping his face while I feared that he might also be hurled overboard, 'Marti! Marti!'

Several blows left his cheeks reddened, while below us another two limp bodies were cast into the sea. As one of the sailors' grunts was heard on the rigging, I almost abandoned hope. At long last, my brother-in-law's eyes finally fluttered, leaving me to haul him upright alongside me. I breathed a loud sigh of relief, as a tear dampened my cheek.

'I can't do this anymore, Abel,' he whispered.

'You must,' I snapped back at him beneath my breath 'Otherwise you'll be cast overboard. Be strong Marti!'

'Where are we?' he muttered at last, as he peered around us. 'The sea is grey for miles around.'

I suddenly realised that the storm had thrust us far out into the ocean. All that was left of the Armada was a handful of other galleys nearby, which sent pinnaces filled with their wounded towards us. When the sailors released us, we climbed back down the rigging towards the boards below, where we learned that five seamen had perished during the storm, with two slaves killed by oar blows. Meanwhile the remaining sails of the Santa Maria had already been raised as she slowly made her way back towards the Spanish coast.

The sailors were still shaking their heads in disbelief at the savagery of the storm, while they led Maerten and I down to the infirmary upon the middle deck. Upon reaching it we were met by a long ward lined with beds and rugs, where there lay twenty wounded men from other galleys, each awaiting treatment. The physicians were nowhere to be seen, as the burly barber surgeon dragged a wooden crate towards us and had us use it as a bench. One of his mates started cleaning Maerten's head with water.

'And what's wrong with you?' he snapped, casting me a dark look.

With a grimace I tried to remove a rag I had placed on my stomach wound, which had turned black from dried blood. The barber surgeon pulled a face before grabbing the end of the cloth and jerking it away from me, causing me to groan aloud.

'Stop your wailing,' grunted a voice from across the deck.

When I raised my head I was shocked to make out the sneering features of Gabri, who was still aboard our ship, recovering from the injury I had caused him. He lay on a palliasse past a few other mattresses, with his sheet pulled up to his chin while he observed everything that happened around him.

'Are you still here?' replied Maerten defiantly. 'It won't get you your arm back.'

A quiver of rage seemed to pass through de Andrés, yet he said nothing as we glared back at him. Meanwhile the barber surgeon picked up another rag and scrubbed the crusted blood off the edges of my open stomach wound. He next snatched up a needle and thread, causing me to squirm in my seat and groan aloud as he stitched it up.

When I turned my face away from my wound, I noticed the ship's physician Don Gaspar de Hurtado and his son Blas. The two men appeared from behind a curtain to our left, which sectioned off a corner of the ward which was reserved for their highborn patients. A bejewelled, pale hand could be glimpsed behind them, dangling over a bedstead. On its fourth finger, I made out the sizeable emerald again, and I sat in silence, spellbound by its gleam and the value which it possessed.

'Will he mend?' called a cocksure voice to the Hurtados.

Both father and son turned to face a pimpled young man who also stepped out from behind the curtain, and who wore a satin garb like his master, the Prince of Ascoli.

'But a bit more bloodletting, sire,' said the elder physician to the stripling, 'and the prince shall soon recover.'

'Are you certain?' asked the knave, turning to face the invalid nobleman behind him.

'Have faith in the art of healing,' said the younger physician, 'for my father has rescued many of high birth.'

The pimpled knave nodded hesitantly, then stepped back behind the curtain which was drawn sideways. It instantly blocked the distant sparkle of the emerald, a sight which left me feeling awed. On an impulse, I looked at Gabri, and my stare became locked with his black, beady eyes. In that instant, I knew that he would also have seen the ring, and would no doubt be craving it. The view of his face was obscured as my eyes closed when another suture was roughly pulled through my flesh. The stinging jab of the needle caused me to unleash a furious oath, which I had learned as a lad upon the wharves of Malta.

'Holy Host of the Madonna!'

'Keep silent you soft popinjay,' snapped the surgeon, 'we've not heard a peep out of your friend here, and the needle's already gone through his forehead three times.'

When I opened my eyes again, I was surprised to find Don Gaspar de Hurtado and his son Blas standing before me. Their faces were as austere as a statue's as they studied me closely, with the younger Blas staring at me intently and his grey-haired father possessed of a worldlier and calmer air.

'A very curious accent for a slave,' remarked Don Gaspar drily.

'What is your name, slave?'

'What's it to you?' I snapped, only to earn a smack in the back of the head from one of the sailors who guarded us.

'Watch your manners scum! And answer Don Hurtado's question!'

'I am Abelardo de Santiago,' I replied since my true identity had already been discovered.

'The Lynx of Haarlem,' shouted Gabri mockingly from his bed. 'Who is also known to shoot his own comrades!'

Don Gaspar's jaw dropped as he raised his eyebrows.

'The galley slave who attempted an escape? I heard you were once a famous marksman in Flanders. What was your crime, slave?'

I met his stare, providing my response in as solemn and truthful a tone as I could manage.

'I am innocent, sire. I was press-ganged into service.'

For a while none spoke. The elder Hurtado appeared to mull over my declaration for a few moments, causing me to momentarily hope for his intervention on my behalf. Then his stoic expression broke into a dismissive grin when he addressed me again.

'That's what they all say.'

Peals of laughter erupted around me, with Gabri doing his best to cackle in a higher pitch than everyone else. I glowered back at the grinning physician, then gritted my teeth and flinched when the needle was pushed through my flesh again. A hoarse coughing was then heard from behind the curtain, and with a swirl of their cloaks the Hurtados hurried off to attend to their illustrious patient. Following this episode, Maerten and I largely sat in silence while our wounds were stitched together, after which Maerten and I were led back above decks and ordered to return to the cock.

'Until our next meeting, Santi', yelled Gabri, and we exchanged a last death stare, while I shielded my stitched-up wound with an outstretched arm from the burly sailors.

'Will they not allow us time to recover?' asked Maerten.

'Move along,' said one of the two burly sailors behind us, 'I've other more important things to do.'

We then found ourselves returned to the platform, where we were chained again before the two sailors left us. Meanwhile our galley sailed back towards the coast, until I sighted ten ships under the command of the famous Don Alonso de Leiva. After joining with his force, we made for the port of Vivero, where urgent repairs on the ships were carried out as we rejoined the main fleet at Corunna.

Once again, the ships had to be careened, caulked and tallowed. Carpenters were tasked with restoring the remaining damage as slaves were led out into the sun to haul at the halyards. In the following days, many stories were traded about the incredible misadventures endured by other ships. Some were said to have blown as far as the English coast, where they caught sight of the English fleet. We were all amazed by this incredible story, yet the following days held another surprise in store. I had barely stirred towards noon to take over from Maerten when sailors were heard shouting in outrage below us.

'Where is it? Who has it?'

'What is going on down there?' I asked in bafflement.

The scenes of tumult below us continued until De Bartulo emerged from his cabin to address the entire crew. To his right stood the pale-faced Prince of Ascoli and, despite the height of our perch, we could tell that the young nobleman looked ill at ease.

'Be it known,' shouted De Bartulo, 'that a ring of the highest material and sentimental value has been found missing. It belongs to his esteemed Lordship, the Prince of Ascoli. Whoever has taken it should surrender it forthwith, upon pain of death.'

None stepped forward as the sailors stared back at him, until the captain ordered that a search of the whole ship be conducted. De Bartulo's men spent two whole days combing every inch of the galley and searching the vestments and possessions of every last man, with sailors even climbing up to the crow's nest to search our clothes. Yet it was all in vain, as was the violent interrogation of sailors of ill repute. Finally, the stir ended when the prince himself reappeared on deck, addressing all those present.

'The ring is an important and treasured heirloom of my house. A precious gift from my beloved mother. I entreat any who have it or possess knowledge of its whereabouts to request an audience with me. I shall withhold all knowledge told to me in confidence and will bestow a reward of ten thousand ducats upon any soul who helps me to locate its whereabouts.'

Maerten sucked air through his teeth at the mention of the sum, which caused a commotion and clamour across the main deck. I stared down in disbelief as the prince made to disembark from our galley, to board a pinnace which would return him to the admiral's flagship.

'Ten thousand ducats,' I gasped, 'just imagine what you could do with ten thousand ducats.'

'Build a road through the sea towards the New World,' said Maerten.

I shook my head in disbelief, then felt a fleeting unease at the thought of Gabri in the infirmary.

'Somehow, I think I know who's behind this,' I said, and Maerten's eyes narrowed beneath the stitching upon his forehead as he stared back at me askance. Upon realising what I meant he nodded his head slowly.

'Nothing would surprise me less.'

We spent the following days in port beneath our blankets as the sun beat down on us. Our spirits rose when we were treated to fresh meat and vegetables which had been bought from the ports of Biscay. When all damage to the fleet had finally been repaired, we were blessed by a brisk southerly which filled our sails. As the huge topsail swelled beneath us, the Tower of Hercules soon vanished to our backs as we stood alongside each other, holding the highest rail as our forelocks flapped in the breeze.

Upon reaching the ocean I realised that another month had been wasted in the port of Corunna. Rumour also reached us that during that time the admiral had done all he could to persuade the king to call off our venture. This counsel had of course fallen upon deaf ears, leaving the Armada to embark on the final leg of its journey to Calais. Throughout the first four days at sea the fair breeze hurried us along to our end. Yet we travelled north with shortened sail, to allow the enormous Urcas to keep up with us.

'Curse those slugs,' said Maerten behind me. 'Without them we would have already reached the English Channel.'

By the fifth day of our voyage, we were almost past the westernmost tip of France, when the wind dropped until noon. Blinding storms raged out of the north once more, putting us through merry hell again until they subsided. When the squalls finally died down, the seams of our galleys were badly strained, so that the admiral allowed all badly leaking vessels to retire. Only a single ship took up his offer, being forced to withdraw from the expedition since she was steadily sinking in the open sea.

I envied the galley's crew as she straggled back to a friendly port, due to my concern about what lay in store for us, and my disquiet only grew further when we at last entered the English Channel and sighted the enemy coast. That night, huge waves tossed the Armada about, as yet another fierce tempest plagued us until the following day. When the freakish elements subsided, it was discovered that no lives had been lost upon our ship, although she had once more been left stranded from the main fleet.

Our long-suffering Santa Maria de Visión was next met with a stiff breeze and calming seas, which allowed her to reach the regathering Armada. All the ships were accounted for, except for four vessels which had been lost during the storm. We waited for them in vain off the coast of England and, after a day of dallying, the admiral ordered that we sail on up the Channel. The squadron of the Levant was placed in the fleet's vanguard, among those ships which would be first to engage in any conflict with the enemy. Preparations for the inevitable clash were by now in place, and a blanket of silence fell across the decks below.

'They're lighting the beacons!' I called down later that day, at the sight of the glimmer that was spreading all along the English coast.

'This will be my first sea battle,' whispered Maerten to me. 'I'm almost excited.'

'There's nothing exciting about battle,' I replied, 'be it land or sea.'

Our ears pricked up the next morning when we heard that we were windward of an English squadron. Loud cries were heard below us, as men readied themselves to grapple with the enemy and trade fire and steel. As the first shots were exchanged, I marvelled at the speed of the English ships which assaulted us. For they were smaller than ours, and able to sail closer to the wind. There followed a short but fierce encounter, with the Santa Maria avoiding the brunt of the exchange with the English ships. During this skirmish two cannonballs hit the side of our galley, with each sounding like the sickening crash of a battering ram.

The English weathered our fire before they changed tack, swiftly sliding past us without appearing to have taken any damage. Rumour soon swept across the ship that the speed of the enemy's movement had greatly alarmed our commanders, who had expected both sides to grapple and board. Men muttered that the king had sent us on a fool's errand, for our galleys could not hook ships which darted past us like the wind.

Not even then did we suspect the amount of misery that would soon be inflicted on us. For in those days Spain was still arrogant and cocky, having tasted precious little of defeat. Barely a decade had passed since she had broken Turkish dominance in the Mediterranean and reclaimed those states in the Spanish Netherlands which had been seized by the heretic. So at the admiral's signal gun, each of the Armada's ships swiftly reformed into a half-moon formation, ready and bristling for battle. Our galley was placed in the crescent's left wing with the rest of the Levant squadron, with the fleet's strongest ships kept to the tips of Spain's imposing naval force.

An English assault followed not long thereafter, with the enemy's attack led by their own admiral's flagship. Several broadsides were traded, causing those below us to pray and curse in different tongues. Amid the clouds of gun smoke a shudder ran through me when I saw an English ship slip swiftly through two Spanish galleys, all the while unleashing an incredible amount of cannon fire. By the time the Spanish galleys had turned towards her another two enemy ships had slid by from out of nowhere, also peppering our ships with shot.

'An incredible sight,' I muttered in stunned disbelief.

'What is?' exclaimed Maerten.

'They have no intention of grappling with us,' I said with grudging admiration, for I could see that not a single enemy sailor carried a hook to fling at our ships. 'The English are not fighting in the usual manner.'

I looked from one enemy craft to another, each of which was swifter than any Spanish galley, and carried more cannons.

'They are relying only on their guns,' I whispered in fascination as their strategy became clearer to me.

Our galleys' oars were soon striking the sea, as our squadron sought in vain to grapple with the enemy. For the whole morning, the two fleets traded fire as our ships tried to close in on the English, only for the enemy's vessels to elude us with the grace of one of our own bullfighters back home. Each time their ships delivered a fierce round of cannon shot and, when the English fleet at last broke away from us, our frustrated admiral ordered that we give them the chase.

We advanced upon the devils in columns, but our foes easily kept their distance while firing the odd broadside. After three hours of toil, Medina-Sidonia called an end to our pointless pursuit. That day our fleet had at least been fortunate, since the enemy's shot had not yet caused serious damage, and only two of their balls had struck the same foremast. Finding himself disgusted and alarmed by the enemy's refusal to engage, the admiral abandoned the fight to lead us up the Channel instead.

Two more ships were damaged along the way. One lost its bowsprit, and a ship named the San Salvador erupted when her stores of powder inexplicably caught fire. The maimed and burned among her crew were transferred to another hospital ship, with the San Salvador left behind with a galleon and four light pinnaces which tried to pass her a cable. Her doom was soon announced by the firing of English guns in the darkness behind us, leaving the other Spanish vessels with no choice but to abandon her and rejoin the main fleet.

Thereafter we made for Calais, with our journey extended by four days due to four more sharp encounters with the enemy fleet. Each of these was but a re-enactment of our first scrap, with the English firing their guns at us from a distance while we sought to grapple with them. During one encounter, the admiral even ordered that our sails be struck to allow the enemy to board us. Even then the heretics refused to engage, instead steering away, and seeking to scatter our shape with their distant gunfire.

After these passing skirmishes, Medina-Sidonia discovered that he had lost close to 170 men, with over 200 wounded passed along to his hospital ships. Howls of suffering could be heard from the main deck, but the admiral had not yet lost a single ship in battle. Under his guidance the Armada approached the French coast in its half-moon shape, a formation which it had always kept in the Channel.

Our journey ended beneath the cliffs of Calais, as the fleet stood to anchor. The men's subsequent relief was soon to be replaced by astonishment, when we learned that the king's orders had been for us to collect Spanish veterans of the Army of Flanders who were supposedly marching on Calais. The Armada was to then ferry these seasoned veterans towards the English coast, where they would in turn launch an invasion. Meanwhile the enemy fleet had anchored a culverin shot away from us, observing us silently as we waited for the Spanish troops to turn up.

'I cannot understand,' said Maerten, 'how we are to collect men without anchoring in a deep-water harbour.'

'Very slowly,' was my grudging reply.

These words were not worth the breath we had wasted to utter them, for the soldiers never appeared at the place of appointment. What did surface, however, were growing rumours of the enemy's intention to use fireships. This hearsay only grew in intensity, with some also mentioning the satanic Federigo Giambelli, the Italian engineer who had built the infamous floating hellburner which had claimed a thousand Spanish lives at the siege of Antwerp but three years earlier. That night my hair stood on end when I saw eight flames in the distance, with each of them slowly growing in size.

'Fireships!' I cried, waking the slumbering Maerten who tossed and turned beside me. 'Fireships!'

My cry was instantly taken up by other lookouts on the other galleys.

'Hellburners! Hellburners! The Giambelli rumours were true!'

Maerten shoved me aside as he hauled himself up against the railing, fearfully scouring the sea ahead of us. Out of the north eight vessels blazed wickedly beneath the light of the moon as they bore down upon us with a startling brightness. Every man on the Armada was soon filled with the fear of God, with a frenzy claiming the fleet at the sight of these flaming vessels. All order was lost as anchor cables were cut and the Armada's ships ran before the wind. We soon found ourselves far out to sea just within sight of the coast, and as her crew members recovered their breath, our hospital ship tarried for a fair while until the distant shadow of a warship could be seen gliding past us.

'Enemy to starboard!' I howled, as a withering volley of cannon fire was unleashed by the English.

The wooden platform beneath our feet shuddered as it was struck by a ball, which left us falling over.

'Abel!' cried Maerten over the clank of our chain, as I slowly rose to my feet to see if the ship had grappled with us.

Yet she was already vanishing from sight towards the distant firing of cannons, with the ripples caused by her passing making our ship swing madly from side to side.

'Double-dyed cowards!' roared a soldier below us, with his grappling hook held in his hands. 'Why will they not engage?!'

I raised myself on all fours and stared after the English warship, grateful that she had left us behind to seek other prey.

'She heads back into the thick of it!' I shouted, then made out a small pinnace gliding at speed towards us.

'Pinnace to port!' I howled to the men below, who each cast me an upward glance before they ran to the galley's left side.

'There it is!' cried one of them, gesturing wildly as the boat slid closer into view.

'Admiral's colours!' I shouted again.

As it drew nearer, I could see Captain De Bartulo's guards below, shoving sailors aside with their elbows as they also hurried towards the port side.

'Make way for the captain,' they shouted, 'make way!'

De Bartulo approached the gunwale, and I could make out his air of discomfort from all the way up near the cross-beam. He looked cautiously over the side of his galley, calling out to the officer who stood upon the prow of the messenger boat, with his hands upon his hips.

'What orders from the admiral?' called our Venetian sea captain.

His voice sounded hesitant and almost sheepish, for he knew that he had cut the anchor's cable without receiving any express order to do so and had not yet made any effort to return his ship to her post.

'I'll tell you what orders!' barked the messenger. 'Who told you to skitter away like a floating turd? The lord admiral's command was for us to slip the cable and then return to anchorage. Now rally to the flagship at once! She's at Gravelines, and there are many who are already wounded!'

'At once, sire!' cried De Bartulo, as he turned towards his crew and roared at them to attend to their tasks.

In the distance, we could make out the solitary galley of the admiral's Santa Maria flagship, locked in a vicious crossfire with the English ships which swept past her like swift sword strokes, each unleashing a terrific fusillade.

'So we are heading back into the thick of it?' said Maerten.

'Yes, it will not be pretty.'

'How can you be so sure?'

I sighed wearily at the shakiness in his voice, being loath to share my thoughts as we approached the raging sea battle. Other Spanish galleys had also returned to the fray, unleashing violent cannonades of their own as they neared the English vessels, which slipped away from them with ease.

'I've not seen a sea battle like this before,' I said.

'Not even Lepanto?'

'No. Lepanto was the usual grapple-and-board affair, so that we were practically fighting on land. Yet the English are relying solely on their guns and will not engage. It is a wise tactic, one which may spell our doom.'

Maerten observed the ships' movements at my words, nodding his head in silent agreement as we drew nearer to the vicious conflict.

'It is as you say,' he whispered, 'they will not engage.'

'And they are closer to their powder stores,' I added, 'which means that this fight is only going to go one way.'

I then turned around to inspect the ocean behind us, swearing a loud oath when I saw two ships sailing towards us at speed.

'Enemy to aft!' I howled below. 'Enemy to aft!'

Instantly the soldiers beneath us ran to the galley stern, holding heavy grappling hooks and brandishing their swords and muskets. They waited expectantly for the English galleys to sail alongside us, yet their hurled hooks only met with thin air. Once again, the vessels steered well away from us, and the usual puffs of smoke appeared along their sides amid a deafening thunder of cannons.

When this first volley was fired, another broadside was suffered to starboard, where the second vessel sailed by and unleashed a withering volley of its own. Beneath us men screamed as balls and canisters ripped across the decks, with another missile thundering into the mainmast and flinging us both to our knees. Once again, our craft swayed violently following the swift passing of the enemy craft, so that it was all I could do not to retch over the railing.

'Cowards!' shrieked De Bartulo beneath us, as he shook his fist at the two vessels which disappeared once more into the surrounding darkness. 'Why will you not fight like men?!'

Maerten grunted with effort as he pushed himself to his feet, to a low rattle of his leg iron. I slowly took his hand as he hauled me up onto my legs.

'We must escape,' I said.

'What? And what of your oath to the captain?'

'Captain be hanged!' I snapped. 'We have already suffered so much misfortune and setback – do you think one broken oath will be our undoing? One taken under duress, no less!'

'So how do we do it?'

I looked over the edge of the railing, going through the makeshift plan of escape which had formed in my head.

'When we free ourselves of this chain, we need to climb down the rigging. Once we reach the confusion which reigns on deck, we must cut that skiff loose and hurl it overboard, then row with all our strength towards Calais.'

When I finished speaking, I could see that Maerten was staring back at me with a doubtful frown.

'As easy as that, Abel? And how do we break free of this chain?'

'I do not know,' I replied in dismay, then dropped to one knee to examine the shackles which bound the iron to our ankles.

Years spent plundering and pillaging towns in haste made most Spanish soldiers experts at picking the locks to chests and strong doors. My decades of service in the Army of Flanders had rendered me something of an authority on the practice.

'They are common enough locks,' I muttered, as my fingers passed over the rough keyholes, 'yet we need something with which to pick them. It must be thin yet strong.'

'Alas,' cried Maerten, 'we have nothing of the sort up here. I doubt that the spoon we stole is strong enough.'

'It's our best hope,' I said drily, holding my hand out, 'give it to me.'

My brother-in-law reached into his tunic and drew out the pewter, which he passed to me. I used it to tease the spring barbs inside the lock, yet each time I applied the slightest strength to twist it, the spoon would start to bend all too easily.

'Curse it,' I said angrily, 'it is of no use.'

'Down Abel!' cried Maerten, and countless cannon blasts filled our ears when he fell on top of me, with a hail of shot showering the railings of the platform.

'They are taking aim at us!' exclaimed my companion in fright. 'It seems De Bartulo spoke true when he said that they knew who you were.'

'Perhaps,' I replied, 'yet 'tis normal enough practice to seek to blind a ship's eyes in battle.'

'Hey, you two,' yelled a sailor beneath us, 'I saw that coming before you did!'

'Stay your tongue!' I called back, 'for we are under fire here too! The ship sneaked upon us from out of nowhere! And yet even now another approaches to port!'

The sailor cried my warning to his fellows before he returned to his duties, then hauled at a halyard while I looked around us in fear. The main deck had been spattered with cannon fire so that dead or wounded men lay everywhere. Some of the injured souls were led down to the infirmary by the few who could spare the effort, and the resounding gunfire grew as we reached other Spanish galleys. Other returning ships joined our number as we made for Gravelines and the succour of the admiral's flagship.

The English had not yet engaged in the usual fashion. Each of their ships still resorted to cannon fire while the larger Spanish galleons sought in vain to throw hooks at them while readying for hand-to-hand combat. Constant fire was traded by cannons and musketeers on both sides, yet the swifter, smaller English vessels were having the better of the exchanges.

'Enemy to stern!' shouted Maerten behind me, and again we cast ourselves upon our faces as more musket fire spattered the wood around us.

When my eyes reopened, I saw that the sides of the mast below us had been shredded by canisters and shot. In that moment I noticed the large splinters which jutted out awkwardly from the end of the damaged wood, and I slowly stood to my feet with another design having formed in my head.

'What wood do you think the mast is made of,' I whispered to my brother-in-law.

'Cedar,' he said, 'definitely cedar.'

'Move this way,' I said, and he stepped over towards me, allowing me the greatest length of chain possible as I climbed over the railing and onto the rigging below our platform.

I desperately reached for a large splinter of wood which was but a few inches away from my fingers.

'Can you move closer?' I called to him.

'No,' he said, 'I cannot.'

I grunted aloud in annoyance, fearing that I might soon be spotted by one of the men below, or slaughtered by shot. A low curse left my lips, when I noticed that the wooden railing in front of him was riddled with holes from all the fire we had endured.

'Push the railing!' I called to him. 'Hard!'

He was going to question me as always, then noted the edge in my voice and did as he was told. As he kept pushing at the railing it slowly broke in two, so that our chain slipped through the crack, allowing me to slide down a little further. I sighed with relief as I clutched the splinter and wrested it free of the mast. It was about the length of a dagger, and I shoved it between my teeth. I was also reassured by its strength as I bit down on it, climbing back towards Maerten.

'Did anyone see me?' I gasped, as I drew the wood from my mouth.

'We'd have heard about it if they did,' he replied.

'True,' I said, then set upon the lock with the piece of wood, which did not bend as easily as the spoon.

Long minutes passed in which I at times despaired of the task at hand, yet at last a spring could be felt moving sideways, as the shackle was undone, leaving the chain to fall away from my ankle. The knowledge gained from the first picking allowed the second lock to be sprung more easily, so that Maerten was almost chuckling when he raised his scarred ankle before him. Then a look of despair overcame him when another English ship could be seen gliding towards my back.

'Enemy to starboard!' I cried, yet it was no use.

Ships without count had gathered around us as we veered close to the flagship, each unleashing one broadside after another and casting a flickering red glow upon the hills behind us. A mad melee of panicked and stricken men could be seen below, with all semblance of order gone as men either fired at the passing ships or helped the wounded to the deck below.

'Follow me,' I said, braving the wild lurch of our ship as I stepped onto the lowest railing and reached out for the rigging alongside it.

'Wait!' said Maerten in dismay, pointing to the shredded rigging further below us, which made any climbing impossible.

For a moment, the sight left me distraught, when I remembered the cord used to pass down the food basket. I hauled myself back onto the platform and snatched it up, then slowly passed it down until it was bouncing against the foot of the mast. Our actions had so far gone completely unnoticed, with the rest of the crew staring in dread across the water or running to and fro to follow their orders.

'Now's our chance.'

I swiftly slid down the cord, feeling relieved that it was strong enough to hold me. I was over halfway down when Maerten also decided to follow suit, leaving me to fear that the thin rope might snap with our combined weight. Yet fortunately the months at sea had rendered us lean and bony, so that no mishap was met until my feet reached the boards at the foot of the mainmast. It was then that I spotted the small mound of dead men, upon which there lay a wounded man holding his entrails.

'A surgeon,' he gasped, 'a surgeon I beg you!'

I ran over towards him, ignoring the stink of ordure as I took his dagger and musket and ran back towards Maerten. Yet another broadside from an English ship had men flinging themselves to the boards as the side of our galley was peppered with repeated cannon fire. When she had passed, a sailor's screech of frustration could be heard from beyond the mizzenmast.

'Where the hell are our damned lookouts?!'

Despite the cry we lay low, while I seized my forelock and hacked at it with the wounded man's dagger.

'What are you doing, Abel?' asked Maerten in bafflement.

'We must rid ourselves of these rowers' forelocks if we are to make it far on land.'

'Oh,' he replied, and I seized his tuft of hair and sheared it off with the edge of the blade.

No sooner was it cut off than I returned to picking the bodies of the dead and wounded. I sliced the clasps on the sides of two breastplates with my knife and we pulled them over our heads, then hauled on stolen boots and donned a pair of helmets. The sea battle still raged around us, as we ran towards the back of the galley. The hospital ship was left to drift alongside the other Spanish warships so that she could pick up their wounded, and her progress towards the nearby cliffs had almost come to a standstill.

We sidestepped panicked sailors as we made towards the rowboat at the back of our ship. None gave us a second's notice as they hurried to their tasks, fearful of their Venetian captain's ire. When we reached the boat, I quickly set about cutting it loose from the galley while Maerten hurried off to find a knife of his own. At the sight of another enemy ship, we both hurled ourselves upon the boards again, withstanding yet another broadside before I resumed cutting the cords. When the first rope was severed the back of the skiff fell towards the water, leaving its hull to clatter against the galley's side.

''Swounds,' I snapped angrily, as the paddles fell into the sea. 'Cut the other rope.'

I passed him the musket and quickly threw off my breastplate. With a deep breath I next dived into the black water below to retrieve the oars, then held the side of the ship as Maerten cut through the other cord which bound the rowing boat's prow. As the skiff fell to the ocean with a loud splash I quickly swam over and pulled it back towards the galley, feeling relieved to hear a loud thud when Maerten jumped straight into it.

'Hurry,' he hissed, 'we must get away.'

I needed no encouragement to do as he said, for already another ship could be seen heading in our direction, with our best hope of escaping the cannon fire being to row towards the front of our galley. After climbing in, I snatched up both paddles and flung myself against them as hard as I could. Maerten dropped his musket and knife, he jumped over the back of the small craft and kicked the water with his feet. In this way, our boat swiftly reached the prow of the hospital ship, before we turned around it. I gasped with relief when we reached the other side of the galley, while the air was filled with cries and cannon shot.

'Now to make for the coast,' I said, pointing towards the distant jagged outline before us, 'and to keep clear of the ships.'

Maerten nodded once and climbed back into the boat, all the while staring at the dark promontory. He suddenly ducked in fright when another cannon shot was heard.

I kept my gaze fixed upon the hospital ship we had just escaped, which stood apart from the main battle that raged to our right. The English fleet still resorted solely to cannon fire, as the lumbering Spanish galleys attempted in vain to get closer to them. Having been spared the brunt of the fight, the Santa Maria de Visión had instead become the target of countless Spanish pinnaces. Each of them ferried the wounded and the dying to her from the ships which were embroiled in the sea battle.

'No enemies in sight,' I muttered, 'and none have noticed our escape. We might yet make it.'

Maerten slumped against the back of the boat with a loud sigh. He then seized up the musket and blew upon its glowing match-cord, having a care to conceal the brightness with his hand. With each stroke of my oars the rolling hospital ship grew more distant, until I noticed a flickering light at her stern. At the same time one of the pinnaces sailed on towards this intermittent glow, and I noticed something eerie about the man who stood at the front of this boat, since the shape of his shadow was all too familiar.

'Abel,' whispered Maerten, 'why have you dropped the oars?'

'Move aside,' I growled at him, 'let me take a closer look.'

Our boat wobbled furiously as I hurried to its stern, nearly knocking Maerten over as I peered ahead into the darkness. A thickset man stood with his leg raised in front of him, holding a halberd as if it were a mark of rank. At his shoulder stood a tall henchman who brandished a *partesana*, his identity betrayed by the slight twitch of his head.

'Bastards,' I muttered beneath my breath, as my throat thickened with rage, 'I can't believe it.'

'What?' asked Maerten in bafflement.

'Ramos and Salva are sneaking Gabri onto their pinnace. And I think I know why.'

'Ramos?'

'Yes,' I replied, seizing up the musket and fitting the glowing end of the slow match between the jaws of the serpentine, 'we must go back.'

'Go back?!' he blurted.

'Row!' I snapped, as I sought to catch Ramos in my sights.

Maerten reluctantly did as I asked, and we were nearly halfway towards the boat when he called out to me between strokes.

'Abel! Another English galley approaches!'

His warning went ignored as I bit my bottom lip in rage, for I lusted to exact vengeance upon the three men I lived only to kill. As the pinnace drew closer to the galley, I could hear the muffle of Ramos's exchange with the cloaked figure of Gabri, who was already climbing over the galley's rail as he readied to jump onto the approaching boat. I angrily pulled back the trigger, and a shroud of smoke engulfed me as I desperately waved it away to spot my next target. When the smoke cleared, I saw de Andrés staring at me across the water, while Salva gestured wildly in my direction with the sergeant also looking on.

'You fired wide,' said Maerten in surprise.

'Cheap garbage,' I said, shaking the musket in annoyance, then refilled its pan as we drew closer to my betrayers.

As the musket was reloaded, Ramos's pinnace veered away from us, and I could hear Gabri's protests rising above the cries from the galley.

'Don't leave me here! Take me with you!'

Yet Ramos' craft had made off without delay, and I was about to take aim at the cloaked figure of de Andrés when the English vessel which Maerten had sighted slid past the port side of the hospital ship. She unleashed a resounding broadside, which had Gabri toppling back onto the main deck.

'Where is our damned lookout!' screeched someone behind him, above the tumult and the cries of dismay.

'Don't stop!' I said, feeling a sudden rush of anticipation. 'Row harder!'

Maerten seemed in a frenzy as he jerked the oars back hard, so that the last yards towards the galley were swiftly covered. When our boat bumped against the hospital ship's timbers, I seized a porthole and hauled myself up towards the top of the gunwale. I climbed over it onto the deck, and no sooner was Gabri rising to his feet than I pounced upon him. A flush of rage was upon me as I seized him by the hair, slamming his face into the boards with murderous abandon.

His forehead almost crashed into the wood a fourth time when he stunned me with a savage punch to the chin. The blow left me sprawled across the boards as he wrested himself free of my grip, stumbling away and reaching for his sword. I shook my head twice to regain my senses when the rasp of steel could be heard from his scabbard.

'Abel!' cried Maerten from the rowboat behind me. 'Abel, what's happening?!'

I ignored his call and shoved myself backwards, just as Gabri's blade struck the planks before my feet.

'Miserable whoreson,' he rasped, 'I'll end this now.'

A deep gash lined his forehead, with blood running across his face all the way down to his chin. I scrambled away from another swing of his blade, stumbling awkwardly over the bodies underfoot. A puddle of blood had me slipping upon a rigid corpse, when my hand met with cold steel. As my fingers closed about it, I could feel the bite of a sharpened edge, leaving me to fumble for the sword pommel. I grasped the blade and raised it just in time, catching Gabri's next thrust as a loud clash of steel rang across the deck.

My assailant grimaced at me with redoubled anger as I bristled with a seething hatred. I shoved him backwards and rose to my feet, regaining the initiative as he stumbled away from me in disbelief. In seeking to take advantage of his disability I clasped my pommel with my hands, using the strength of both arms to swing at his one-armed defence. My third stroke all but dropped his blade from his grasp, and I leant in towards him until I could smell his chain mail.

'Such bravery against a one-armed man,' he jeered, seeking in vain to push me away.

'I thought you hated a fair fight,' I replied, shoving him against the mizzenmast.

Men drew away from us for fear of being struck, when a cry went up from near the prow.

'Reload the cannon, another devil approaches!'

Soldiers hurried past as they rushed to arm the ship's guns, loading them with shot as another English ship could be seen veering away from the main battle. Our rolling galley was in her sights as she drew ever closer, and I grunted in frustration when she slid past. I broke away from Gabri and flung myself upon the boards underfoot, just as the first shots were heard.

The entire deck was shrouded in a momentary red glow, with the whole port side showered with shot as men around us were ripped to shreds by shards of canister. Before our own guns could reply, one of the cannons was struck by a ball, sending it spinning with its heavy carriage into various sailors amidships, leaving a trail of injured men in its path.

'Tie that thing up!' yelled the bosun.

I rolled away from the cannon as it thundered across the upper deck, jerking my head from side to side as I sought Gabri out again. Just then a fierce thrust struck my blade from out of the darkness, sending it flying from my hand towards the jostle of sailors behind me.

'Adios Santi.'

De Andrés spat his farewell as I tried to regain my footing, only to fall in a crumpled heap as I slipped on the blood and faeces beneath me. The one-armed musketeer gritted his teeth as he leant over me, and shut my eyes as his blade descended, when my attacker issued a loud cry which rose above the din on deck.

'Marti!' I cried, upon opening my eyes, for he had buried half his dagger in Gabri's shoulder.

A burst of blood spattered Elsien's brother as he looked back at me askance, before an elbow from my assailant sent him sprawling. A roar of rage was next heard from de Andrés, with his next sword swing only just missing Maerten, who staggered against the gunwale in shock. As the ship rolled my brother-in-law missed his step and was about to regain his footing when Gabri kicked his legs from beneath him. As he stumbled the youth clutched at thin air, then fell through a wide crack in the ship's rail towards the ocean below.

Gabri hardly had time to smirk in triumph for I threw myself at him, seeking to also hurl him overboard. As my hands met his back, he drew himself aside, leaving me to fall towards the fissure in the side of the ship. I saved myself from going over by seizing a dislodged deck board, then saw Maerten in the water, clutching torn rigging from the mainmast that floated alongside our galley.

'Hold on!' I yelled, then rolled sideways as a swing from Gabri's blade almost brained me.

I kicked at his right leg with both feet, dropping him to one knee as I snatched up a dead man's sword. Once more our blades met with a resounding clash, as we stumbled over bodies amid the odd thrust. We both ignored the chaos on deck as another three English ships slid past, releasing more broadsides. Men fell around us as our mortal duel unfolded, with each of us struggling against the galley's violent sway and driven by mad hatred as we endeavoured to serve the last fatal blow.

Our struggle took us towards the steps which led below decks. Gabri struggled to catch my doublehanded thrust before I shoved myself against him and pinned him against the side of the stairs. I pushed my blade hard against his, seeking to dislodge it, while my right elbow jabbed at his tender left ribs. A grunt of agony was heard from him, and amid the mad tussle his wooden arm became unsecured, falling to our feet as he looked after it in despair.

'The ring,' I cried, upon spotting the prince's bauble which had also fallen from his body.

I instantly realised that the scoundrel had stowed it in the space between the wooden claw and his severed arm, knowing that no one would have asked to look there twice.

'The ring!' he also exclaimed, and then shoved me backwards.

My heel hit the invaluable trinket, which was sent rolling towards the open hatchway.

'No!' he cried, running past me, and his hand almost fell upon it when it rolled through the opening and down the steps.

We both gaped at its descent until I hurled myself at my old comrade, with my sword stroke missing his head by a hair's breadth.

'Double-dyed cur!' he roared, incensed by his loss, 'I'll be rid of you now if it's my last act!'

His subsequent thrusts were relentless as he assaulted me with a speed born of huge frustration. I did my best to counter him, feeling as enraged as he was by his deceitful thievery. Once more our blades clashed amid the firing broadsides, as we again sought not to lose our footing. Our fierce fight brought us towards the ship's waist when my back met with hard steel. A backward glance revealed the damaged cannon behind me. It was the same gun which had been struck by enemy fire, whose carriage had been secured with two cables to the mainmast and foremast.

I fended off another sword thrust as he forced me against the gun, then shoved my sword point at him again. With expert deftness he refrained from a parry, instead choosing to let my sword point pass between the iron bows of his sword hilt. When half my blade followed, he jerked his wrist hard so that my sword blade snapped, reducing the weapon to a quarter of its length.

'Just die!' he roared, as his cloak fluttered about him.

I somehow met his next sword blow with my broken blade, yet his strength left me sprawling across the gun carriage. I threw myself away from his next swing, which cut through one of the ropes binding the cannon to the mainmast. As the huge gun was partly unsecured, I fell along one of its carriage wheels, then crawled beneath it towards the other wheel. Behind me I could see Gabri diving to the boards when another enemy ship appeared to port, spattering the decks with cannon fire. He then jumped back to his feet when the English warship slid past, rushing at me with his blade held before him.

With my death appearing imminent, I was seized by a desperate idea, what with the hospital ship swaying madly from side to side, and the single rope that bound the cannon creaking aloud as the great gun rolled towards port. Just as the ship's rocking was momentarily suspended, I leant back towards the other side of the gun, hacking through the rope that bound it with what was left of my blade. I next met a thrust of the musketeer's sword beneath the carriage, then rolled out from under the gun and tried to parry his next savage blow, which sent my broken sword flying overboard. His face lit up as I knelt before him defenceless, until I snatched up an end of his fluttering cloak and passed it under and over one of the gun's axles twice. I next hauled it back with all my strength to jam it tightly between the wheel and the carriage.

'Die you bastard!' he cried in a blind rage, as the ship swayed violently towards starboard, leaving me to release the end of his mantle.

Gabri's sword point nicked my breast, and he would have run me through had he not flown after the gun carriage which lurched towards starboard, leaving him to fumble madly with the clasp at his neck as the cannon rumbled on towards the ship's rail. The galley's gunwale was well riddled with shot, and a crash of wood was heard as the gun carriage smashed through it, hauling my foe over the edge with it.

'Santi!'

The musketeer's piercing cry was followed by a loud splash, as I turned onto my back in disbelief, gasping heavily as I surveyed the smoking ruin of the main deck which was piled high with bodies.

'Abel!' cried a familiar voice, and I raised my arm to my brother-in law who ran over towards me, dripping wet from the ocean.

'Are you hurt?' he asked, as he fell to one knee, staring at the scarlet blotch on my chest.

'No lad, pricked is all.'

I grabbed his hand and was gratefully hoisted to my feet when I remembered the prince's ring.

'The bauble,' I exclaimed, 'we must take it.'

'What bauble?' he replied, when a loud voice was heard behind him.

'What are you two bastards doing down here?'

We both turned in fright to see the contorted features of Captain De Bartulo, who was surrounded by his guards.

'Allow me to explain,' I said, pulling Maerten behind me.

'Don't!' he cried. 'I've heard enough tall tales from you! I'll clean the whole hull of this ship with you once we pull into port, but until then, you shall return to the oar!'

'No!' cried Maerten as the captain turned away, and I raised my arm after the Venetian as we were caught in the iron grip of his men.

'Wait! We had to leave our post! We found the prince's ring!'

'And I'm the queen of England!' called the captain, as our weapons were taken, and the breastplates and boots hauled off us.

We were then forced towards the stairs, and back down towards the hell of the lower decks. De Bartulo's men treated us without care, shoving us forward as they held us in a firm grip. As we passed through the infirmary, the physician Gaspar de Hurtado looked at me furtively, then showed me his back as I called out to him.

'The ring! Did you find it? It fell down the steps!'

'Move along,' growled one of De Bartulo's sailors, before we found ourselves back in the stinking hold, where we flinched at the sight of Dimas and his wardens.

'What is this?' asked the overseer, with a malicious grin. 'Have my flown lovebirds been returned?'

'Shut up and chain them back to the bench,' said a sailor. 'Captain's orders.'

'With pleasure!' cried the Portuguese sadist, and our skin crawled as we were led along to our old rowing bench and seated back alongside Esteban and the two negroes.

At that moment Georg appeared with his head still bandaged. The German did not say a word while he quietly proceeded to unfurl the length of his whip, then served us with a merciless hiding until our backs were left striped and bleeding from countless lashes.

'That's for Lisbon,' he snarled, 'and only the start of payback.'

He next showered us with a gob of spittle and made his way back up the catwalk, leaving us shuddering in agony.

'Got off lightly,' said Esteban when the German was gone. 'What's happening outside?'

'W-we are doomed,' I managed, shuddering from the whipping we had received. 'The English carry more cannons and will not engage.'

'That is strange,' said the Algerian strokesman, pulling a face.

'N-no,' I stuttered, as I took in the horror of our surroundings, while cursing myself for returning to the hospital ship, 'that is shrewd.'

Outside we could see countless pinnaces streaming towards our galley, still ferrying the wounded from other vessels that battled the English. Before long no more of the maimed and the dying could be taken aboard. In the meantime, the attacks of the enemy ships carried on unabated, with the furious thud of cannonballs heard against our ship.

'Down!' I howled at Maerten, seizing him by the shoulder and pulling him onto the filth underfoot, as the last cannon shot produced the loudest crack we had yet heard.

It was followed by another ball, which was the first to break through our deck, tearing through flesh, hair and bones. As I held down my brother-in-law, another shot screamed past our bench which tore through two galley slaves in the bench in front of us.

'Christ's bones!' I yelled, lying in piss and fresh spew, but the blood was barely wiped from my eyes when Dimas appeared with his whirling lash once more.

Amid flying oars and jabbing elbows, we set about turning the galley, steering clear of an enemy ship which peppered us with shot. The English dodged our burly galleys with ease, as they unleashed round after round of gunfire. The Armada was taught a hard lesson in sea battle that day, by a swifter and better equipped rival. Yet the Spanish fleet was prepared to fight until its last ship went under, so that the clash raged from two hours past dawn until late after midday, by which time a spent Dimas had toppled onto the steps from sheer exhaustion.

'God spare us,' I muttered beneath my breath, as yet more cannon fire riddled our flank.

Just when it seemed that we would be sent to the ocean's bottom, another tempest forced the two fleets apart, as blinding torrents of rain screamed over the sea, scattering ships of both sides in all directions. When at last it cleared, we were made to row back towards our flagship to loud grunts of effort, then gasped in disbelief when we saw the smoking Spanish warships striking their sails, ready to engage with the English once more.

It was a scene of typical Spanish bravery, which verged upon the insane. For most of our ships had gaping holes in their sides and had leaked a few feet of seawater into their holds as their decks creaked beneath mounds of corpses. The ensuing clash was to be nothing other than a last stand, and as the Spanish ships slid into position an officer was heard above deck, nervously speaking to one of his peers.

'They say our powder is almost finished.'

Yet the English showed no desire to fight again, being merely content to shadow our movements. Meanwhile a sailor could be heard shouting at Dimas, who lay exhausted across the catwalk.

'We've been crushed, Luis. Most of our ships are leaking, and all of the vessels have lost spars and rigging.'

The decks were littered with wreckage while the scuppers choked with the blood of dead bodies. One of the large Biscayans had gone under, as we foundered up the coast early in the night. Two more ships abandoned the fleet and staggered back towards the Spanish Netherlands, struggling to remain afloat, and an armed merchantman disappeared below the sea the following morning.

Worse perils lay in store when the English fleet drove us towards the low sands of Zeeland, in an attempt to shipwreck the whole Spanish enterprise. Maerten lay against the galley's timbers in detached silence while I glared around me, jerking in vain against the steel chain at my ankle while rumours abounded that the whole Armada was about to go under.

'We must try and escape,' I uttered to Esteban, who glared back at me suspiciously.

He had been injured by a large splinter during the crossfire and held his bleeding side.

'How the hell can we escape?' groaned a huge Berber behind him.

'Overpower an overseer, take advantage of the confusion!' I replied.

A general murmur of unrest passed over the benches, until Dimas descended the stairs with his wardens. They brought their whips down on us with furious abandon, almost as if they had sniffed out our mutinous sentiment.

'Silence curs!' roared Dimas, as his whip flickered like lightning. 'Shut your mouths and stay your tongues.'

The suffering Esteban was roused with a furious growl as two lashes caught him in the chest, and I threw myself upon my ailing brother-in-law and caught four of the best on my back, head and shoulders. The lashes left my ear bleeding badly and a deep gash across the back of my neck, while innumerable prayers were heard all over the ship as we were pushed closer towards the reefs. Then, as if by a miracle, a late change of wind spared us from going under, as for once the weather turned in our favour.

We were flooded with relief, and even Costa could not help grinning when he whispered to us that another council of war had been called by the admiral, in which he declared that at the first change of wind the Armada would reengage the enemy or seize an English port. Yet after four days the gales had still not turned, so that it was instead decided to make for the Sea of Norway, prior to attempting a return to Spain by sailing around Scotland and Ireland. Our sails were full for the next two days as we made north, when we learned that the English fleet had turned away from us.

All along the benches we huddled in our threadbare cloaks and shivered in the growing cold. The black oarholes betrayed only darkness outside, and we sailed along a coastline that was largely unknown to us. Relieved from hauling the oar, I lived only for scraps of gossip, always praying that our heavily leaking ship would not sink beneath the ocean. For as galley slaves we had a strong attachment to our vessel, with the iron rattle at our feet a constant reminder of this.

VIII

ATLANTIC COAST
OF CONNACHT, IRELAND

14 September 1588

'What day is it? The fourteenth?'

Maerten squinted at the calloused fingers on which he kept count. 'It is... by my reckoning.'

I slumped forward onto our oar handle and sighed aloud. A drop of seawater fell off my forehead and trickled down my nose, then flew off my lips when I whispered again.

'What a mess.'

My brother-in-law sighed too.

'If Ramos had but finished us off in Seville...'

Maerten's eyes had turned dull, and his sallow features barely reminded me of his sister's face anymore. Our recent troubles had also quenched his youthful spark, for ever since we had reached Scotland, our homeward journey had turned all the more wretched. The Santa Maria de Visión was in a piteous state, with cables passed under her keel to keep her from falling apart. Shot holes close to the waterline punctured her side, and barely enough rations were left to see us home.

Our hopeless plight was only worsened by the admiral's black mood, since Medina-Sidonia had not been gracious in defeat, nor had he forgiven his captains for scattering before the English fireships at Calais. On our journey north, his orders were no sooner ignored again than he sentenced twenty sea captains to death by hanging. One of these officers was said to be his own neighbour from Sanlúcar in Cadiz. Yet the admiral was resolved to make an example of the man, whose corpse was strung up on a pinnace and paraded ahead of the fleet as a warning.

This act sapped the spirits of the Armada's crewmen, so that morale became as low as our supplies of water. This last shortage was of greater concern to the admiral, who ordered that all horses and mules, whose thirst was greatest, be cast into the sea. The shrill neighs and braying above decks were distressing to hear, although the act saved our dwindling rations. Each day we were only permitted a pint of water and a half-pint of wine with which to wash down eight ounces of rock-hard ship's biscuit.

Yet water shortages were to prove the least of our troubles, for we had hardly rounded Scotland when an outbreak of dysentery claimed the lives of men from all ships. Around us our fellow rowers toppled from their benches like drunks, including the two blackamoors on our bench. They too were dragged up to the ship's waist and swung overboard. Our barber surgeon was also killed by the flux, so that hair prickled our undergarments for the first time in months, and growth a week old sprouted upon our heads.

Once Scotland was behind us, we sailed on towards the western coast of Ireland. Throughout our journey, the fleet was plagued by a south-easterly wind that hindered our starboard tack, until great storms broke our formation. Amid roars of thunder, we were cut off from the main body of the fleet, though we joined two other lost galleys the following day.

'Looks like the bastard won't see out the day...' said my Brabantian brother-in-law, as Esteban's head swirled away from us.

Our ship lurched sideways, when the sound of footsteps was heard. We threw ourselves upon our oars and feigned sleep, when Costa appeared down the hold. We immediately made out the enslaved cook wobbling like a drunken sailor, as he clumsily sidestepped the rowers who lay in his path.

'Hey there, Costa!' hissed Maerten. 'What news from above?'

The cook bit his lower lip as a sign for us to keep silent, then tottered over with a crate held in both hands. He placed bowls of maggot-strewn curd on our bench, but Maerten flipped them over without a second glance. Costa ignored my brother-in-law's gesture, for the one-eared slave had himself advised us to starve rather than touch the putrid servings.

He next looked furtively over each of his shoulders, before reaching inside his cloak and holding out a palm full of sawdust. Maerten and I greedily picked the weevils out of it and swallowed them whole, while the cook muttered to us beneath his breath.

'Confusion still reigns above deck. There is one hell of a tempest brewing.'

Maerten hung his head and sighed.

'Will the captains not press on past Ireland?'

Costa cast yet another wide-eyed look over his shoulder, then whispered his last words to us.

'I must away. I swear I heard the devil's voice.' So saying, he turned on his heel and scampered off.

We dared not utter another word, for his reference to Dimas left us feeling terrified. Maerten and I strove to nod off for a while, but our attempts were foiled by the increasing roll of our ship. We leant onto the shaft in front of us to quell our seasickness, with our bodies huddled closely together for warmth. A gelid fear had claimed my insides at Costa's mention of Dimas, so that even my beating heart sounded too loud for comfort. When the madman did not appear, my brother-in-law resumed his ranting.

'Who knows what's become of Pieter. My poor, long abandoned brother. How will we ever return for him now?'

'Maerten,' I said, 'do not despair.'

He grabbed my shoulder and rasped desperately in my ear.

'Promise me, promise me that you'll return for him!'

'Of course I will,' I replied, 'but we shall do it together Marti!'

My brother-in-law released his grip and sighed aloud.

'I wonder if those fools will ever make a decision.'

'Still awake, are we?'

I jerked our oar away in fright, unintentionally shoving its end into Dimas' teeth. The scoundrel had crept up behind us from starboard, so that my bad ear had not picked up his approach. Maerten drew a sharp breath when the overseer fell like a brick, causing a huge splash. As the overseer rose from the knee-high bilge water, he held his fingertips to his bloodied mouth, which soon widened into a cruel smirk.

'That was your last miserable act, Santiago!'

He made to rise onto his feet, when it occurred to me that he finally had the excuse he needed to be rid of me. My escape from his clutches would never be forgotten, and for days on end he and Georg had provoked me at every turn, hoping that I might strike back at one of them. In their view, my time in the crow's nest had been nothing less than a reward for my misbehaviour, and they both itched to make a grim example of me if I so much as questioned their authority again.

Yet the overseer's tumble had also dented the impression, strengthened by his day-to-day inhumanity, that he was some invincible scourge in our lives. As I looked at the other wretched slaves across the benches, it dawned on me that there would never be a better time to break free. Dimas lay alone at our feet as our ship fell apart during yet another gathering storm. Meanwhile a foreign land lay just over two miles away, which might easily be reached if we stole away on pinnaces or ran the galley aground.

'Take his keys!' I yelled out in Sabir, feeling like I spoke the thoughts of most present. 'Take his bloody keys!'

Dimas' eyes widened as I stood off the bench and pointed at him, still shouting at the other slaves to act. As the overseer made to speak, a brawny arm suddenly curled itself about his throat, which belonged to a hefty Berber strokesman. The enormous slave nodded at me once, then spoke to the rowers alongside him.

'Get the keys.'

He then bent over sideways and shoved the stunned Dimas underwater. The crazed overseer kicked with his feet and twisted and turned, yet it was all in vain as the bulging muscles rippled in the arm of his victim turned aggressor. Meanwhile another slave had already reached Dimas's side and undone his huge belt, with the heavy clanking keys passing through many hands as the overseer stopped kicking. The large Berber then pulled Dimas's head from the bilge water and wrung his neck for good measure.

'Keep silent,' he boomed across the benches, 'and let none escape without my command!'

Having emphatically declared himself the leader of the slave revolt, the giant then turned his tattooed face towards our side of the deck, waiting for us all to be freed. When the last shackle was undone, he strode towards the steps ahead of us, crying out to the surviving rowers who already milled behind him.

'Whosoever craves freedom, join with us now!'

A roar was returned as most hurried after him, with only a handful still clinging to their benches in fear. I flung Esteban away as Maerten and I hurried out, scarcely believing our luck as we ran after the fleeing jostle of slaves. A swish of bilge water was heard at our feet before we made up the steps, and as we hurried through the infirmary, I could see that it was choked with wounded men, who groaned aloud at our passing while the physicians and surgeons stared at us in disbelief.

Upon reaching the main deck we were greeted by a flash of lightning, which streaked the nightly heavens. The sight left us startled as our ears were deafened by a roar of thunder. Our galley continued to lurch leeward as the end of great waves spattered our decks. The scent of the open ocean left me feeling halfrevived, as I took in the chaos which Costa had mentioned. Ahead of us, guards beat back mutineers before they too were set upon by the Berber and his freed cohorts. We all swayed to the growing throes of the ocean, and at the fo'c'sle a despairing nobleman flung gold doubloons overboard and cried out in despair.

'Forgive us, oh Lord, for we have sinned!'

Furious pleas echoed within the officers' cabin behind us, to what sounded like the loud beating of fists upon a table. A second bolt of lightning cut the sky in half, when another thunderclap drowned out all the shouting. Black waves rose as high as the poop deck, pounding the hull with a fast-growing fury. When I turned my head, I could see that the winds tore rigging off the mainmast as if it were lace.

A hand then wrapped itself around my throat, and I turned and saw Georg. As I grappled with him, he cried out to the other wardens, with his face turning as dark as the clouds gathered above us. Two of his men seized Maerten, who pushed and shoved at their grasp like a fiend. Amidst our struggle the galley was shoved towards land like a squealing child led by the ear, causing us to wobble across the slippery boards underfoot. Our mad dance was soon ended when a burst of seawater scooped the five of us over the ship's rail.

'Christ wept!'

The oath left my throat as I seized the edge of the gunwale. Hailstones the size of small pebbles pelted my head, and my shoulder was half-wrenched from its socket as one of the wardens grabbed hold of my ankle. When I looked down, I recognised the gaunt face of Georg who returned a fierce glare, while trying to reach for my cloak with his other hand. I kicked at his face until he finally let go, dropping with a howl into the dark swirl below.

'Abel!'

I raised my head towards Maerten, being flooded with dread as I saw him dangling by the ledge alongside me.

'Hold on!' I cried at him, trying to reach for his tunic with one hand.

Having lost her mooring, the Santa Maria sheered shoreward, as another westerly screamed across the ocean. We teetered violently along the ship's side, until Maerten's grip was loosened, and he fell into the furious waves.

'Marti!'

With a howl, I released my hold and fell in after him. Breath burst from my lungs as I plunged deep into the black icy ocean, with its salt burning my wounds and grazes. I struggled back to the surface for a gasp of air, seeing the youth struggling for breath alongside me.

'Marti,' I cried again, as we snatched each other's forearms.

'Abel...' he groaned, meeting my frantic gaze as an ocean wave crashed into the hull and flung us in different directions.

When I lost sight of him, I cried his name again and again while desperately trying to keep afloat in the raging sea. In the corner of my eye, I spotted a wayward plank of wood, and no sooner did I grab it than I was borne to the heavens upon a white crest, coughing up the water that flew into my face.

When the wave toppled, I clung to the wood like a barnacle, finding myself pulled far below the surf by a vicious current. My left shoulder was slashed by a reef edge before I was hurled back above water, with my cries muffled by the roaring thunder. A last moan left my throat amid the screaming of other drowning men, when the current dragged me down again and whirled me in all directions.

Great sea swells tossed me landwards as my hold on the board began to slacken. The waves next shoved my driftwood onto some low-lying rocks, and the collision sent me flying onto a shallow bank of sand. Amid the rush of seawater, I somehow hauled myself onto my feet, entirely uncertain where I was and shivering violently from the cold.

Dozens of other castaways staggered onto the ashen sand around me, and a swirl of cloaks ahead of us revealed men running in our direction. They were at least half our number, natives who appeared scrawnier than us and of an even wilder cast. For a moment, I took the approaching band to be rushing to our aid, when one of them flung a rock at the closest Spaniard. A loud thud was followed by a roar of agony, and we quickly scattered as the bandits fell among us, beating men senseless and rifling their garments.

These thieves were swiftly rewarded for their lawless efforts, since the king of Spain had paid his men before the Armada had set sail for Calais. Even the poorest officer had gold doubloons stitched into his garments, but most Spaniards were too stricken by weariness and disease to provide resistance. Some sank silently to their knees as they were beset with cudgel and fist. A handful of others fought back, throwing in the odd punch before they were themselves stunned with rocks and branches.

Other robbers soon arrived to swell our aggressors' number, as they also ran towards the sea like fishermen at the start of the salmon season. Their advance was hindered by the Atlantic winds which screamed across the beach, as I span about and fell over. The castaways around me were being beaten senseless, so that my thoughts turned to survival alone. In the distance, I could make out rushes billowing to my right, which presented a forlorn hope of escape. More Spaniards were washed up as more robbers thronged among us, when the waves spat a boat across the beach, which battered all unfortunates in its path.

After a moment's hesitation, the brigands gathered about this craft, cracking its caulked hatchway open as if it were a walnut. From within the broken vessel, they pulled out a few highborn Spaniards who coughed and spluttered, as well as the corpses of those who had drowned in the heavily leaking boat. Some of the nobles yelled furious commands at the rogues who seized them, only to be knocked out and stripped to the skin.

The robbers howled with delight when handfuls of jewels and crown pieces were also pulled out of the boat. I took full advantage of the attackers' distraction, heaving my body through the dunes and making my way past a dazed sergeant-major who had suffered a blow to the head. Just ahead of me I could also see the blood-soaked face of a dead sailor. Other bandits tore at his doublet and hose, pushing each other and squabbling over every last gold coin in the garments' stitching.

I crawled on, inch by inch, covering the few yards that remained between me and the rushes. A glimpse over my shoulder revealed other corpses being pulled from the sea, which were also stripped and searched. The sight pushed me to redouble my efforts, when strident cries heralded the arrival of more robbers running down onto the beach. I lay low as they tore past me, thinking that I was safe until I heard one of them cackling aloud behind me.

I caught a glimpse of him in of the corner of my eye, a scrawny beggar in a tattered browned tunic who held aloft a silver plate which he had plucked from a dead Burgundian's jacket. For a moment I could also see him taking a step towards me, when he was set upon by two of his ragged fellows who bickered wildly over his prize. Their quarrel allowed me to creep forward some more, with the fluttering grass ahead of me teasingly close. The anguished protests of the three robbers could still be heard behind me as I made my way over the harsh grains of sand.

I had hardly reached the edge of the rushes when the cry of a pursuer was heard behind me. A low groan of dismay left my lips, as I crouched lower in the undergrowth to peer over my shoulder. A youthful vagabond could be seen approaching me at a loping gait, having strayed from the main scenes of looting. He appeared slightly hunchbacked and brandished a knife.

I leant back upon the ground, feeling utterly spent from my efforts, when the hunchback reached me amid loud snorts of excitement. The malformed youth tugged at my cloak to turn me towards him, with his blade raised over my chest. I fumbled for something with which to strike out at him, and in that moment my fingers closed around a black rock. My backward swing was aided by a sudden burst of wind, with my assailant caught on the temple as he whirled about and fell onto his back.

Shrieking gales drowned out all sounds, but I knew that his skull had been cracked. I lay back on the ground for some time thereafter, struggling for breath while I relieved myself where I lay. The warmth down my thigh brought some relief in the biting cold before I reached out for the cloak of my fallen pursuer. After wresting the garment free, I wrapped it around me to ward off the merciless cold. My chafed lips then widened enough for raindrops to land in my mouth, with each of them burning the back of my crusted tongue.

When I had swallowed almost half a mouthful of rainwater, I lifted my head above the bush that concealed me. The rout of the Armada's castaways still raged ashore, and upon the ocean the three carracks were being tossed landwards by the elements, spilling both men and flotsam into the waves. The reefs off the strand of beach resembled a sea monster's fangs, with the rocks crushing the ships' wooden hulls, amid a mad swirl of driftwood and torn rigging.

For close to an hour the galleys were hurled to and fro until at last their seams came apart. A few brave sailors still fought to save their ships, only to be hauled beneath the relentless waves by their lifelines. Soon all that remained of the galleys were large mainsails that briefly trailed over the sea. I watched the floating canvas in disbelief, sick from the realisation that all hopes of a swift return home had been dashed.

In truth, the foundering of the Santa Maria de Visión should have filled me with joy since she had been my prison for over a year. But I was crushed by the thought that Maerten might also have gone down with her. A tear streaked my cheek when I realised that I had probably lost him, as my sodden cloak flapped in the wind. His likely reunion with Elsien in death was of little relief to me, and I also felt ravaged by loneliness, lost in a land of which I knew nothing.

New cries could soon be heard from the brigands on the beach, when staves, barrels and caskets bobbed towards the shore. Men clung to them howling in fear, with their fates decided by the fickle winds that crushed some against the rocks and sent others sprawling over the beach. Scores more Spaniards stumbled dizzily out of the waves, wearing golden chains or silver crosses and saints. Their feet had hardly left the shallows before they were struck down by the natives, who did not leave a shred of metal or a piece of cloth upon the castaways' bodies.

I watched on in dismay until well beyond dusk, and it was an hour past midnight when a scrabble of hooves was heard. The noise announced the arrival of a large body of armoured horsemen, who seemingly appeared out of nowhere as they charged the robbers upon the shore. Between the light of the moon and the flashing torches I could just make out the scarlet mantles which flapped behind these riders, who also wore iron corselets over tawny and blue cassocks.

I estimated there to be over a hundred white shields, all of which were emblazoned with the red cross of St George. Startled, I ducked behind a clump of rushes, as the English troopers scattered the native brigands who fled from the beach at full pelt, dropping coins and jewels behind them. After killing both native and Spaniard, the troopers then galloped on towards the water, slaying more of the newly beached men who splashed about helplessly as they emerged from the sea.

Not a single pistol shot was fired by the riders, who despatched their Spanish foes by cold steel. In the time it took to recite an Ave María, the water ran red off the grey sand around the kicking hooves of the enemy's mounts. I beheld the slaughter that unfolded in horror, crushed by the realisation that my newfound freedom had been achieved in a land where the heretic held sway.

When their deathly work was done, the troopers dismounted to seize those clothes which struck their fancy. Velvet caps were whisked from the water while gloves and boots were pulled off the bodies of the slain. Helmets of every sort could be seen scattered everywhere, with Milanese sallets and burgonets also snatched up by those on horseback.

Feeling overwhelmed by the sight of this mounted force of enemies, my head fell back onto a small mound of sand. I felt half-dead from exhaustion and must have resembled a corpse beneath a cloak. My bleeding shoulder still throbbed in agony as the gales screamed across the cloud-scudded sky. They were the last sounds in my good ear before I passed out.

IX

COUNTY SLIGO, IRELAND

15 September 1588

A loud beating of wings woke me with a start. I pulled the mantle away from my face, which sent a black crow shrieking towards the grey sky above. For a few moments, I stared at the rushes around me, with my deep breaths of salt air relieving the bitter taste in my mouth. When the rest of my body was bared, the blanket came away reluctantly, for it was stuck to a patch of dried blood on my shoulder. The bruise around the wound seemed to have doubled in size, so that my upper arm was near violet in colour.

'Marti,' I gasped, remembering the events of the previous night, 'Marti...'

I ignored my discomfort as I slowly raised my head above the dew-covered rushes. Loud squawks were heard from the beach, and the moon was but a faint glow upon the horizon. Its light was soon replaced by that of the rising sun, which revealed hundreds of corpses across the iron-coloured sand.

Crows and gulls fluttered among the rows of the dead, pecking at carrion. Small groups of men could also be seen in the distance, picking through the bodies which lay between the clumps of seaweed.

My heart quickened at the sight, which was rendered more sinister by the low hum of the sea breeze. As I slowly stirred, I turned towards the body of my assailant from the previous night, thinking to search it for a weapon. The wretch was sprawled over the yellowed grass, with a welt the size of a fist upon his forehead. I averted my eyes from his glazed stare and blue lips, and sand fell from my cloak as I shuffled towards him to search his rags.

I had hardly taken two steps when my nostrils picked up a stink of raw flesh. A shaggy head was raised from among the rushes, and I froze before a tawny eye which blazed in my direction. The wolf issued a low growl as its black lips quivered around its fangs, causing me to fall back into the long grass with my hands held out in front of me.

'Mother of God...'

The cur's muzzle was red with blood, and I saw that it had ripped open the dead hunchback's throat. One of the dead youth's legs had also been gnawed down to the bone. For a few moments the one-eyed wolf and I beheld each other, as its ribs twitched beneath its grey hide. As the daylight grew it eventually occurred to me that it was not the largest wolf I had seen, and was in fact a starving, sorry creature guarding its prey.

I slowly crawled away from it, hoping to find some branch which I might use to defend myself. A loud yelp from the beach reminded me that wolves scarcely travelled alone, and another glimpse at the sand revealed that the distant figures

I had mistaken for men had tails and pointed ears. At my retreat, the wolf fell silent and returned to its feast, yet I dared not give it my back until I had stepped further away from it.

Behind me were hundreds of bodies strewn across the sand, and despite my wretched condition I was resolved to learn it my brother-in-law had also reached land. With a slight shiver, I crouched low on the ground, skulking over the corpses like a scavenger as I sought in vain to find him. For well over an hour, I called his name and hobbled across the beach from end to end twice over, feeling overwhelmed by the scenes of slaughter and a growing sense of despair.

My search was rendered more desperate by hundreds of crows, which pecked at many more disfigured faces then fluttered away from my feet. Wolves issued low growls whenever I trudged past them, clenching entrails or limbs between their fangs. At all times, I readied to strike out at them, yet each time they turned their attentions back to easier pickings. Twice I stumbled across the body of a dead slave, leaving me to groan in dismay as I turned them over.

For each time an unknown face gaped back at me, leaving me to close the glazed eyes which were not yet pecked out. At last, I fell to my knees in front of the lapping of the water, staring at some of the flotsam and sails which had gathered along the distant rocks.

'Marti,' I whispered, as the pang of loss hit me again, 'Marti...'

I regarded the ocean in quiet disbelief, praying that it had granted him an end that was swift and painless. Then boiling tears overtook me again, and I angrily wiped them away as I berated myself.

'I failed you again Elsi, all over again. And you too Marti. I failed you all.'

My anger then had the better of me, and my bunched fists throbbed as I remembered the men who had caused us so much mishap and setback.

'If they yet live...,' I whispered, as my voice shook with fury.

For a moment I despaired that they had indeed perished, and that I would not slay them by my own hand. The passing of Cristó and Gabri had somewhat eased the pain of my loss, yet my desire for vengeance seared me deeply as I yearned to claim the lives of Ramos and Salva. Yet to do so I first had to save myself, and I reluctantly struggled to my feet, ever fearful that the English troopers from the previous night might return. I sidestepped the countless bodies in my path and then trudged through the sheltering rushes once more, making for the countryside further inland.

As I left the beach behind, a lagoon shimmered ahead of me, and beyond it a flat-topped rise at the end of a long mountain wall jutted towards the sky. These heights were magnificent, with their heather-clad ridges resembling the crenellated battlements of a tower house. They were also surmounted by high crests which were feathered by low-lying cloud.

An eerie calm seemed to hang over the land between us, which consisted of a jagged pattern of rushes and high grass, that was only broken by large swathes of forest. My grumbling stomach demanded that I forage in the woodland, so that I struck out along the rim of the brackish marsh in front of me. I tottered along until a path became clear through the grassstrewn plain. The ocean had claimed my shoes the previous day, which hindered my progress over the stubbled tract, soon reducing it to an awkward hobble.

Ever watchful for signs of others, I passed over a ridge overlooking the beach. The crescent of sand grew and then shrank before the incoming waves. Although the storm had abated, the Atlantic seethed and hissed through the black rocks which studded the grey sand below me. The growing sunlight had finally overtaken the whole of the horizon, affording me a glimpse of the distant islets which lay across the water.

Then the old soldier's instinct for survival returned as I studied my position, looking from left to right. I strenuously climbed a gentle bluff, often casting a swift glance over my shoulder. Each time I was met by the far-off sight of the slain soldiers upon the shore, and of the restless waves that rushed through the reefs in front of the headland. The sound was soon replaced by the distant rumbling of thunder as I made my way further inland, with the rocks beneath the grass hindering my steps so that I often stumbled and fell.

'Keep close to me,' I snapped, by force of habit, then recalled with deep dismay that Maerten was no longer with me.

My spirits were somewhat lifted as I climbed further up the rise, and the strand had long vanished behind me when a small monastery appeared ahead. The sight spurred me to hasten my pace, just as the first drops of rain could be felt on my head. I was soaked through by the time I reached the forlorn abbey, with its gabled walls thick with creepers and weeds. The door fell open with a loud creak when I rested my hand on it, then sagged sideways like a flap of skin on a wound.

I cautiously stepped inside in the hope of obtaining warmth and shelter, only to find myself facing a row of empty hearths.

Each of the abbey's windows from the nave to the chancel had been shattered, and my mouth fell open when I saw that all the images of the saints had been burned. At the cracked altar, I glimpsed a band of men sitting cross-legged beneath a headless statue of the Virgin.

I turned on my heel and made to depart, only to bump into a portly man-at-arms who barred my path. The snarling soldier was as broad as the doorway behind him, and upon colliding with him I fell back onto the ground. A broadsword was held out in front of him, which left me cowering in fear at his feet.

'Mercy, I beg you!' I whimpered.

A look of surprise appeared on the brute's face, and he called out to the men that were seated on the other side of the chapel.

'Upon my oath, he speaks our tongue perfectly.'

As I lay in the dirt, I counted close to a dozen Spaniards near the damaged altar. A few of them were stark naked and shivering as they huddled closely together. They were seated around the only one of their number who wore a scarlet sash across his breastplate. The officer was as white as a sheet and lying on his back, with a nasty gash on his forehead. One of his men studied me keenly, with narrowed eyes beneath the long black curls which fell over his unshaven face.

'Spare him, Nando,' he said after clearing his throat, 'he's one of ours.'

'Are you sure, *Pelo Polla*?' asked another of the shivering Spaniards.

'Can't you tell?' replied the curly-haired man. 'His accent is unmistakeable. Yet we should watch him closely, for outlaws are never to be trusted.'

'How do you know he's an outlaw?' shouted the burly Nando, as he glared down at me and raised his drawn sword.

Pelo Polla rolled his eyes at the question before he replied.

'He wears the tunic of a galley slave, and his ankle is scarred by a manacle.'

My mind raced as I followed their conversation, while praying that the giant Nando would heed *Pelo Polla*'s order to extend mercy.

'Unruly whoreson!' exclaimed another Spaniard, 'I can smell his shameful lawlessness from here!'

'In truth,' remarked Nando, 'he smells of piss.'

'What's your name, Spaniard?' cried the curlyhaired man they called *Pelo Polla*.

'Juan de los Hospitalarios, sire,' I replied, choosing to use my long-abandoned childhood name.

'Juan of the Hospitallers?' asked yet another castaway, wearing a puzzled frown. 'Whatever does that mean?'

The curly-haired Spaniard sighed aloud.

'Isn't it obvious? He's the bastard son of a Knight of Malta.'

Pelo Polla then returned his attentions to me.

'Why are you not at the bottom of the ocean, slave?'

I cleared my throat and made up a false reply.

'I was ordered to man the pumps, sire.'

He fell silent for a few moments, as he paused to wipe the rain from his face. The heavy storm had caused the roof of the abbey to leak more heavily than that of a wayside inn, so that the curly-haired man shielded his eyes with one hand when he spoke again.

'Did you see any officers upon the beach?'

'Only dead ones, sire.'

One of the naked Spaniards paused from his fevered shivering long enough to issue a loud snort.

'What would a galley slave understand about officers? All he knows is the oar! Get him to start a fire, I'm freezing my balls off!'

'Indeed,' agreed *Pelo Polla*, as he himself barely restrained a shiver, 'get him to work Nando.'

I winced in pain as the burly swordsman hauled me to my feet by my injured shoulder. He then shoved me towards the door as the other Spaniards resumed their fevered discussion.

'What in God's name are we going to do?' cried one. 'The admiral warned us not to land here!'

'We should have followed that woman!' protested another. 'She seemed friendly enough.'

'Nonsense!' spat *Pelo Polla*. 'A woman should never be trusted in times of peril. Besides, these savages are no friends to us. Need I remind you of what befell us yesterday?'

Loud grunts of assent followed, when another survivor piped up.

'*Pelo Polla* speaks truth, but we should have at least taken her cow!'

'No,' replied the naked man, 'we should have left with Fernández. *El Perro* and Ramos were right to go with him.'

'Ramos?' I exclaimed, turning towards them.

Nando scowled at my dithering, before he dealt me a hefty smack on the back of my head.

'Silence, slave. Do not speak unless you are spoken to.'

A burning rage welled up inside me, but I took a deep breath and issued a grovelling apology. I bit my tongue when Nando ignored my gesture, while pulling my cloak off my back and wearing it himself. When he kicked the door open to lead me out, the other Spaniards were still squabbling over what to do next. One of the fools shrieked that they should defend the monastery with their lives, and another yelled that I should also be sent to forage for them, since a slave's life was worth the risk.

I would have gladly done their errands had it guaranteed my safety. Yet given their precarious situation, I was not disposed to be their servant any longer than I had to. So when we exited the abbey, I bustled about collecting twigs and branches under the watchful eye of my burly minder, all the while forming a sense of the countryside around us.

As the storm subsided, I paused to wipe the rain from my eyes, then studied the beginnings of a nearby wood that reached the foot of the flat-topped mountain. I thought of Ramos heading towards it, and my anger grew again when I thought Salva might still also be alive, with the evil pairing having survived the raging storm and the previous night's mishap upon the beach.

'Cursed, double-dyed bastards,' I growled beneath my breath, 'I'll yet consign you both to hell.'

As I picked up another branch, I saw that Nando had pulled down his hose to relieve himself against the church wall. The path to the woods was just over a bowshot away, and its call was more inviting than that of a siren. Of a sudden, I was overwhelmed by the realisation that I was no longer a galley slave chained to a rowing bench, and that there would be no better moment to flee into the open country. The bundle of twigs fell from my hands as I shuffled away from the chapel.

To my good fortune Nando had not yet relieved himself, and I was more than halfway to the forest when muffled whinnies reached my good ear. The ensuing thud of hooves revealed a distant band of troopers to my right, whose mounts lunged towards the decrepit monastery. My fear at the sight of them spurred me to limp hastily until the cover of forest, when angered cries were heard from the chapel door.

'Come back, slave! Are you mad? The heretics will kill you – if I don't get you first!'

I grimaced at the sound of Nando's shouting, which would only serve to hasten his death. In that instant, I felt like I was passing between two worlds, leaving my Spanish past behind as I made for the unknown shingling of forest leaves before me. I pushed on through the thickening trees without a backward glance, and my heart quickened when a piercing neigh was heard from the direction of the chapel, followed by a crash of steel.

An agonised cry reached my ears, but it died away as I shuffled into the dim wood over a rough path littered by stumps and sharp stones. My shirt was poor protection against the cold, and though my shoulder twinged and throbbed painfully, I wrapped my arms tightly around me for warmth. Twigs cracked as I ran, and my bare feet were gouged by all manner of sharp ends.

I pressed on with gritted teeth, since my best hope of safety lay in the haste of my tired legs. Whenever it seemed that my strength might fail me, the galley's drumbeat and Dimas' shrill whistle returned to my mind, bringing a rhythmic, dogged pace to my faltering steps. In this way, I covered significant ground as the stunted trees to my right receded, until I could make out the billows on the distant ocean.

When my attentions returned to the path, I saw two men running ahead of me, whose hair fluttered wildly in the wind. Their torn doublets and hose revealed them to be other Spaniards, and I had hardly spotted them when I heard the jingle of reins behind me, along with the pounding of heavy hooves. A mad panic seized me as I swivelled madly and sprang into the brush to my left. An awkward landing had me rolling across the branches on the forest floor before my stomach came to rest on a bed of nettles.

I bit my lower lip in pain as the mailed riders crashed past me, their red mantles fluttering over their steeds' haunches. They were no more than twenty in number, and the fresh blood on their boots and trews revealed them to be a roaming search party. It appeared that they would soon be well clear of me, when a rider at the back cried out as he wheeled his mount around. The other troopers reined in their chargers at the sound, amid the odd curse in their guttural tongue.

The tarrier swung off his horse and handed his reins to another trooper. My heart quickened when he crouched down low, edging ever closer towards me as he prodded at trampled leaves on the stretch of path between us. He was evidently some sort of tracker, and I shuddered when he shuffled closer, with his wizened face resembling that of a ferret on the scent. When he picked up the ends of a broken branch, I trembled in the low grass but a few paces ahead of him, thankful for the fat log that shielded me from his line of sight.

My breath tightened when he took another step in my direction, while his hand fell upon his sword pommel. Sweat prickled my forehead at the realisation that I was unarmed, with no rock or branch close at hand with which to even attempt a defence. I made ready to fly at his next step, then hesitated but an instant when a distant rustle was heard. The trooper's head shot sideways at the sound of hurried footfalls, and he quickly turned away and ran back to his horse.

The noise was caused by the two Spaniards I had seen running ahead of me, who had also hidden along the side of the path. As the pair darted off a clamour rose among the troopers, whose mounts wheeled around wildly before charging after the fugitives. With my head barely lifted over the brush, I could see the pair of Spanish wretches scrambling downhill past some stunted trees. As the heretics' raised sabres pricked the air behind them, I pushed myself to my feet and rushed into the undergrowth, while the strident shrieks of the pursued were heard behind me.

With ragged breaths, I crashed through the trunks and slipped over the rocks that littered the forest floor. Dread filled my gut at the rustle of every leaf and at the sound of each twig that cracked underfoot. Thereafter I shunned the path like the plague, as I resolved to stick to the surrounding trees instead, fearful of other perils lurking in unfamiliar countryside. After a time spent pushing on through the wood, it soon dawned on me that my shortness of breath would prove a greater foe than the heretics, since my days spent aboard the Santa Maria de Visión had increased my strength but reduced my agility.

Before long I reached a small clearing, where I fell to my knees at the roots of an oak. My hands ripped up the grass around it, and I bit off dirty root ends to ease the aching groan in my stomach. Their bitter taste made me cough up the soil upon them, before I leant towards a puddle, straining my parched lips towards the muddy water. When at last my thirst was slaked, I fell back against the tree trunk, gasping for breath while the oak's boughs shielded me from the rain. As I lay on the ground, my bruised feet throbbed from my exertions, and I was also plagued by a growing loneliness.

'Oh Marti,' I said with a deep sigh, 'what would I not give to have you back again?'

I lay in a half-trance for what seemed like an hour, when a snapping sound turned my attentions to a crooked ash ahead of me, where someone was watching me from behind a trunk. A sallow face with puckered cheeks next appeared, when a bony youth stepped out from his hiding place, swathed in a linen tunic which was secured by a rope belt at his waist. When he turned his head towards me, I could see that his eyes were covered by a long, auburn fringe that nearly reached the end of his nose.

The stripling observed me carefully as his lips formed an abrupt smile, which was as cruel as it was discomfiting. His stealthy approach gave me gooseflesh, leaving me to shuffle against the bark behind me as he raised his staff over his head. He next spoke in a sharp and lilting tongue, stretching a grimy palm out towards me as he raised his weapon over his head.

'An t-airgead geal s'agatsa?'

I trembled at his gesture from the gnarled foot of the tree, staring at him in panicked disbelief as I tried in vain to understand his words. At my silence, his lips were drawn back in a snarl, and he brought his staff down upon my wounded shoulder, issuing a roar of agony from me that sent birds fluttering from the trees. The pain exceeded that of a knife thrust, and my mind was further clouded by agony when I blocked his next swing with my forearm. My attacker seemed heartened by my distress, as he spread his grassstained legs and brought the staff down again. I caught most of the blows on my arms, although two struck me in the head.

In a daze I tried to scramble away, but he was a sprightly devil and as strong as an axeman. My fingers and forearms were further bruised when I heard a low rasp from behind us that ended the youth's swinging. My whole body trembled as I lifted myself off a bed of dead leaves. When the blood was wiped from my eyes, I could make out the buttocks of a cow, which stood alongside an old woman and a small girl.

A russet mantle was pulled over the crone's pleated shirt. It was a white tunic that reached down to her ankles and was fastened across her breast by a bodkin of bone. Silver hair appeared at the sides of a linen headdress, which had been doubled over before being swaddled around her head and tied to its front. The little girl, who bore an uncanny resemblance to the crone, wrapped her arms around the waist of the elder. Seemingly ignorant of the danger she was in, the brave old woman wagged her forefinger at the savage who stood over me, appearing to scold him for his acts of violence.

For his part, the brute hardly seemed ruffled but, after a few moments, he looked from the crone to me and then back again, then raised his bloodstained weapon and took a step in her direction. I grunted aloud and struggled to my feet, but before I could intervene, the woman whipped a strange dagger from her belt. Our actions prompted the coward to desist from his approach. After a few moments, he snorted aloud and strode off into the trees, with the sounds of his footsteps soon dying away.

I stood still, uncertain what to do, while the two natives observed me with a sombre expression. Their cow nudged the forest floor with its nose and lowed, as the crone studied me from head to foot. Her hazel eyes lingered on my tunic, which had been darkened by the bleeding gash in my shoulder. When she spoke, my good ear picked up her Latin.

'Thou Spain?'

'Aye,' I nodded to her quickly, 'aye.'

'Thou make haste. Horse of enemy here. Follow Grian. Follow'.

She then tugged at the cow's halter as she struck a path into the forest, with the girl following close on her heels. I uttered a silent prayer of thanks to the Holy Virgin as I made after them, envious of the rough brogues on their feet as I stumbled barefoot over more rocks and twigs. My unlikely guides made swift progress, so that it was a struggle just to keep within sight of them. Only once did they refrain from their remarkable progress, when Grian turned to call out to me again.

'Haste, Spain. Haste.'

We pushed through the cover of woodland until it thinned out near the foot of the mountain. Ahead of me the crone shuffled along with her staff, with the little girl following her so closely that she seemed joined to the older woman's hip. I gritted my teeth against the cold and protected my face from the whipping branches with a raised and shivering arm. It was all I could do to keep up, and it was not long thereafter that the distant pounding of hooves had my knees buckling again.

The fleeting look of terror on Grian's face left me bereft of hope. The crone spat commands at her young charge, then hurried over to me without a word, seizing me by the arm and shoving me after the child. My feeble objection was dispelled by a low growl in the woman's throat that shocked even the protesting girl. Before I knew it, I was hurrying after both girl and cow as Grian rushed off in the direction of the hoof beats without a backward glance.

The girl put an arm to her face as she ran, and I soon realised that her cheeks were ruddy and swollen with tears. Now and then she would stare back at me with an accusatory scowl as we ran, her eyes blood-red with rage. When a piercing shriek was heard far behind us, the girl fell to her knees and began to sob furiously.

I collapsed in a heap beside her, my legs aflame from toil and my head spinning from both horror and weariness. As I lay but a few paces away from my little guide, I realised that I was not only pursued by the enemy, but also a grave threat to any wretch that would help me.

X

COUNTY SLIGO, IRELAND

15-16 September 1588

When the child ceased sobbing, she decided to resume our journey. The trees became sparser as we drew closer to the forest's edge, when we saw a settlement that stood almost at the foot of the nearest mountain. Tendrils of blue smoke arose from the thatched roofs of sod-built huts, and cattle loitered around them between a dozen minders. These men appeared to be native herdsmen, who each bore two javelins and a curiously long knife at their waists. At their appearance, my step faltered, but my guide pressed on towards them.

The tribesmen beheld the girl's approach in grim silence, until one of them stepped forward to take the cow's halter from her hand. The deftness of his movements surprised me, for the men wore fringes that reached down to the points of their noses, so that I wondered how they could see at all. Their hair was also as long as a woman's, and the ends of their beards reached down to their chests. From their backs hung thick woollen mantles which they wrapped around their linen tunics, the ends of which reached down to about a handspan over their knees.

Another tribesman also approached the girl, as he uttered their strange language in a questioning tone of voice. My little guide offered plaintive replies, and her face turned crimson as tears ran down her cheeks again. The twelve men beheld me in awe as they listened to her garbled words, then proceeded to raise their weapons while forming a ring around me. I held my hands out before me to stem their fears, as their feet were parted to make ready for their spear throws.

My hesitant smile was not returned, nor did the men's severe bearing ease when a resounding gurgle was heard from my stomach. After the girl had finished her speech, one of the men called out an instruction to his fellows, who stepped away and beckoned to me to pass through them. I took up his instruction with a sigh of relief, hobbling after the girl who made for the clustered mud huts and cattle pens.

The young lass ignored the other natives in the settlement, a few of whom called out to her. but I could not feel as indifferent after more than a year spent at sea. My eyes quickly strayed towards a few of the maidens among their number, whose ringlets of hair were bound up in knots, or wreathed around their heads and interwoven with bright-coloured cord. Most of them were beautiful in the extreme, whether they were red, dark or fair headed, and I had often encountered their kind before, since many an exiled Irish whore had trailed the Spanish army in the Netherlands.

Yet the breed of Irishwomen before me was entirely different, having not been plucked from their lands to wait on the mercy and attentions of foreign strangers. The older ones watched their children at play, with the crowns of their heads wrapped in linen headdresses like the one Grian had worn. There were also younger, bareheaded damsels, who knelt over their quern stones and flax, with their bare ankles revealed at the end of their smocks. Despite my battered appearance and torn clothes, the bolder ones cast me unguarded smiles, seemingly smitten by the sight of a swarthy foreigner.

My attentions returned to the little girl when she stopped to enter a crude abode built of sods and tree branches. After pausing to point at the pallet by its entrance, she retired to a corner of the hut and threw herself onto a straw mattress of her own. I silently entered after her and crumpled onto the pallet she had indicated to me, grimacing from the ache in my worn legs. For a while thereafter, her sobs were barely restrained, and her head bobbed up and down near a small pile fishing nets made of vegetable fibres.

After several deep breaths, I opened my eyes again to study my new surroundings. Specks of sand and seashells could be made out in the wattle walls, and a blackened hearth lay at the centre of the hut. Fresh logs were piled alongside it, and the chimney hole in its roof revealed the grey sky overhead. By the time the girl had wept herself to sleep, a faint drizzle of rain could be heard outside.

'Hispania, Hispania,' chanted small voices behind me, and I turned to the entrance to see a handful of brats staring at me with cavernous eyes.

The Latin word which they used must have been learned from their elders, and I was half-inclined to return their cheeky grins. After all I had endured, the scrawny children were a heart-warming sight, and one of them drew a small blade from his belt, slashing the air before him as he repeated the word that they hurled in my direction.

'Hispania! Hispania!'

The children scattered when a middle-aged woman walked up to them and seized the loudest one by the ear. She scolded him aloud as she led him away, reappearing not long after with a smoking faggot held out to her and a mantle of sheep's wool folded over her other arm. Upon entering the hut, the woman handed me a lice-ridden blanket. She then placed some of the logs on the hearth, under which she wedged the bundle of flaming twigs.

After she left, other visitors also stopped by the cabin, silently passing on scraps of oaten bread and handfuls of rancid butter. I snatched them up and wolfed down the lot. The little girl stirred long enough to eat the food brought to her before she returned to sleep. An old man was next to enter our hut, with black and grey locks falling from his balding head like torn curtains. Unlike the other natives in the settlement, he wore shoes of hide, and I also noticed that his tunic had many more folds of linen to it. A large wart bedecked the middle of his long nose, behind which there blazed a pair of keen brown eyes.

'Ah, the latest Spaniard,' he remarked, then drew a small cup of fat from within his tunic and dipped his fingers into it.

As he wiped them across my chapped lips, I drew my head back at the touch, which drew a low growl from him.

'Do not stir, friend. This is the fat of the great sea beasts. It shall heal you.'

The whale blubber was indeed soothing, so I did not move again as he continued to apply it onto my red-raw knuckles, which soon glowed with warmth. When his cup was emptied, he next produced a small bottle of verdant salve.

'Where did you learn Spanish?' I croaked, then winced when he applied the salve to the bruises on my head and the gash across my shoulder.

'I was a sailor in my youth,' he replied. 'You Spaniards are wily whoresons, yet always paid well for our skins. I am now the chieftain of this *túath*... we once all earned our living from the sea.'

'Tuath?' I asked, puzzled by the word.

'My family,' he explained after a few moments' thought, then nodded at some of the natives outside the hut.

'You mean all of the people out there?'

'Yes,' he said.

'Yours is indeed a large family,' I replied between groans, as he wrapped a long strip of linen around my damaged shoulder.

Another moan left me when the ends of the cloth were bound into a tight knot, which earned me a glare of disapproval.

'Of the eight castaways that we've succoured,' said the old wart-nose, 'you are certainly the fussiest.'

'Other Spaniards?' I said with a start, instantly thinking of Ramos and Salva. 'Where are they? Tell me!'

He fell silent at my reply, staring past the crackling flames at the small girl napping on the other side of the hut. Finally, he rose to his feet, whispering to me with a frown of concern on his face.

'You'll meet with them soon enough. Until then, get some rest, Spaniard. I fear you will need it in coming days.'

'But where are they?' I called back, only to see him walking out of the hut.

I struggled to get to my feet, then threw my head back and fell into a deep slumber. For the first time in months, I slept with a full belly, woken but once when loud shouts and singing were heard at dusk. Through the doorway, I could see the glow of campfires outside, and the whistling wind filled our hut with the scent of broiled cowflesh.

My head turned groggily from side to side before it fell back again, and I passed out with a mouthwatering scent in my nostrils and the warmth of the popping fire beside me. My dreamless repose lasted until morning, when a deafening screech had me rise from the ground with a start. I soon realised that dawn had been heralded by the chirping of countless birds in the nearby wood.

'Christ's wounds,' I croaked, upon taking a deep breath, 'that is one hellish din.'

After the horrors of recent days, my hands trembled slightly until my nerves were steadied. I then thought to seek out Ramos and Salva, until I realised that it would be useless to do so without a weapon.

'I still need a damned knife,' I said to Maerten, then chided myself for again forgetting his absence.

A small shuffling noise reached me from across the glowing embers, and I watched the little girl playing on her knees with bits of driftwood and twisted fragments of metal. As I beheld her in pity, I could see that her cheeks were still ruddy from the tears that she had spilt the previous day. It was not long before she noticed my attentions, and after serving me with a dark stare, she rose to her feet and stomped out of the hut, leaving behind her trinkets disgorged from the sea.

A deep sigh left me as I pulled the sheepskin over my back, to shield myself from the chill air. Sleep quickly returned, and it was only rowdy singing a few hours past midday that roused me once more. The hut had by now turned darker and colder, with the ashes on the hearth having long since cooled. When I wriggled over towards the dwelling's entrance, I saw a party of natives marching through the huts, bearing a chest over two feet long which was adorned with the eagles of Imperial Spain.

As curious onlookers gathered around these singing new-comers, a hint of silver winked from inside the heavy coffer, revealing more booty stolen from other Armada survivors. No sooner had the chest's bearers reached the middle of the village than the trunk was dropped to the ground with a loud crash. The tribesmen quickly set upon the treasure hoard within it, snatching up pieces of eight and silver plate as the old wart-nose walked up to them.

The leader of the tuath held a staff in his right hand and shook it wildly at the gathering as he shouted in their tongue. Most of the natives appeared bewildered by the tirade, and a couple of the men made a timid protest before staggering off reluctantly. Their aged leader stepped over to the Spanish chest and slammed it shut, then snorted aloud as he walked towards my hut. Behind him, the trunk stood alone in a new drizzle of rain, and the chirp of grasshoppers filled the air as dusk set in. Old wart-nose shook his head in annoyance as he stepped in beside me, grumbling beneath his breath.

'What ails you, friend?' I asked nervously.

The man was still in a huff as he beheld me angrily.

'A pox upon you Spaniards! Those spoils shall only bring us grief, for we have no use for such trinkets. They should have been left behind on the beach.'

His indifference to the chest's contents stunned me, when a knave appeared in the hut's entrance to pass wart-nose an earthen bowl. The old seadog held it out to me, and I gaped at the charred strips of flesh within it, amazed by the sight of meat after weeks spent eating hard tack and weevils. The old man seemed bothered by my hesitation as he proffered the bowl towards me again.

'Here, eat. One of us has gone without to afford you this portion.'

My voice was thick with awe when at last I managed a reply.

'Your people are most generous, friend.'

'Perhaps more humane than your masters, slave. Do not look so surprised, for I have travelled far enough to recognise the garb of galley slaves and cannot imagine the horrors you must have endured at sea.'

I took a piece of meat from the bowl and placed it in my mouth. It was tough, but I chewed on it furiously, while wart-nose stared at me with his eyes twinkling. The taste of the food did much to improve my spirits, and my host's knave knelt in the door of the hut again, passing me a small bowl of goat's milk which I drained in one gulp.

After collecting the empty earthenware, the servant knelt at the fireside, placing logs and twigs upon it and setting to work on them with a piece of flint and a dagger. All the while, the warty-nosed seadog beheld me with a faint smile and his hands clasped before him. His silent presence left me feeling awkward, until he finally spoke.

'You are fortunate to have survived the slaughter on the beaches.'

'It appears so,' was my reply.

'What will you do now?'

'Seek my revenge,' I said, without a moment's hesitation.

Despite his many years, the old man seemed taken aback at my words.

A brief silence endured between us, until he spoke again.

'That is most curious,' he said. 'Given your current plight, I would have thought that survival would be your first priority.'

'My life is worth nothing to me,' I replied, 'for I live only to avenge my family.'

'Oh,' he said absently, before asking, 'what family?'

Memories of Reynier's household returned to me then, and I bristled with rage, remembering the loss of the old miller, as well as his son and daughter. My hand covered my face as I struggled to collect myself, while feeling distressed by my last memories of both Elsien and Maerten.

I then recalled my promise to Maerten, during our last conversation on the ill-fated hospital ship. An oath to return to the last place I wanted to see again in my life, to find the boy who we had so blindly abandoned to the war-torn disaster of a once-thriving country. To return my younger brother-in-law to a world of new hope. At the memory, I met the old seadog's stare and answered his question.

'My late wife's brother, Pieter.'

'That name does not sound very Spanish.'

'He is my brother,' I replied defiantly. 'He was left behind in the hell of the Netherlands, and I must return for him.'

'After your revenge,' replied the man observantly.

'Yes,' I said, glaring back at him, and wondering if he had just mocked me.

Yet there was not even a hint of a smile from the tuath's leader. He refrained from asking me anything further, and in the lingering silence I wondered whether it was his people's custom to expect their guest to make conversation.

'The girl,' I said, as I nodded at her trinkets upon the ground, 'is she your daughter?'

His brows crinkled sorrowfully at my question, and his lips trembled slightly until he could reply.

'She is the daughter of Grian's son. He once shared that mattress with his wife.'

He jerked his head at the palliasse on which I lay and stuttered when he spoke again.

'I am... I am all she has left in this world.'

'A fair child, sire. Are you her grandfather?' A wan smile appeared on the man's face.

'No, slave. I am but a poor widower who is charged with leading his flock in these troubled times. In recent years Grian and I... lived together.'

'What happened to her son?'

My host fell silent at my question. I wondered whether I had offended him, and I avoided his distressed gaze by turning my attention to the sparks of flame produced by his knave's efforts.

'The same thing that killed her,' he answered at last. 'Sassenachs.'

Our eyes met at the last word he had uttered, as I tried to guess its meaning.

'You mean the English soldiers that...'

'Sassenachs,' he repeated with a snarl, 'are not merely regular soldiers. They are butchers who break every rule of combat, even dishonouring parleys.'

The severity of his expression left me feeling unsettled, until I uttered the word myself, struggling to imitate his accent.

'Sassanas,' I said with a curt nod.

'Sass-uh-nock,' he repeated sharply, 'and you would do well to remember it. Even now they are searching the coast for castaways, killing all Spaniards and any who would help them. They have spread all manner of lies about your countrymen, so that many Irish renegades are also hunting you down.'

At his last words, a crackle was heard by the hearth, and I shuddered upon recalling the slaughter I had seen on the beach only the previous day. My thoughts were distracted when the servant cupped his hands over some flaming kindling, gently growing the fire by blowing faintly upon it. Outside our lodging, the wind hummed among the huts while the heavens grew darker, with the treasure chest standing alone on the grass in the middle of the settlement. Tribesmen bustled around it without giving it a second glance, as they started other larger fires on which to cook their dinner.

'What am I to do?' I asked, 'until I met Grian, everyone in this land was hostile. Those brigands we first met on the beach...'

The old seadog swiftly raised his head, and his fists were bunched in anger while he interrupted me once more.

'But common robbers!' he spat, before wiping the slight dribble from the edge of his lips.

His chest heaved as he regathered himself. There followed a terse silence, in which his knave rose to his feet and left the hut, having grown the small fire to twice its size. Seeming satisfied that there was no one within earshot, my host addressed me again in a low voice, his brown eyes smouldering behind his warty nose.

'It is the Sassenachs' doing. They have destroyed our trade in exports and broken our spirit through war and famine. Many of our kin serve them in secret, while many more have been reduced to thieves who would as readily rob their own countrymen. For these men faith no longer matters. All that they prize is their own survival.'

His words left me fearing that I might lose my life as swiftly as my freedom had been regained. Outside the hut men were grouped around their open fires, and the unworldly smell of their cooked meat grew with dusk.

'What shall I do if I cannot tell friend from foe?'

The tuath's leader bit his lip at my question. He closed his eyes again, and his brow creased in thought as he whispered softly to me beneath his breath.

'Rare is the man who can outrun his own fate. And make no mistake Spaniard, your immediate fate appears dire. For the enemy wants all Spaniards tortured and killed.'

I held his stare for a few moments, worried that the English might yet rob me of my revenge. Old wart-nose mistook the concern on my face for terror, as he quickly tried to relieve my fears.

'Yet do not yet abandon hope, for my tuath pays tribute to the O'Connor Sligo. He was once a powerful chieftain but can no longer guarantee his people's protection from the enemy. They say that both he and the O'Hart have become restless because of the landings of so many Spaniards. Such a momentous event has not befallen *Éirinn* since Desmond's second rebellion.'

His eyes slowly closed, and he shook his head, as if banishing dreams from his harsh reality.

'No, no, it will all end in bloodshed and tears. You Spaniards cannot match the strength of our enemy. I fear that you must flee north, slave.'

'North?'

My host's eyes assumed a hazel glow in the growing firelight, and when he spoke again it was in a fervent voice.

'Yes, north, to the lands of O'Rourke. They still resist the yoke of the Sassenachs there and refuse to pay tribute to the Crown.'

'How will I find them?'

My host sighed.

'Tomorrow my kinsman will lead you to Keeloges, where others have succoured your countrymen. The O'Rourkes should take you in, for it is said that their chieftain is allied to the king of Spain.'

His words were a huge comfort to me, although one which was to prove all too fleeting. For I had hardly opened my mouth to thank him than another knave scrambled into our hut with mud stains all the way up to his knees. We beheld him in shock as he struggled to speak amid ragged breaths. The old seadog turned pale as he listened to the boy, who made ample use of the word Sassana.

'What of the Sassanas?' I asked, grabbing the sleeve of my host's tunic when the messenger scrambled back out of the hut.

He beheld me grimly.

'They are riding here. You must leave.'

'What?' I exclaimed, 'now?!'

'Be quiet! Hide your face away, and do not stir until my return.'

He shook my hand off his wrist and left my side, stepping out of the hut towards the growing rumble of hooves. Around the fires the natives bowed their heads and nervously traded low whispers, the same word playing upon their lips like the growing hiss of a serpent.

'Sasanaigh, Sasanaigh...'

I searched all over the hut for a weapon, inwardly cursing the man for having left me defenceless, before realising that I had not even asked him what his name was. While the old wart-nose treaded through the campfires, the fearful gibber grew around him like some incantation of doom.

'Sasanaigh, Sasanaigh, Sasanaigh!'

A trumpet blast was heard, and another peek through the hut's doorway revealed the sinister outlines of domed helmets. In my helpless condition, I shivered at the sight of the approaching horsemen in the gathering dusk, who moved through the settlement at a gentle canter amid the clank of iron. The hood of their leader's mantle was pulled closely over his eyes, with the steel half-champron on his horse's face suggesting that the man was also heavily armoured. The blazing torches held aloft by other riders revealed a mocking smile between his sallow cheeks, which bore the slightest of auburn beards.

The natives cowered away from the score of arrivals who each bore the crest of Saint George on their breasts, as well as on shields strapped to their shoulders and waists. To my horror, severed heads could also be seen dangling from the troopers' saddle straps, and as my gaze passed over the shrivelled skin on these trophies, I recognised the contorted features of Nando and Grian dangling from the leader's horse. The flickering torchlight also revealed a dozen bound Spanish and Irish captives, who were led in halters behind the heretics' mounts like chattel.

My aged host hobbled out towards the riders with an outstretched hand, earning himself a frown from their hooded leader who jerked at his horse's reins and signalled a halt. The riders' mounts stamped the ground and blew up clouds of mist, and for a few moments, all that could be heard was the distant chirping of crickets and the whinnying of the horses. My warty nosed host craned his neck up towards the foremost rider and addressed him in the Irish tongue, which caused the trooper to regard him with a scornful sneer. The rider then released a disdainful sigh before replying to the old seadog in Latin.

'The vile words thou speakest are forbidden by law,' he said in a reedy drawl, 'I am Sergeant Treasach Burke, assigned to Lieutenant John Gilson who serveth the Sheriff of Sligo. Thou shalt address me in the tongue of civilized men.'

My host made a grudging shift to Latin, then spoke again.

'Thy name is known to me, Sergeant. What dost thou seek?'

'Thou shalt surrender all aliens unto me.'

A few moments passed in which the old man shuffled awkwardly from one foot to the other.

'Alas, our laws decree that we grant them refuge.'

Burke cast him a glare of deep outrage.

'Thou art a fool, old man. These aliens are enemies of the Crown, and the law of which thou speakest no longer holds sway in these lands.'

Despite his hazardous predicament, the tuath's leader made a last attempt at dialogue, seemingly ignoring the gruesome sight of Grian's head which dangled before him.

'Surely thou couldst spare a mere handful of men? They are but a few helpless castaways, saved from the ocean, who pose no threat to anyone. Long hath it been said in this land, that under the shelter of each other, people survive.'

A ring of steel was heard as Treasach Burke drew his sword, to loud gasps from the native bystanders.

'The sheriff hath received orders from the Viceroy in Dublin,' he said. 'The Crown accordeth me the rights of seizure, torture and execution of Spaniards and of all those who would help them.'

My host took a deep breath, as the whole tribe hung on his next words. The old seadog next startled everyone by resting his hand on the face of Grian, its lips parted in a silent scream. After gently withdrawing his fingers from the severed head, the old man spread his legs in a defiant pose and rested his hands upon his hips.

'Thou wouldst threaten me before my own people?'

The sergeant's voice descended to a pitch barely above that of a whisper as he slowly uttered his reply.

'Thou wouldst do well to accept it.'

His armed riders appeared to tower above the tribe's leader, who stood as crooked as a willow before them. My host took a deep breath and stepped forward, pointing a gnarled finger at the mounted Burke.

'Why raise arms against thine own people, Treasach? Why persecute us for aiding the needy? What of those robbers upon the beaches? Shouldst ye not also deliver justice to them?'

The Irish renegade appeared to ignore the old seadog as he raised his sabre.

'I shall not ask thee again...'

With a scowl, my host gestured to the Spanish treasure chest on the ground behind him.

'Take that trunk and begone, Iscariot. We know what it is that thou truly seekest.'

So saying, he turned on his heel and walked off, giving his back to the hooded sergeant. Yet Burke was swift to recover from the slur, as he flicked his reins and wordlessly rode in alongside the natives' leader. It took but a moment for him to stand in his stirrups, before plunging the length of his sword between the old man's shoulders. A strident howl tore through the gloom outside the hut, as Burke kicked my host off his blade. Blood and piss sprayed the seadog's flailing limbs as the sergeant next proceeded to belt out an order.

'Smoke them out!'

Burke returned his sword to his scabbard and drew two flint-lock pistols from his belt. He raised them at two tribesmen who rushed towards him, and a loud crack was heard when both guns went off. The mounted troopers streamed towards their sergeant, cutting down natives and flinging torches onto the thatched roofs around them. At the sight, I kicked off my blanket and tore out of the hut, cursing aloud when I tripped over a ewe.

'Christ's blood!'

Large hounds stirred at the sheep's bleating, their baying filling the night air as the screams around the settlement grew louder. I got to my feet and shoved my way through the throng of natives who had rushed to their huts to fetch weapons. Men ran out of their dwellings armed with spears and staffs, their mantles whipped off their backs and wrapped around their forearms to serve as shields. A passing woman startled me when she tossed me a long dagger, then hurried off, pushing a small boy ahead of her.

As I fumbled in the mud for the weapon, another score of enemy riders closed in on us from another direction, their torches like fireflies in the dark. The new wave of heretics broke through pens and crashed over hovels, then turned onto the tribesmen. Before me, a swinging sword rent a boy's head from his shoulders, and other riders could be seen rounding up livestock.

Amid the cries of assailed women, I shrank behind a hut, when a sword blade whipped the air just above my head. The thrust sent me sprawling upon my back, and I felt a stinging sensation in my scalp. When I put my fingers to my hairline, they were left sticky with blood, and my crown had been sheared clean of hair. All around me the natives' battle cries were defiant as my flight was resumed.

I had not run five paces when a dismounted trooper sprang in front of me, the point of his blade missing my nose by a whisker. As my assailant raised his sword again, I hurled myself at him, wrapping my arms around his waist as we both crashed onto the ground. His helmet rolled away as I climbed atop him, crashing my forehead into his face again and again.

His screams soon died off, and his weapons fell to the grass as his writhing stopped. With the immediate threat averted, I staggered over his lifeless form and snatched up his sabre, then scurried away from the huts with my lungs ablaze. I darted back towards the forest, the jagged rocks underfoot slowing my flight. Hoof beats pounded in my ears when a rider bore down on me, his horse tearing up the ground until its breath was almost upon my neck. The butt of the trooper's sword pommel then struck me in the back of the head, which sent me flying headfirst into a puddle.

As I rose from the water, I could see the horse's gallop being slowed to a canter, and my pursuer threw himself off the charger and walked up to me. In the moonlight he cast a sinister, growing silhouette, until he was so close that I could see the twitches of mirth at the sides of his lips.

'Not so fast, my rabbit,' he said in accented Spanish, and the blood rose to my head when the malign whisper revealed him to be the renegade sergeant, Treasach Burke.

Mud dripped off my face when he gestured to me to stand up. 'On guard, cur!'

In a fury, I fumbled for the sword in the darkness, then rose to my feet when my fingers had closed around its hilt.

'Come on then, you bastard.'

Within an instant our encounter was over. Treasach Burke was not as tall as me, which gave me the longer reach and meant that I could press for the advantage. Yet he sidestepped my first thrust with ease, before his pommel was slammed into my bandaged shoulder, hurling me onto all fours with a yelp. A blow of his knee across my chin left me writhing in the sludge again, coughing up dirt in anguish. The sound of a cocked pistol followed as the renegade pressed the mouth of his gun against my temple.

'Get up, rabbit.'

My head was still throbbing as I was led back to the cabins, with a cold dread growing in the pit of my stomach. All resistance had been quelled in the settlement, where we sidestepped the corpses of natives which were sprawled over the smoking remains of the huts. Among the carnage I also spotted a dead trooper, before two of Burke's men appeared and wordlessly led me away from their smirking sergeant.

After they had bound me hand and foot, I was forced onto my knees. The men rifled through my rags for booty, then rammed their gloved fingers down my throat until they had brought up my dinner. This vile prodding was repeated again and again, until my captors were satisfied that I had not swallowed any precious trinkets. With their search over, the troopers flung me into a cattle pen with their other prisoners, where my raw gullet had me seized by violent coughs.

Despite the dark of nightfall, I could make out from the muted whispers that eight other Spanish captives also shared my quarters. To my dismay I knew none of them, and they ignored my presence upon noticing my humble rags. A wounded Basque lay among us holding his spilt entrails, and his groans were as prolonged as they were distressing. His agony lasted for at least another hour, when furious protests were heard from the few remaining huts where Burke and his men were billeted. At these cries, one of our guards waded into the makeshift gaol, and drew the length of his sword across the dying Basque's gizzard. The brutal gesture brought an end to the moans but none of us could sleep thereafter.

The troopers reentered our pen at dawn, jabbing us with their sword points and booting us to our feet. In the growing daylight, the Sassanas appeared a ragged and unkempt bunch, not dissimilar to the forlorn troops of Imperial Spain who lived by their own means in the far off, forgotten forts of North Africa. Like all troops in a distant frontier, our captors wore unstarched shirts and ill-fitting armour, and were most likely brigands who had been pressed into the service of the English Crown.

As they led us away from the huts, Burke rode up and reined his horse in alongside his prisoners. A deep dread overcame me as the sergeant studied us, and it was all I could do to keep from shaking when he pointed out four of our number. This unhappy quartet was tasked with bearing the heavy treasure chest which had been brought to the settlement the previous day. After lifting their burden off the ground, the wretches stumbled ahead of us to muffled grunts and loud oaths, as our captors hurled burning brands upon the thatched roofs of the huts. As the settlement smoked behind us, we were herded out into the open countryside, with the rustled cattle tightly hemmed between Burke's riders.

After an hour, our path revealed the streaked flank of the great mountain range to our left. We were driven over a lush pasture until almost mid-morning, when we caught sight of another village of bog-wood huts. The Sassanas paraded us through it to piercing blasts of the trumpet, then dismounted to demand food from the natives who lived there.

We were left to collapse beneath a large cross, being too tired and hungry from our forced march to pay much notice to the mythical animals that were carved into it. A tall tower rose from among the thatched huts before us, which captured my attention until I passed out from weariness. More trumpet blasts woke me towards noon, which announced the arrival of another force of heretics.

'What are they saying?' rasped a Catalan sailor, as snatches of talk were traded by the troopers around us.

'They speak of a lieutenant's arrival,' replied an Irish prisoner who knew our tongue, 'one John Gilson.'

This haughty officer soon appeared in his highcrowned hat and his glistening breastplate, astride his black destrier. He rumbled through the village at the head of a band of troopers, leading a dozen Spanish captives who were bound up in halters like wild asses. The small detachment of troopers dismounted but a musket shot's distance away from us, where they proceeded to hitch their steeds. Burke could be seen emerging from a hut and bowing to the lieutenant, who strode past him to enter the dwelling, with the sergeant swiftly following him in. Meanwhile I carefully studied the faces of the newly arrived Spanish wretches, yet I could not make out either Ramos or Salva among them.

'They always had the luck of the devil,' I grunted beneath my breath, so as not to be heard by our guards.

It must have been over an hour later when Gilson and Burke approached us with their thumbs hooked into their belts and six of their men behind them. As they drew nearer, I could better make out the lieutenant's features beneath his hat, which consisted of a cropped fair beard which grew on a handsome face which was also pockmarked. At his order, Burke and the other troopers picked out the dozen Irishmen from among our number. These natives were dragged away from us by their tunics as they squirmed in their bonds, struggling to shove off the grip of their captors.

They were led away kicking and screaming towards a makeshift gallows which had been hastily erected a few feet away. The Sassanas had them strung up one by one, which left me to clamp both my hands over my good ear to stifle the sound of their passing. Meanwhile Burke and Gilson turned their backs on the killings they had ordered, being caught up in a heated debate as one lifeless body after another was cut down behind them.

The gruesome spectacle was repeated nine times, before Sergeant Burke despatched the last three natives in person by his own blade. With this deathly work finished, bugle blasts pierced the air again when Gilson ordered another march. I was kicked to my feet, finding myself part of the next foursome forced to carry the bulky treasure chest. Within minutes I was grunting aloud from the toil of bearing the heavy load, hobbling madly over stony paths until we came to a river.

Upon reaching the stream our captors immediately proceeded to ford it. As we stumbled through the icy water, an old Spaniard collapsed with a splash, but the attempts of other captives to help him were met with the jabbing butts of our captors' spears. The fallen prisoner was left to drown, until the stream of bubbles from below the water disappeared downstream. My head sagged forwards and tears pricked my eyelids at the effort it took to keep the heavy treasure chest above water. When we had crossed the stream, I released my grip on the chest and fell to my hands and knees. Both my arms burned from strain, but the first blows of a spear end upon my back prodded me to return to my feet and lift the trunk once more.

Our captors travelled in a grim silence throughout our journey, watching our surroundings at all times and swiftly relighting the match-chords on their muskets. They were clearly uneasy about some everpresent danger that lurked in the open country, and I remembered wart-nose telling me about tribes which were hostile to the English Crown. The lieutenant often called abrupt halts whenever sounds were heard from the undergrowth, and in these moments, the heretics' guns were held at the ready as their heads shifted from side to side.

Ahead of me, Burke's head turned as swiftly as a barn owl's at the slightest sound, and when his eyes met mine, I swiftly bowed my head, fearful as I was of provoking him into new barbarity. Meanwhile the other Spaniards about me trudged on like corpses risen from the grave, all skin and bone like long-abandoned strays. To a man, their faces were as ashen as those of convicts condemned to the gallows, with each of their heavy steps looking like it might be their last. Now and then, the odd boundary of privately held property could be seen during our forced march, with rows of stones followed by turf walls.

When yet another river was forded, we tramped towards a far-off stump of flat-topped mountain ahead of us. It stood on a coastline that stretched along the ocean to our right, and Lieutenant Gilson's men appeared to relax their guard as we drew nearer to the coast. Before long, loud cheers broke out amongst them while the sea breeze played with the hair of the captive ahead of me, obstructing my view. When my head was jerked sideways, I caught my first glimpse of the garrison town.

XI

Sligo Town, Ireland

16 September 1588

A wall of stone greeted us outside the garrison town. An array of severed heads was displayed atop it, with curled tongues hanging out of them almost mockingly. The rampart was flanked on both sides by ugly hedgerows of stakes, which had been erected between high mounds and deep ditches. To the north, the garrison was also shielded by a river that wended its way through the town itself, bearing rain from the mountains into the sea.

Upon reaching the gatehouse, Gilson ordered a halt while Burke rode ahead and called out the watchword. When the stout wooden doors ahead of us creaked open, we were greeted by loud sounds which were typical of a cattle enclosure. Upon our entry we were met by several corrals and stables that were choked with livestock. The rustled cattle in our party issued their own lowing and bleating, as they were led off to their confines by their new minders.

The rest of us approached yet another gate within the inner walls of the garrison, which defended the town itself. A grizzled veteran stood alongside it, drilling fresh-faced charges in the use of wooden swords. He only paused their training to jeer at us as the portcullis behind them was opened. Once we passed through the gateway, we were next led over a wooden bridge, with our own steps muffled by the deafening rush of the river which served as yet another barrier behind the walls.

At last, the town itself stood before us, and our nostrils were filled with the tang of salt and herring. As my stomach rumbled at the smell of dried fish, I observed the wooden houses around us. Many of them had a facing of rubble and lath, standing over two storeys high. Slit windows could be seen in the facades of unwrought flint, with sombre, unwelcoming faces leering at me from behind them.

The cobbled avenues rang as other troopers rode past us towards the bridge, casting dark glances in our direction. We were next met by the sight of a bevy of townsfolk who had gathered at the other end of the street. Most of them appeared to be traders and merchants, dressed as they were in gaudy, silk embroideries and peaked shoes. Our awe at their finery was replaced by horror when we saw the six Spaniards hanging from the gallows behind them. The heads of the dangling castaways were surmounted by a plaque which bore the Latin word *idolatres*.

Some of the traders shouted insults at the strung-up corpses, while I studied the faces of the dead, seeking the ones of my former comrades. Meanwhile a few patrons had emerged from one of the town's alehouses, watching us with their large tankards of double beer resting upon their bellies. A group of children were also gathered alongside them, who appeared better fed than the young natives I had seen in the raided settlement. They were also far better dressed, with rich mantles of rug wrapped around their shoulders and soft leather shoes on their feet.

From among the gathered crowd, a bearded man strode towards us with a hateful expression, wearing a Jewish skullcap. His open revulsion at the sight of Spaniards declared him a descendant of the unconverted Jews who had been expelled from Spain and Portugal at the end of the last century. A hawking sound came from his throat before he showered those captives closest to him with his spittle, then formed a fist and shook it in our direction.

I was filled with dread as we were led on towards the castle which loomed ahead of us. It was a structure that dwarfed the buildings alongside it, the menace of its grey battlements reinforced by the dozens of corpses which were strung up from them. There were no Spaniards among their number, and I averted my eyes from the malign sight as we stopped in front of the mottled doors of the keep. I dropped to one knee, while my hands quivered around the handle of the accursed trunk. Gasps of relief could be heard from my fellow trunk-bearers, which turned to agonised grunts again when the door creaked open.

Lieutenant Gilson led us into a small courtyard, which was full of grim-faced troopers who bore all manner of weapons and armour. Many a punch and blow was received when we passed through them, as some accused us of being papist idolaters, while referring to the infamous Saint Bartholomew's Day massacre of Protestants in Paris.

After the last blows and kicks had been received, we were at last relieved of the cursed chest. The guards took it from us before we were next led down a dark staircase, which brought us deep into the bowels of the keep. Our captors cast us into foul, dripping cells, in which sunlight was as scarce as fresh air. My ears throbbed as my head spun in the dank, suffocating dungeon, where I was cooped with other wretches who had also been caught by the heretics.

I toppled to the ground, heaving deep breaths, with my back aching from all the miles spent bearing the treasure chest. When the door of the dungeon was slammed shut, the silence around me did not endure for much longer, when some of the haughtier Spanish captives began to loudly bemoan our plight. One rose to his feet and hobbled furiously across our cell, with his loud muttering marking him out as a proud son of Andalusia.

'God curse the fool who talked me into departing Spain with this enterprise! Sea battles never favour us, we've been cursed ever since the Emperor's setback at Djerba!'

Another sighed wearily from the ground.

'Why has the Lord abandoned us to this predicament? We are Spanish troops, it is the heretics who should be rotting in cages.'

Behind me a low voice was heard, which was possessed of a Florentine accent.

'That cursed Regiomontanus was right, after all. Now we shall all swing from the hangman's noose.'

The pacing Andalusian gibbered in fear.

'We must attempt an escape. There are over thirty Spaniards in here, without counting men of other nations.'

'Escape where?' retorted the Florentine behind me. 'We don't even know the tongue used by the savages!'

A greying Galician piped up, his brow heavily furrowed by decades of service.

'I know the tongue they use. When they are not begging for alms, then it is most certainly their native Irish.'

Nervous chuckles were heard despite our miserable plight.

'The thieving bastards,' spat the Andalusian. 'I cannot believe our treatment on the beach. We should have attempted a landing and put them all to the sword, instead of waiting for that storm to shipwreck us!'

No sooner had he spoken than he looked about furtively, so as to ensure that no guard was stealing up on us. Another prisoner showed no such concern, as he spat on the ground and snarled aloud.

'Perhaps God has indeed forsaken us.'

He then issued a spate of the darkest blasphemy that only the Sicilians were capable of. It even exceeded the foulest tirades I heard from Dimas during my last days on the Santa Maria de Visión. When his broadside had ended, a few moments of stunned silence passed, until another inmate passed a dry comment from the cell opposite ours.

'You have hardly won back His favour.'

'What are we to do?' said the Andalusian, resuming his aimless tread. 'Should we merely surrender and swing from the gallows?'

'The gallows would be a small blessing,' said the Florentine behind me, stretching his lanky legs out before him. 'These heretics are known to be quite vicious.'

The Andalusian cast him a fearful look. 'How do you mean?'

'Verily it is said,' replied the Italian with a sigh of resignation, 'that those who fought in the Low Countries have heard all manner of dark tales...'

'There are tales and there are truths,' shouted the Andalusian nervously. 'This is not the time for your old wives' tales!'

'Well,' said the Florentine with an injured tone, 'we know that they go to great lengths to make their prisoners' tongues wag. There was this Jesuit we once rescued from the English in the Spanish Netherlands, who had been forced to wear the fire boots.'

'Fire boots?' stuttered the Sicilian blasphemer in a small voice. 'What devilry is that?'

'Why, nothing more than their name implies. Shoes of cast iron that are locked about your ankles and placed on an open fire. I'll not tell you what the poor priest's feet looked like.'

An uneasy silence followed his words, which was broken by a collective gasp when we heard the clank of heavy keys turning in the prison doorway. The haggard faces of guards next appeared in the flickering torchlight, and they unlocked our cell and stormed into it, seizing the Andalusian who beheld them in shock.

'No! Not me! What have I done?'

His cries were stifled by a punch to the mouth, and he clawed desperately at the ground as they dragged him away from us. His fingernails scraped my swiftly withdrawn ankle as we cowered before the burly gaolers, and he screeched his head off as he hurled all manner of curses at our captors. His screams were drowned out when the dungeon door was slammed shut, and in the dreadful quiet that ensued, I rubbed the deep scratches upon my ankle. In the next hour, more inmates were removed by our captors until one of the younger prisoners voiced a question none had yet dared to utter.

'Are they killing them all?'

'It depends,' remarked the burly, greying Galician.

'On what?'

The older soldier snorted at the youth's simplicity.

'Why on their rank, of course. Officers are always ransomed.'

The youth turned pale in the dungeon's half-light, when the next rattle of keys had us swiftly cowering into the tight corners of our cell like mice in the hold of a sinking ship. In the ensuing scuffle of men and rats in our cage, I could see Treasach Burke striding through the corridor with a wizened little priest at his back. A Spanish inmate hissed and spat at the bowed cleric, until the renegade sergeant drew his sabre and hacked at the spitting Spaniard's outstretched hand, which was swiftly withdrawn to an anguished howl. Burke frowned at the three severed fingers which had fallen at his feet, before kicking them across the tiles. He next cleaned the edge of his blade with a swiftly drawn cloth, as he rasped at us in his accented Spanish.

'Keep silent, you ungrateful curs!'

The ensuing quiet was only broken by the grumbling of stomachs and the low whimpering of the inmate who had just lost his fingers. The sergeant sheathed his blade and spoke up again as he eyed us with unmasked contempt.

'In his Christian goodness, the sheriff of Sligo offers the ministry of his confessor to the miserable misbelievers in his gaols. That you might obtain salvation before your despatch. Be warned that I shall not have the good clergyman suffer the dungeon's steps again. So those of you who would recant your papist heresy must speak up now, for you'll get no other chance.'

For a few moments none responded, but then a collective howl broke out, so strident that it would have drowned out the wailing of newly widowed wives. For although our lives were forfeit, our honour remained dearer to us than life itself. I knew it from my time spent soldiering, that despite their numerous sins and trespasses, every last Spaniard would have gladly embraced death rather than abandon the faith they were sworn to protect.

'Curse you and your false witness!' cried a captive.

Most prisoners cursed aloud and spat at Burke and his priest, flinging themselves against the bars of their cages in furious ire. The sergeant shrugged at our defiance as he made to leave the dungeon, dragging away the shivering priest, who looked like he was on the point of recanting himself. At the renegade's order, three gaolers hurried into the dungeon with their maces, slamming them against the iron bars and felling prisoners to the ground. In this way the Spanish outcry was soon ended, as men tumbled around me clasping cracked heads and nursing fractured fingers.

As this latest stir unfolded, I cut a silent figure in the corner of my cell, caring little for the religious conflicts I had long sworn to trade for the New World. My limbs ached after the long march south, and my only desire was to spend my last living moments in peace, that I might find the strength to die an honourable death at the gallows.

A deep dismay had also gripped me, since I had been robbed of the chance to avenge Elsien and Maerten. In those moments

I would have given anything to earn my freedom, for the chance to hunt down the sergeant and corporal who had destroyed our lives. Yet my longing was pointless, and I fell back against the wall crushed by acute disappointment, grudgingly accepting that Maerten had died in vain, and that Pieter and I would never reach the Americas.

The lull in the cells did not last much longer. Men cowered like small children when the gaolers reappeared, dragging yet another captive behind them. After opening our cell door, they hurled him among us, as if he were some rabid animal and not merely a whiskerless youth. Rats screeched in protest when he rolled over the floor, towards another prisoner who raised a foot at him.

'*Pardiez*! Get away from me!'

Our new inmate stank to high heaven, and the dim light in our cell revealed branches and twigs in his tousled hair. He was but another native youth with a bloodied brow. At last, the old Galician was moved to pity, and reached out with his torn shirtsleeve to dab the gash across the lad's forehead. The youth's eyelids fluttered once before he pushed the old soldier away.

'Leave me!'

The lad's Spanish was perfect, leading me to suspect that he was one of the many Irish sea hands who had sailed with the Armada. To my further amazement, his bunched fist nearly caught the Galician in the jaw, so that the old Spaniard pushed the young inmate away in outrage.

'Be still, fool! We are your friends!'

The old soldier had barely spoken when one of our gaolers entered the dungeon and stood at the bars of our cage, causing us to whirl around and behold him in terror.

'Silence, curs! Do not fret, for your hour is soon at hand.'

His threat spread further distress among us, and I was relieved when he finally walked away, leaving the other Spaniards to resume their hoarse whispers. Upon regaining some calm, the Irish inmate told us that his name was Killian, before being interrupted by loud noises through the grate in the castle wall behind us. The Florentine shot to his feet to peer through the small opening, where a flurry of shadowy hooves and men's boots could be seen.

'What is going on out there?'

Killian sounded downcast as he dropped back onto the ground.

'It is the sheriff, George Bingham. He has arrived in Sligo Town from Ballymote Castle. The Sassenachs must be preparing a raid.'

The Galician's curiosity was piqued.

'Against whom?'

'The northern rebels.'

'Who?'

Killian sighed wearily at the old man's ignorance.

'The wild Irishry who do not recognise the English queen.'

For emphasis, the young Irishman formed a circle with his thumb and forefinger.

'The tribes that pay her this much tax.'

Some of the Spaniards sniggered nervously, but their laughter was cut short at the sound of other footsteps and the clank of keys. When our captors reappeared, a frightened murmur was heard among some of the prisoners in another cell, where men trembled in corners like sheep about to be culled. Their cage door flew open before the burly gaolers entered it, shoving the other Spaniards away as yet another prisoner was plucked from among them. His hands were struck with a bull's pizzle until his fingers came away from the cage bars, with the wretch's final cry being half stifled when the dungeon's iron door was slammed shut.

'For Thomas More-!'

Killian's low whisper could be heard a few moments later.

'An English Catholic. You cannot envy his lot.'

The lanky Florentine grunted.

'My head is done in, what with English who are papists and Irish helping heretics. In Florence we are all Catholics. Over there, we argue over women instead.'

A few laughed grimly at his words while others discussed the scene which they had just witnessed.

'Why are they doing this?'

All ears were strained when Killian replied. For we knew nothing of the ways of the land in which we found ourselves and, if nothing else, he had taught us the name of the town in which we awaited our end.

'They are leading prisoners off to interrogation. The Sassenachs have been terrorised by the Spanish landings. I fear that this confinement is the best treatment that we can hope for, although it shall not last for much longer.'

'Rats in a trap,' said another inmate. 'How can we threaten them if we are already gaoled?'

Killian sighed.

'They are afraid of the wild Irishry who inhabit the woods and mountains, men whom they consider uncivilised monsters and animals. You must believe me, for I know this land well. Even now the rebels will be readying to rise up against the heretics. And much as the heretics fear you, they are more afraid of you joining forces with the rebels.'

After Killian had spoken there was heard no reply, for his intimation had been understood by us all. Finally, someone asked him how he had been captured.

'Oh, believe me, I ran like the wind! But these days one cannot tell friend from foe. I was tricked by some Iscariots who sold me to my doom. May they burn in hell!'

'Wherever they are,' I added from the shadows behind him.

Killian turned and observed me curiously, having not paid any heed to me before.

'What's your story, Spaniard?'

I refused to answer, for various spells in gaol had taught me that the ears of one's captors could be anywhere when one was imprisoned. I did not doubt for a moment that at least one of our inmates was planted among us by the enemy, with orders to spy for information. Yet some of the younger Spaniards spoke freely, telling Killian how Grian's lover had afforded them shelter before he had perished by Burke's sword. The Irishman listened intently to each part of their tale, then shook his head with a scowl at the mention of Burke.

'Ah, Treasach Burke. That Judas. Many in this land curse his name, for he is said to be a man as dangerous as he is ruthless.'

One of the Spaniards then gibbered on about the natives' kindnesses towards us, and I almost told him to shut his mouth when he pointed at me.

'You shared the old man's hut, didn't you? I saw him bearing a bowl of meat there.'

Killian's grey eyes widened as he fixed them on me again.

'Truly, Spaniard? What did he tell you?'

The attention of every last inmate had turned to me, and I fumbled for a reply that dripped with sarcasm.

'The old man promised to introduce me to a native castaway. One who knew his own land so well, that he would lead me straight into this very dungeon.'

For a moment, my listeners batted their eyelids at me, then the Florentine burst out laughing, closely followed by the other Spaniards. In the meantime, Killian's face reddened and a vein in his temple throbbed with unspoken fury. His voice sounded terse when he spoke again, and it also held a hint of malice.

'Perhaps you are right, Spaniard, that I do not know the whole of this land well enough to flee the enemy with ease. For it has been my lot to spend most of my life among your proud and haughty people. Long enough for me to tell a cultured accent when I hear it.'

Upon saying this he issued a shrill whistle, and a puzzled lull descended until our gaolers flung the iron door open and made for our cage. They had not even unlocked it when Killian casually got to his feet, as if he had just met two close friends, then walked out of the cell a free man. I stared at him in disbelief, as he left the dungeon with a small chuckle. Then the iron door slammed shut again and its heavy bolts squeaked into place. One of the younger captives in our cell sounded baffled.

'Why do they spy on us? Are we not already dead?'

The old Galician snorted at the youth's naivety but sweat prickled my forehead. In a corner of our cell, the Sicilian spat and blasphemed some more, then sighed aloud in resignation.

'The sparrow has flown. But when will the cats return, I wonder?'

He had hardly spoken when Treasach Burke reappeared in the company of his gaolers. His tone was ironic as he gently patted a wooden club upon his thigh, his reedy voice akin to the hiss of a snake as he glared right at me.

'Your presence has been requested by our betters, my rabbit.'

When the cell door opened, I scrambled away towards the bars that surrounded us, wrapping my hands around them and kicking at the enemy like a prodded mule. With a loud oath, Burke fell onto my back with an outstretched knee and dug his gloved fingers into my wounded shoulder. I howled and seized his bloodied gauntlet with both my hands, but he swiftly withdrew it as his thugs hauled me towards the door by my ankles.

My fingernails scraped every last floor tile, before my wrists were roughly bound behind my back by the gaolers who led me towards the winding staircase. The renegade sergeant seemed stirred by my anguish, excitedly sucking air through his teeth as he slipped in behind me and pushed me ahead of him.

My toes were stubbed against the same staircase I had descended earlier, and after making our way up another two storeys we reached the fresher air of officers' quarters. We trod across the rush-strewn floor of the castle, passing beneath barrel-vaulted ceilings until a heavy oaken door was reached. Burke stepped towards it and knocked once, which prompted a knave's head to appear from behind it moments later. He took one look at me and gestured us in, when I was shoved into a grim, grey dining hall.

Upon entering, I saw the fair-haired Lieutenant Gilson seated at the table in front of us. He appeared entirely ignorant of our presence, seated as he was among a handful of richly dressed burghers, and passing bills of exchange to two of his subalterns. Behind him a short scribe sat at a desk, ready to take notes with a quill brandished in his ink-stained hand.

Wolfhounds the size of colts snarled at the diners' feet, and their yellow fangs glistened between thin black lips. One of them growled when Burke winded me with a punch to the stomach, which dropped me to my knees once more. The renegade's fingers closed tightly around the back of my neck, as he snarled into my good ear.

'On your knees before the sheriff, rabbit.'

I dared not raise my head, then heard the squeak of leather boots which announced the presence of someone behind us. A chair was dragged backwards before it creaked beneath the weight of the new entrant.

'So… you are one of those found near the Abbey of Staad?'

The gruff voice spoke in an accented Spanish that was near perfect. Burke jammed his club beneath my chin and raised my head with it, forcing me to look up at the man who had addressed me.

'Face the Sheriff when he speaks to you!'

A shiver ran through me when I beheld the short, broad-chested man with a neatly cropped brown beard. Sheriff George Bingham observed me stoically from his seat at the head of the long table, his back straight as a scouring stick as he calmly peeled off his black gauntlets. The high rank he held was emphasised by his fine livery, which eclipsed that worn by the other officers at his table. A collar of gilded steel was fastened around his throat, worn above a black doublet with a peasecod belly. Two cold blue eyes studied my face from behind the end of his pointed nose, and his smile was that of a man who was secure in his power to torment others.

My stomach rumbled when a bowl of steaming beef broth was placed in front of him. Bingham then nodded to a freckled knave who walked over and produced his own spoon, which he used to help himself to the sheriff's serving. After swallowing one mouthful the taster then withdrew to a corner of the room, where he was watched for a few minutes, long enough to confirm that the sheriff's meal had not been laced with poison.

I stood as still as I could, not daring to utter a sound, when I noticed a woman striding silently towards Bingham. As her ringed hand slid onto his arm, I could see that she was a striking beauty, fair-haired and with skin as pale as alabaster.

Her clothing revealed her to be a Frenchwoman, with the high neck of her bodice fastened with ribbon ties down the front of her breast and surmounted by the frill of a petticoat. Her expressions mirrored his within an instant, with her lips parting into a smile whenever he displayed contemptuous mirth and being pursed tightly together whenever his expression turned to one of anger.

Meanwhile the stinking, double-dealing tosspot of Killian stood behind her, his arms held to his side and his head bowed as the sheriff fondled his wench with one hand. Bingham finally released her behind, reaching instead for a silver spoon when he addressed me.

'I once fought under the banner of your King Philip. Saint Quentin was my first battle abroad.'

He refrained from speech when one of the men at his table proceeded to say grace. The prayer was not yet finished when the sheriff lifted his spoon and sipped at some of the soup, and his guests swiftly followed his lead amid a loud clink of cutlery. When he had chewed an end off a hunk of bread, George Bingham returned his attentions to me.

'Times change, as do princes and kings. I have since fought against Spain and aided the heretics in the Low Countries. I also defeated the Pope's troops at Smerwick in Kerry.'

Broad smiles appeared on his and his wench's faces as he recalled the last event.

'That day we put six hundred Spaniards to the sword.'

His words sank in like dagger thrusts. In my shock I twice attempted to utter a reply, when Burke prodded my shoulder to urge me to speak.

'When did you change sides?'

Bingham's smile quickly turned into a scowl, and he watched me closely as he dabbed at his lips with a napkin.

'I see that you have fetched me a glib specimen, Sergeant Burke. Albeit one who is ignorant in matters of politics and dominion. I never once changed sides, Spaniard, for surely you know that your king was once also ours?'

Another prod from Burke spurred me to blurt my thoughts.

'Then you understand my frustrations.'

Across from the sheriff, the short scribe jabbed furiously at a page with his quill, while Lieutenant Gilson frowned at my unabashed attempt at familiarity.

'You say that Spaniard,' scoffed the pockmarked officer, 'yet you still served him willingly. No doubt you were keen to repeat the atrocities of your Spanish fellows in the Netherlands, those butchers who still ruin the lives of countless innocents.'

'But I – I -'

I was about to protest my innocence, by claiming I was but a mere galley slave who had been pressed into joining the Armada illegally and against my will. Yet in that instant I recalled what the old Galician had said in the cells about ransoming high born prisoners, so that my teeth were clenched tightly about my tongue. For a wild idea had already formed in my mind, one which I thought might improve my chances of survival. So when all present regarded me curiously following my broken outburst, I said the next thing that came into my mind, which left me sailing perilously close to the wind.

'I – I meant to say that the Irish indeed appear a happier lot than the Netherlanders.'

Gilson fell silent while Bingham glowered at me while he appeared to consider if there had been any mockery in my reply. When he spoke again his voice quivered with annoyance.

'They would be happier still, were it not for the flames of rebellion fanned among them by your king. A few of the savages still resist the queen's law and order, having elected to ignore their pacts with the Crown. But in time they will pay, one and all, no matter how long it takes to bring them to heel. Every last sottish traitor among them will be beaten out of every last bush.'

He returned his attention to his soup, sipping his last spoonfuls before speaking to me again.

'There is an able axeman in the yard who can spare you a hanging. You may earn yourself a swift death, Spaniard, if you do not waste my time. I have few enough men as it is. And as you can see, I must also attend to my duties during meals.'

'What is it that you would know?'

The sheriff's cold eyes met mine as the empty bowl was whisked away from him and swiftly replaced by a serving of roasted mutton.

'Everything.'

Since I was reluctant to unleash any further ire against my person, I told him of the slaughter on the beach and of what I had found in the defiled church. The sheriff chewed on his meat as he listened to my account, his eyes meeting mine but once when I mentioned how the natives had borne a chest full of valuables to the settlement before they were put to the sword. When I had finished, Bingham crossed his arms and looked at the ceiling above us, weighing up my narration of events. At last, he spoke again, almost as if to himself.

'Indeed, a heart-rending tale. Yet one that is already known to us.'

Just then, Killian piped up from behind the sheriff's wench.

'He has refrained from telling you all, sire.'

The sheriff looked almightily displeased, and I flinched when Burke whacked me on the thigh with his club. Bingham next proceeded to take bites out of a lamb shank which he chewed slowly, thereby prolonging my dreadful unease. The interminable silence was ended when he flung what remained of the leg to his wolfhounds, leaving them to rip it to shreds as they fought over it, their tails whipping me in the face. My attentions were drawn away from the dogs when the sheriff growled at me accusingly.

'I told you to tell us everything.'

'What more would you know?' I asked hesitantly.

'The Irish rebel, what did he tell you?'

'Which one?'

The strength of Burke's blow to my crown left my mouth hanging open, while the sheriff's voice trembled with rage.

'The friend of the crone Grian! What did he tell you?!'

I delved into my memory as my head throbbed with pain, attempting to recall the few words I had exchanged with the brave tribesman.

'He spoke of an escape path.'

Bingham leant towards me like a viper as he studied my face intently.

'Did he reveal the whereabouts of other Spaniards?'

'Yes, he did.'

'How many? Were they northward bound? Tell us all and we might yet spare your hide. Labourers for my new gatehouse are in short supply.'

Enraged by the treatment I was receiving, I could not keep a hint of defiance from pervading my voice as my eyes narrowed in fury.

'He said that they were headed south,' I lied.

The sheriff's back straightened in shock at my words, almost as if he had been repulsed.

'South? How is that possible? Why in heaven's name would they go south?'

He swiftly entered into a fevered debate with Gilson and the other men who surrounded them, then addressed me again as he jerked his head at Killian.

'I have questioned enough of these treacherous, back-stabbing vermin to be able to tell a liar from a mile away. You had best speak the truth, for I am fast losing my patience with you.'

My tongue loosened and I sang like a bird released, telling him every single lie that I could come up with. After a few minutes of my ranting, the sheriff seemed appeased, gesturing at me to hold my tongue. He exchanged words with Burke in their guttural tongue and addressed me again.

'Before you receive our mercy, there is but one more thing you should tell us.'

He beckoned to an earthenware bowl at the centre of the table, which his confessor passed to him with a trembling hand. I tried not to slaver as Bingham shuffled through the browned apples and plums contained in it and picked the least bruised plum. Distracted as I was by the plump fruit, he caught me on the back foot with his next query.

'Indeed, it was at Saint Quentin that I first heard the speech of our Spanish commanders. It was an accent that differed markedly from that used by the common troops, an accent not quite unlike yours. Who are you, Spaniard?'

My bloodied appearance and calloused hands hardly allowed me to pass for one of gentle birth. Yet during my interrogation I had used the finest of stresses on my words, in the hope that I might be spared for ransoming and buy some more time in which to attempt an escape. Seeing that my bait had been taken, I played my hand further.

'I am but a defenceless castaway who has been taken prisoner, sire.'

At the sight of his master's annoyance, Burke hauled my head back by my bad ear, twisting it mercilessly while he drew a dagger and slipped it beneath my chin. No sooner was this done, than Bingham proceeded to utter his next words very slowly.

'Your name, Spaniard. Tell us your name.'

Everyone stared at me as I took my last gamble, croaking a reply through my constricted throat.

'I am Don Blas de Hurtado. Son of Don Gaspar de Hurtado, the head physician of the Santa Maria de Visión.'

XII

Sligo Town, Ireland

16 September 1588

For a while, none spoke at the declaration of my false identity, which left me to wonder if my ruse had worked. I observed the faces of those gathered at the table in front of me, thinking that Bingham would be smirking at the prospect of ransoming a highborn prisoner. Yet the sheriff's face had turned a hue of scarlet, and his words seethed like hot coals as they left his lips.

'Your father told us that you were dead.'

My heart quailed when I learned that the old physician had been taken alive, realising that my gamble might soon cost me my life. Yet the dice had already been cast, so that I mustered as much gall as I could, somehow managing to hold Bingham's menacing gaze. My voice quavered when it left my throat, which might have been mistaken for elation.

'Father... is alive?'

The sheriff seemed deaf to my question until he asked me one of his own.

'Where is the ring?'

'The ring?' I replied in bafflement, uncertain what he meant.

The sheriff sprang from his seat and dealt me a punch that launched me across the straw-strewn floor.

After a few moments of dizziness, I raised my head, to find myself faced by one of the huge dogs. I rolled away in fear at its low growl, when Burke seized me by the ear and hauled me back onto my knees.

'The prince's ring, damn your soul!' barked Bingham. 'Where is it? Give it up, or I'll have you gutted like a fish!'

The thought of my entrails hanging over my waist had me gape back at my captors in wordless silence. The sheriff's mention of 'prince' and 'ring' brought to mind the Prince of Ascoli's emerald bauble, and I blurted the suspicion which had lingered with me ever since my fight with Gabri.

'Father has it!' I wailed, closing my eyes to stem my weeping, for fear of the horrors that would befall me once my falsehood was discovered.

The sheriff glared at me in silence, clearly unmoved by the tears that streaked my cheeks.

'You Spaniards force me to resort to uncivilised means. But we will find out which one of you is leading us a merry dance.'

His guests along the dining table shared his scowling, except for the mole Killian who stared at the ground, either out of guilt or fearful deference. Meanwhile Bingham issued Burke with what sounded like curt orders, as he smoothed his ruffled doublet over with the flat of his hands and then turned his back on me.

Burke gripped the neck of my tunic and twisted it around his fingers, before hauling me out behind him. My last memory of the dining hall was the fear in Killian's upraised eyes, Then my injured shoulder hit the door jamb as we made our exit, causing me to groan aloud as I was shoved back through the hall. As we returned down the stairwell, I could make out the familiar wan light at the entrance to the dungeons. Yet Burke hurried past the door to the cells without ever acknowledging the gaolers who were seated outside.

'Where are you taking me?' I croaked.

My question went ignored as the renegade sergeant turned to the steel door down the passageway and kicked it open. When he pushed me through it, I fell upon sticky tiles which made my hair stand on end, and in the haunting dimness, I could make out the first signs of a torture chamber. A rancid stench pervaded the room, and numerous fingernails and teeth littered the flagstones, as they gleamed dully in the faint torchlight.

'Not the strappado!' I cried, as I noticed a man dangling before me by his wrists, which were in turn bound to a chain slung over a hook in the ceiling.

By the light of the guttering torch, I could see that the captive had been terribly mauled by all manner of flames and sharp implements. The tormented prisoner issued a low groan, leaving me to stare on in horror when Burke walked past him towards a cogwheel upon the wall to my right. Upon reaching the device he dislodged a stave from within its teeth, which in turn freed the chain that rattled shrilly through the hook as the captive was brought crashing onto the ground. The face of the fallen victim was so charred and lacerated that I could barely tell that it was human, except for the single, perfect eye that fluttered at me, and the drool that slithered through broken teeth.

Burke removed his helmet and dropped it onto the ground, before walking over to the wretch. He rifled through his rags, then snatched a silver chain from around his captive's neck, meeting my gaze with a mischievous wink.

'For safekeeping.'

The renegade sergeant next stowed the valuable in the lowest powder charge of his bandolier, in the manner of soldiers who scavenged the bodies of those fallen in battle for trinkets. When he had finished searching his captive, Burke frowned in concentration at the grime-splotched floor, patting it with the palms of his hands until a handle was located. Upon finding it, the sergeant raised a trapdoor with a loud grunt, releasing a foul waft of air which all but had me retch.

Anguished moans rose from the uncovered pit, leaving me shocked that any living being could survive such a hellish malodour. My jaw dropped when the sergeant released the hook from his mauled victim's bonds and flung him through the stinking hole. The heart-wrenching groans from within it were silenced when the trapdoor was slammed shut again. It was a scene which left me feeling rigid with fear, and I beheld the sergeant in disbelief when he rose to his feet and turned towards me with the freed hook in one hand.

I swiftly recoiled from his approach, rolling onto my back and kicking out at him. Burke sidestepped my lunges with a mocking grin, before he raised his cudgel and beat me half senseless with it. I made a last struggle to get to my feet, when a fist to the chin left me spent and sprawling over the tiles again.

Blood trickled from my nose onto my broken lips, as the renegade grabbed one of my ankles and dragged me over the flagstones' rough edges.

My hoarse pleas for mercy were drowned out by the clank of the chain attached to the hook in Burke's hand. After hauling me over the trapdoor he released my leg, then passed the chained hook through the cord which bit into my wrists. Iron rings clinked when my hands were dropped back onto the floor, and I watched the sergeant hurry over to the cogwheel on the opposite wall, which he proceeded to spin around madly.

The wheel's teeth caught the rings of the chain, which were in turn pulled through the iron loop in the ceiling. Burke groaned with toil as he savagely strained at the wheel. As the chain was raised towards the ceiling, my arms and body were next to shoot up into the air, followed by my feet. When my bonds met the loop in the wooden beam overhead, I was left to dangle like a lifeless pendant, barely able to raise my chest enough to breathe. I kicked at the air in a last desperate lunge, only to be left swinging from side to side.

Meanwhile the sergeant had jammed a wooden stave through the cogwheel's teeth, before opening the chamber door and calling out to someone down the hallway. One of the gaolers promptly arrived, placing a glowing brazier alongside the trapdoor, and hurrying out again without a backward glance. My eyes were shut at the fearful sight of the coals, as I fervently commended my soul to God.

Burke next hurried towards the tools which hung from the wall behind him. I stiffened at the sight of so many devilish devices, while my tormentor gently passed his hands over the array of blood-encrusted tongs and knives. A warm trickle ran down my thigh when he plucked an evil-looking instrument from the wall.

'This should help curb your homesickness,' he chuckled, as he held up the hellish device, which was known as the Spanish spider.

The deepest unease flooded me at the sight of the pair of steel claws, used by the Holy Office of the Inquisition to rip out women's breasts. What it would do to the shallower chest of a man was not a thought I dared consider. Burke frowned with effort as he snapped them together a few times, producing a dull chomping sound, and I wriggled furiously when he addressed me again, with his malice hanging on his every breath.

'You seem anxious to be elsewhere, friend Hurtado. Is the fair land of *Éirinn* not to your liking?'

'Erin?' I gasped. 'Is that what you call this hell?'

'Oh no, Spaniard,' he said, walking over to me with the instrument held out in front of him. 'That is what the mere Irish call the Queendom of Ireland.'

He laid the rusted claws upon the brazier's red-hot coals, grinning openly as I beheld them in fear. I cursed beneath my breath, almost wishing that I was back upon the rowing bench of the Santa Maria de Visión.

'Some cry to their mother,' he said at last, 'others to God. Yet in the end all comes away, flesh, hair and nails. In truth you will be left amazed, for there are more parts to you than you would ever have thought possible.'

At his words, my thoughts returned to his disfigured victim who had been hurled through the trapdoor beneath my feet. Meanwhile the sergeant set his cudgel aside and returned to his devices on the wall, where he drew a whip and unfurled the length of it with a loud crack.

'Burning tongs make the flesh come away much more easily,' he remarked, 'but until they are hot enough, your tongue might be loosened in other ways.'

My slow swinging turned into a mad whirl when Treasach Burke vanished behind me, placing his hands on my sides to still my movement. I cringed at their touch before I felt the edge of a blade between my neck and shoulders, which ripped open the back of my tunic. The low hiss of my tormentor reached my ear like the tip of a snake's tongue.

'It appears that you have already tasted the lash,' he observed drily, 'yet these are indeed curious scars for the son of a Don.'

The cave of my mouth turned dry at his casual remark.

'Why are you doing this?'

He withdrew his clammy hands and sniggered as he stepped away from me.

'Did you think that we would welcome invaders, Spaniard?'

'Your people have always called us allies.'

The renegade sergeant snorted.

'Liberators come to help Irish beggars?' he said, when his tone turned more menacing, as he loosened his whip, 'I know your kind well, Spaniard, nearly as well as I know this land. It is you who are the strangers now, and I shall hunt down every last one of you. None shall escape me.'

A wheeze left my chest when I strained at my bonds to snatch a quick breath. The sergeant appeared before me, seizing my throat and shaking it as he raised his voice.

'Speak, Hurtado! Where is the ring?'

I averted my eyes from him and fixed them upon the ceiling, barely managing a breath of the fetid air.

'With my father...' I gasped, not knowing whether I had uttered truth or falsehood.

Burke nodded once, then released his grip and vanished behind me. A vicious flogging began, with each stroke of the lash so hard that we were almost brought face to face. He sneered aloud at my cries, putting his back into ten lashes which left me dazed. Yet before I could swoon, he stood in front of me again, jabbing my ribs fiercely with his whip handle, as flecks of spittle flew against my cheeks while he shouted.

'The ring, Spaniard! Where is the ring?!'

My arms burned and my vision was blurry, while blood filled the searing stripes on my back. Burke's chin was barely a handspan away from mine, and in the torchlight I caught a glimpse of the scar which ran across his cheek and over towards his upper lip. The flesh above his mouth had once been badly stitched back together, so that it resembled a harelip.

'Speak the truth, Hurtado,' he growled. 'Spare yourself another flogging.'

'I have done,' I barely managed, teetering upon the edge of unconsciousness.

Burke's lower lip trembled for a few moments as he sought to regain his composure. Then his hand fell to the leather handle of the Spanish spider on the brazier before him.

'Have you heard of Saint Agatha?' he asked.

Stunned by the cruelty of his taunt, I stuttered in reply. The sergeant raised the steel claws and held them a hair's breadth from my chest, a gesture that straightened my back with a jolt. Trickles of sweat seeped down my forehead, and the palms of my hands turned damp when I swung back and then forwards again. My body was shaking as I twisted about madly, to try and frustrate his attempts to touch me with the claws.

'As man has marked me,' he whispered, 'so do I mark others.'

A roar left my lips as the white-hot steel met my left breast, my howls growing louder as the spider's eight points sizzled against my burning flesh. Burke's grin widened as he drove the steel into my breast, drawing the claws more closely together. I barely noticed the door opening when the evil tongs were wrenched away from my chest, leaving me to gasp for breath, wholly baffled by the unlikely interruption. When I opened my eyes again, I saw the sheriff striding into the chamber, followed by a heavyset gaoler who dragged a wretched captive by a halter.

'A new prisoner,' remarked Burke, in Spanish. 'Was he brought in with the last catch?'

'This is Don Gaspar,' declared the sheriff, then seized the wretch by the neck and flung him to the ground.

Despite his bruised cheek and black eye, I recognised the greying captive as the elder de Hurtado, the head physician of the Santa Maria de Visión. My supposed father was a far cry from the richly dressed and haughty nobleman who had once mocked me in the presence of his true son. He was trussed in torn rags, yet as he looked around him the old *prado's* eyes burned with indignation. The ageing physician also had the stomach to shrug his gaoler's hand off his shoulder after the latter attempted to seize him.

'What is this horrible hole?' exclaimed Don Gaspar, before receiving a hefty smack in the mouth which toppled him backwards.

The sheriff ignored his gaoler's treatment of the physician, seeming more concerned by my condition. Upon studying my appearance, he barked orders at Burke, who swiftly dropped the Spanish spider back into the brazier and hurried to the cogwheel against the wall. The torment in my arms and chest was greatly relieved when Burke released the chain a few notches, lowering it enough for me to balance myself on my toes.

My breathing eased as I drew deep gasps of fetid air, while Burke strode across the chamber to lift the single torch out of its sconce. I flinched when he held it close to my head, as I blinked furiously in the glaring heat. Meanwhile the sheriff glowered at the old Spaniard upon the ground and leant over to tug at the rope around Hurtado's neck as if it were a dog leash.

'Do you recognise this man, Spaniard?' he growled.

Hurtado glared back at Bingham in disgust, then grabbed the rope around his neck which was reddened from the blood that dripped from his mouth.

'Father,' I desperately gasped, in the hope that the old man might play along with my lie.

Don Gaspar squinted once at the torchlight held before my head, then proved himself as sharp-eyed as a hawk.

'Who in God's name is that? Is he another heretic sodomite?'

At this insolent reply the sheriff nodded once to the heavyset gaoler, who raised a bunched fist against the *prado*. Hurtado cowered before the portly trooper, quickly shielding his face with his arms.

'Wait! You would strike an old man again? Damn your souls, what is it you want from me?'

The gaoler stared back at the sheriff in puzzlement, awaiting further instruction since he did not understand Spanish. George Bingham furiously chewed his whiskers, and his voice seethed with impatience when he pointed at me again.

'That man, Spaniard! Is he your son?'

A chilling fear overcame me when the old *prado* stared at me again, and a tear ran down his cheek when he lowered his eyes in disappointment and glanced at the gaoler's raised hand. When he looked at me once more, I returned a forlorn gaze, for I had abandoned all hope that he might buy us both time. Yet after studying me for a few moments, Don Gaspar dropped his head and sighed.

'Yes.'

The sheriff bristled at the old physician's answer.

'And does he have the ring?'

'What ring?'

Bingham's mantle flapped around him as he swooped upon his prisoner and seized him by the collar.

'Do not play the fool with me, old man!' he roared. 'Our spies heard you and your lackey speaking of it in the cells!'

Hurtado raised his arms in front of his face, since he clearly feared another blow to the head. Following the sheriff's last outburst, the *prado* craned his neck in my direction and glared at me for a few moments.

'Yes, he does.'

Bingham hurled Hurtado away, then whirled around and strode up to me, pinching my chin between his gauntleted fingers.

'Liar!' he snarled as his eyes bulged out at me.

'Where is it?!'

'I do not have it,' I croaked. 'He lies, I swear it.'

Bingham pushed my chin away and drew his sword, then turned around and placed its point against Hurtado's throat.

'I want the truth of it, old man! Only the truth! If you are lying...'

In that precise moment, the door of the chamber burst open once more as a pimpled knave appeared. The boy seemed both alarmed and winded as our attentions turned to him, before he blurted out a message amid a series of ragged breaths. The three heretics were left speechless by his words, until the paling sheriff sheathed his sword and barked at Burke.

'Use any means to learn the truth of it, Sergeant, until I return.'

With that, he darted out of the chamber like a hound on the scent, brushing past the messenger who slammed the door after them. At the sergeant's instruction, the portly gaoler forced his fingers down Don Gaspar's throat, and Burke himself seized up the iron claws from within the brazier. His attempts to return them to my chest were frustrated as I swung wildly from side to side, until a fist to my stomach left me dangling helplessly as the Spanish spider inched towards me again.

The steel had barely singed my flesh again when a piercing shriek caused the sergeant to turn away from me. We looked on in disbelief at the gaoler who was bent over double, struggling to pull his hand out of Hurtado's mouth. In his rage, Don Gaspar bit into it rabidly while he rose to his feet, reaching with his bound hands for the gaoler's sword.

Burke ran towards the old *prado* with a curse, landing a vicious kick against the captive's bent knee which produced a sickening crack. The gaoler's hand was at last released when Hurtado fell away from him, clutching his twisted leg in both hands and throwing up a spurt of vomit that caused the sergeant to quickly skip away from him.

Low moans were then heard from the physician while our enemies inspected his spew which glistened across the ground. Both of them stooped over it and picked out the odd coin and ring, when the wide-eyed gaoler pointed at the tiles and uttered a cry of disbelief. Meanwhile Hurtado reached out to them with a shaking hand.

'Leave it, I beg you!'

The Sassanas ogled at the object of their attentions, until the sergeant bent over to pick it up. When Burke rose to his full height again, he held the item out before him in both hands, his mouth hanging open at his discovery. A high-pitched giggle escaped the gaoler as he also beheld the prize, his pudgy cheeks pinched by a triumphant grin. With a desperate effort, Don Gaspar rose onto his good knee and hissed at Burke in accusation.

'Thief!'

The sergeant turned and kicked him across the face, which flung the old Spaniard across the ground and left him twitching like a skewered eel. Burke then approached the throbbing light from the brazier in which the claws had been placed. In his grimy palms a golden ring could be seen, its mounting bearing an emerald which was the size of a man's knuckle. Its crisp, verdant glow stole what little breath I had left, and a sharp radiance refracted through the gem's vitreous lustre, casting a green sheen upon the sergeant's pale fingers.

He twisted and turned the trinket playfully between them until his hand closed around it. Burke next shut his eyes for a few moments and turned to face the gaoler who grinned foolishly in his direction. Without a moment's hesitation, the sergeant strode up to his fellow Sassana and whipped out his sword in a rightward arc. Its edge slashed open the space beneath the gaoler's double chin, and Burke hopped away as the wounded man crashed onto the ground. Blood spurted against the walls while a sharp hiss escaped the victim's severed gullet.

'Another deserter,' muttered Burke to us, as we observed his thrashing victim, 'and also another deadpay, which never goes amiss.'

Upon witnessing this shameless murder, I struggled in my bonds, as Burke reached over to the dying gaoler and dragged him towards the trapdoor. The sergeant's design was not lost on anyone, and to my left Don Gaspar was already crawling away, with the rope at his throat slithering behind him. He reached the cogwheel within moments, where he noisily wrestled with the stave caught in its teeth.

The squeak of wood against steel soon alerted Burke to the old *prado's* movements, causing the sergeant to issue a low snarl as he dropped the dying gaoler to the floor and approached Don Gaspar with undisguised anger. As I tottered helplessly upon my toes, the physician jerked wildly at the wooden spar until it wobbled over and bounced upon the ground. The chain above me issued a brief clank before I fell over and landed upon my side with a loud curse.

'Holy host!'

At the sound of my fall Burke looked over his shoulder towards me, raising his sword again when a muffled thud was heard. A loud crash followed when the sergeant's blade fell from his hand, and his head sagged forward as he stumbled from one foot to the other, then collapsed onto the ground in a heap. Behind him Hurtado cast me a befuddled frown from the shadows, with the stave from the cogwheel held out in front of him. His swing of the post had instantly knocked Burke out cold, and we regarded each other in stunned disbelief as we mulled over our next moves.

'Who are you?' he called out to me, in a voice both proud and haughty.

'Certainly not your son,' I rasped from the ground.

Hurtado's mouth fell open at my impudence as he cast me a dark glare. He then crawled towards the limp form of Burke and searched his body while I thought to ask him a question of my own.

'Do you know the whereabouts of Sergeant Ramos or Corporal Ortiz?'

'I know not of whom you speak,' he snapped, as he searched the body of our stunned tormentor.

I sighed wearily at his reply, then summoned what strength I had left and crept over towards the body of the fat gaoler. A loud clank was heard when I moved, which came from the chain that was hooked to my bonds. I rubbed the leathers around my wrists against the edge of the gaoler's sword blade until my hands were freed, then rose to my knees and studied the chamber, my head clearing as I regained some regular breathing.

Although my stomach churned with hunger and fear, the years spent skirmishing behind enemy lines allowed me to reason with a relative calmness that would have been beyond most fugitives. After a few moments I set upon a course of action, as I snatched up and wore the sergeant's long mantle and helmet. I next grabbed the gaoler's ankle and pulled him with a growing frown towards the trapdoor, with tears gathering on my eyelids from the effort it took me to shift the heavy corpse a few paces.

'What are you doing?' snapped the *prado* from across the room.

'Be quiet,' I hissed back at him, then dropped to one knee and searched the floor for the trapdoor's handle, frowning with effort until it was raised.

I swiftly turned my face away from the evil-smelling waft out of the pit below, which was filled with dispiriting groans of the half-dead and the squeak of rats.

'What a horrible stench!' protested Hurtado. 'Are you trying to choke us to death?'

At his outcry I bit my lip in frustration, then pulled the rigid corpse of the gaoler across the pit, almost falling in after him when I pushed his belly down with my foot. I then dropped the grimy trapdoor back over the hole, with the physician still bleating complaints about the hellish reek which had filled the chamber.

Don Gaspar finally ceased his loud ranting when a look of distress overcame his proud features. He cast his head around from side to side, then crawled across the floor to search the unconscious sergeant's body. I thought that I should try and help my fellow captive to his feet, yet my hand was hardly rested upon his arm than the old halfwit jerked it away and gestured wildly across the room.

'The stone,' he howled, dropping Burke's fingers from his hand, 'the stone! It must have skittered away when he fell!'

I frowned at the *prado*.

'Even now you would worry about the blessed ring. We must get out of here, old man!'

His lower lip quivered when he turned to face me, and he clutched my hand in desperation.

'Return it to me, I beseech you!'

The sound of muffled steps could already be heard from behind the door. Don Gaspar and I beheld each other in fear before I scowled at him and rested a forefinger upon my lips. When the sounds had finally abated, the *prado* bleated again from the ground.

'The ring, I beg you!'

I snorted at him in disgust, then hobbled off to fetch the guttering torch from across the chamber. I cast its radiance over the ground as I patted the crusted flagstones with my fingers, flinching whenever they met pieces of flesh and other human parts. When my hopes of finding the trinket were all but abandoned, something winked at the stunned sergeant's foot. I picked up the ring and held it out to the aged Spaniard, who snatched it from my hand without a word of gratitude. He stooped over his right leg, which was unnaturally bent before him, kissing the prize as if it were some long-lost lover.

For a few moments I beheld him in awe, relieved that I had finally silenced him. I then swiftly returned my attention to escaping, as I hauled Burke's boots off his legs and proceeded to strip the dazed sergeant of his sword belt and bandolier. My hands were clammy with fear as I undressed the renegade, feeling ever fearful that the sheriff might return at any moment.

Meanwhile the *prado's* joy at being reunited with the gemstone was finally being transformed into words, amid his muffled sobs.

'Thank God, I have recovered it. My beloved son may be lost, but the prince's heirloom will help restore the fortunes of our house!'

'How did the enemy learn of it?' I whispered, as I undid the sergeant's shirt buttons.

'A fellow prisoner, a spy, betrayed me in the cells. I swallowed it before they came for me.'

I nodded back at him empathetically, for Killian's treachery was still fresh in my mind. A few moments of welcome silence passed, in which Burke was also relieved of both his shirt and breeches. To my fortune the renegade sergeant's clothes fitted me well, and I scowled as my bruised and swollen feet were forced through his leather boots.

I next swung the sergeant's bandolier over my shoulder, then rammed his pistols through the belt I had stolen. After securing both guns, I grabbed him by the foot and dragged him towards the pit, holding my breath as I raised the trapdoor once more. Burke's eyes flickered but once as I pulled him towards the hell of his own creation, then dropped him through the hole and slammed the trapdoor down after him. In the ensuing malodour, I covered my nose with my arm, and Don Gaspar beheld me in awed silence when I walked over to him.

'You look like him,' he said, as he finally understood my design, 'and yet, it is dark in here.'

His words went ignored while I inspected the weapons I had taken from the sergeant. I primed both of Burke's wheellock pistols before slipping them back into the belt at my waist, then attempted a couple of swings with his heavy sabre. Meanwhile Hurtado attempted to rise to his feet, then fell back onto his backside with an agonised gasp.

'Arrrgh,' he groaned, 'I cannot take another step'.

I ignored his grumbling, as I sought to quell the fear which threatened to cloud my mind with panic. It took several deep breaths to steady my nerves as I stared at the door, feeling as though I was about to storm a breach in an enemy held fortress. Just as I had calmed myself enough to take my first step towards it, the *prado* spoke up again and delayed me further.

'Wait, slave! What is to become of me?'

With a snort of frustration, I drew my sword and spun on my heel towards him. The Don blanched when I seized him by the collar, holding the point of Burke's sabre against his throat.

'Say your last prayers,' I snapped, 'but be quick about it.'

He pushed the blade away, clearly disturbed by my lack of hesitation.

'There is no need for that! Surely these curs will ransom me?'

I stepped away from him, outraged by the further delay he was causing me.

'Then farewell, Don Gaspar. Unlike you, my only hope lies in my feet.'

Hurtado's beard was caked with blood, and his yellowed jowl sagged from the blows he had suffered. In that instant my eyes fell upon the ring he held in his hand, which would fetch a reward of ten thousand ducats. I remembered the rumour I had heard below decks, of how the Prince of Ascoli had disembarked before the terrible sea battle at Gravelines, to summon those Spanish troops in the Netherlands who were meant to board the Armada's ships.

'Ascoli still lives,' I muttered to myself, recalling the great ransom he had offered for the ring.

I also knew that the ring would fetch a small fortune in the dark corners of Venice or other Italian capitals. For it was a prize which would certainly not be short of buyers, what with many of the Turkish Sultan's agents stationed across Mediterranean, keen to feed their master's passion for gems of all sizes.

The brilliant stone held the promise of untold riches, of a life free from all financial burdens, in which the cold, rain and filth of war would be unknown. Great plains full of cattle appeared in my mind, and I imagined myself standing before them like a New World lord, holding Pieter by the shoulder and surrounded by guards I had hired as protection against the Indian savages. The *prado's* hand closed tightly around the ring when he saw me gaping at it, for he was visibly disturbed by my longing stare.

'Give it to me,' I said suddenly.

'No!' he protested. 'You do not realise the worth of this thing!'

'Oh, and you do?' was my reply, as I leant over towards him to take it.

'Don't you dare,' replied Hurtado, drawing his bunched fist away.

A mad struggle ensued, in which I found his grip to be fiendishly strong. Heavy blows from my fist rained down upon the back of his head, and his cries echoed against the singed and dirtied walls, until he was knocked half-unconscious, and I snatched the ring from his hand. Without giving it a second thought, I placed the trinket upon the back of my tongue and swallowed hard, when the dazed *prado* spoke again.

'Ingrate!' he hissed from the ground, 'I released you from bondage!'

His eyes were red and rheumy as he glared at me.

'You are no better than them,' he continued, 'just another honourless cut-throat...'

With a scowl, I angrily spat on the ground before him.

'For all your airs and graces,' I replied, 'you are no better than me. I would have returned this ring to the Armada's commanders in a heartbeat, yet you kept it for yourself, you honourless hypocrite.'

His mouth fell open at my words, and he nervously hesitated before responding.

'I did not steal it... I took it... for safe keeping.'

'That's what they all say,' I snarled, somewhat bemused by the drastically changed circumstances in which the words were expressed.

The *prado* was in a dishevelled state as he stared back at me. His messy hair hung over his ragged clothes, and a week-old stubble sprouted around his well-trimmed moustache and beard. The physician's feet and hands were black with filth, so that I even pitied him for a moment. Then a loud thud against the trapdoor had me bolt out of the chamber, and Hurtado's cry echoed against its walls as I slammed the door behind me.

'Stop, thief! You'll never make it out of here alive!'

XIII

SLIGO TOWN, COUNTY SLIGO
IRELAND

16-17 September 1588

The dark passage reappeared, devoid of life. To my left, a flickering light revealed a group of gaolers seated at the end of the hall. I stiffened at the sight, yet there was little time for hesitation. I pulled Burke's hood over my face and took a deep breath of air, which was already much fresher than it had been in the torture chamber. My gauntleted hands fell to my weapons, and I clenched them tightly as I imitated the sergeant's gait as best I could, despite the ache caused by the sores on my feet.

My short walk proved a prospect more daunting than the Camino de Santiago, with my heart pounding ever faster as I drew closer to the stairwell at the end of the hall. I studied the gaolers from beneath my lowered hood, ready to draw my weapons at the first sign of trouble, while resisting the urge to run as I clung to the unlikely hope of escape. At my appearance, the men lowered their heads and fell deathly silent, so that their fear of Burke allowed me to reach the stairs unhindered.

I had made it to the first floor when a dozen troopers were seen running at me, leaving me rooted to the spot in disbelief. My hand was already on the sword pommel when they suddenly veered towards the castle door, their heavy armour jangling as they tightened the straps of their cuirasses. When one of them called out to me, I gazed back at him wordlessly, then hurried on up the stairs as more soldiers appeared in the hall.

During my ascent I prayed that I would not encounter any more troopers. My fears had somewhat subsided when I reached the second floor, and I marvelled at my silhouette against the flint walls, which was eerily similar to that of the renegade sergeant. For a moment I berated myself for not cutting his throat before flinging him into the pit, when a loud snore at the end of the dimly lit hallway drew my attention to a heavyset trooper, asleep on a stool.

I loosened the sabre at my side, half-drawing it from its scabbard as I slowly approached the guard while trying to make as little noise as I could. He was a burly specimen with drooping whiskers, whose size offered a serious physical threat. As I softly stepped past him, I noticed a door to my right, which was slightly ajar. I quickly surmised that it must lead to a room overlooking the battlements, with windows through which I might attempt an escape.

I cringed when the door creaked open at the touch, then quickly stepped inside. A finely furnished bedchamber appeared before me, with a lustrous bathtub at its centre that filled the room with strong fumes of lavender. Of a sudden, I felt like some filthy barbarian who had just intruded on a spotless, Roman bath complex, when I noticed a handsome woman near the windows staring back at me in disbelief. I immediately recognised the sheriff's wench, who I had seen less than an hour earlier, whose hair was held by a handmaiden armed with a brush.

The image of Sergeant Burke gaped back at me from the mirror behind her, and for a few moments I forgot that it was my own reflection. At my sudden appearance, the wench rose to her feet with a wave at her servant, who fled from the room after the briefest of curtsies. When we were left alone, I could not help feeling a slight stirring, for the woman wore nothing beneath her chemise of gossamer, so that her curves and endowments were plainly visible.

When she strode up to me, I could better appreciate her striking, fair-haired beauty in the light that streamed through the window. Blue eyes sparkled like sapphires, set above high cheekbones that twitched handsomely when she grinned. Upon reaching me, she placed a hand upon my breast, and her eyes were filled with desire when she caressed my good ear with a sensuous whisper.

'*Tu me manquais*, Treasach.'

Although I was not conversant in French, I knew enough to realise that the man whose clothes I wore had not been idle behind his master's back, having clearly dallied with the sheriff's precious bed warmer. The woman's beauty left me feeling entirely entranced, so that I could not stir when she pursed her lips and brought them towards my face, as her hand left my chest and raised the tip of my hood. Her yearning expression swiftly turned into one of shock, and her eyes narrowed when she beheld my face instead of Burke's.

She took a swift step back, as if faced by a viper, and my hair stood on end as a scream left her lips, until I stifled her cry with the back of my hand. The blow caught her across the jaw, sending the wench hurtling to the floor. Her lips had hardly parted again when the point of my sabre was brought to rest upon her collarbone, with the forefinger of my other hand placed across my lips as a warning to her to keep silent.

I seized a handful of her hair in my free hand, as I scoured the room for a length of rope with which to restrain her. I dragged the whimpering harlot towards the windows, where I used the sergeant's sword to cut the tasselled cords around the Flemish curtains which were used to bind her wrists and ankles. All throughout her binding, the wench did not offer resistance, which allowed me to steal glimpses of the town between the wooden astragals in the window before us.

In Sligo's streets, a mighty bustle of troopers and armed townsmen could be seen rushing over the bridge towards the direction of the bawn. Fierce hand to-hand combat took place along the ramparts, between the garrison's sentinels and men who wore long tunics and embroidered jackets. I recognised the invaders as the Irish natives, who had stolen over the town's defences to try and break into the garrison.

I next looked nervously across the room, seeking a compartment in which to stow the whore while the pell-mell of the attack lent me cover and secrecy. I stuffed a damp bath sponge into her mouth, and I had already dragged her halfway across the floor towards her large wardrobe when a creak was heard from the door behind us.

'Mother of God,' I cursed, as the heavyset guard I had left snoring in the corridor appeared in the doorway, having stirred at the broken scream of his ward.

With a furious oath, he charged into the chamber, resolved to make amends for his oversight. My sword was not yet raised when he barged into me and bowled me off my feet. We collapsed in a deathly struggle against the edge of the bathtub, causing the vessel to wobble violently and douse our legs. My assailant proved as hard as nails, hardly seeming to notice the punches I aimed at his head. With a snort, he wrapped his arms around me, snug as a barrel hoop, then found his footing and lifted me into the air, holding me over the bathwater.

A desperate tussle ensued, in which my limbs flailed all over the place as I struggled to free myself from his iron grip. My knuckles still throbbed from the blows I had dealt him, yet the trooper's hold did not slacken, and he had all but swung me into the tub when he tripped over, landing both of us against the basin's edge so that we upended it amid a huge splash. I swallowed a mouthful of sweet water as a mad scramble ensued, with our soaked forms slipping and skidding across the ground until the brute had me pinned against the wall. His thick fingers formed a fast-closing noose around my throat, and as my neck hit a chest of drawers behind me, I heard an object rocking over our heads.

A quick upward glance revealed a huge earthenware pitcher that tilted treacherously above us. With a last gasp, I gritted my teeth and shoved my injured shoulder into the chest, then reached out for the wobbling jug which fell over towards us. I brought the vessel down on the trooper's head with enough force to brain a wild boar. A loud crack was heard as the jug was smashed to pieces, with my assailant's grip on me being instantly released. My throat ached terribly as I squirmed out from beneath the huge, lifeless form, grateful for the slice of luck which had delivered me from death's doorstep.

In the corner of the room, the bound figure of the sheriff's wench could be seen slithering towards the open door on her belly. With a hoarse curse I got to my feet and pulled Burke's hood over my eyes, before striding up to the harlot and dragging her back towards her open wardrobe. The bitch beheld me in dread as she was flung among her many dresses, then I shut the doors of her closet and bound their handles together with a silken sheet from her bed.

With the wench taken care of I next staggered over to the window, where I could see that the defence of the town was still raging. The sentinels upon the walls appeared to have had the better of the invaders, with many of them already leaving their posts to make across the bridge in the direction of the enclosure. Large billows of black smoke rose ahead of them, clouding my view of the country as they climbed towards the grey sky overhead.

As I watched the soldiers rushing towards the bawn, I was struck by another idea. In minutes I had removed Burke's boots and soaked pistols, then stripped the cuirass off the dazed guard's body and hurled my neck and arms through it. The large breastplate drooped over my waist, for it was an ill-fitting piece of armour, albeit one which would allow me to blend in among the ragtag frontier troops. I next twisted the torn shoes off the trooper's feet, which were bound to their soles by strips of rag tied in crude knots.

After assuming my new disguise, I seized the body of the unconscious guard by the shirt, cursing inwardly as I dragged it towards the huge double bed and pushed him beneath it. I also hurled Burke's cloak and boots after him, followed by the sergeant's helmet and gauntlets. Upon realising that my bared hands and face might betray my identity, I next ran over to the wench's dressing table, where I applied generous amounts of Venetian ceruse to them from a small pot that was full of the whitening pigment.

Finally, I seized an empty goblet and filled it with some of the remaining water in the bath. As I poured it down my parched gullet, the bitter aftertaste of lavender caused me to splutter aloud. I was still coughing when I ran out of the wench's room and over to her guard's stool, where I hoped to find his helmet. In his hurry he had left it behind, and after pulling it onto my head I tore towards the staircase down the hall. In my haste to flee I jumped down the steps two by two, and all but screamed in relief when I ran into the blinding light between the keep's open doors.

None stepped forward to bar my path. The sheriff had spoken truth when he said that he was short of ablebodied men, for most guards had abandoned their posts to repel the invaders at the cattle-filled enclosure. Yet my relief was quickly dispelled, when a half-dozen sentinels called out to me, as they descended the ramparts to my right. Across the street, a band of townsfolk had gathered with all manner of implements, ranging from pickaxes to rusted swords. Finding myself caught between the two groups, I heeded the cry of an officer who led his men in the direction of the bridge.

I drew my sword as I ran towards this force of troopers, who followed their leader at a brisk jog with fast reddening faces, their guns and blades held out at the ready. We made over the narrow crossing in pairs, charging so tightly together that I could even smell the rancid sweat on the men. It lingered in my nostrils until we had reached the enclosure, where the fighting upon the bawn was fiercest. A desperate confusion reigned at the outer gate, where the right door was already in flames and being violently jolted by some force beyond the wall.

The town's defenders flung themselves at the gap in the large wooden doors, where they hacked and slashed at the moustachioed faces of the rebels who attempted to force their way into the town. The ground beneath the melee was littered with the bodies of both troopers and natives, and the ramparts above us were also strewn with corpses. Fierce fighting raged up on the walls, with troopers stumbling over the dead at their feet as they struggled to repel the bearded rebels in their yellow and white tunics.

These Irish braves set upon them with sword and spear thrusts, undeterred by their enemy's guns and crossbows. The viciousness of the natives' attack was stunning to behold, with a pair of these invaders even returning to their feet despite being struck by crossbow bolts. with many of their fellows roaring their war cry as they set upon the bewildered defenders.

'*O'Conchobhair Abù!*'

We gathered in front of the flaming gate alongside dozens of other troopers, filling the spaces created by those who had been felled by their wild Irish assailants. Lieutenant Gilson soon appeared in his high-crowned hat, bawling orders at his men, who swiftly abandoned the gate. I was confused by their retreat as I followed them into the enclosure, when a side-long glance revealed two cannons which had been hauled out behind us. Between them the sheriff could be seen scowling upon his chestnut gelding, which kicked and snorted as the heavy oxen used to draw the demi-culverins were led away. I shuddered at the sight of these guns, which when fired could each unleash almost a dozen pounds of shot, rock shards, canisters and a few lengths of chain.

At Gilson's orders, a subaltern sounded a trumpet blast, and we withdrew behind the cannons in a halfcircle. To a man we held our ears as the invaders' blows unhinged one of the burning doors, before they charged us to murderous cries and flooded the enclosure. As they passed through the gate, I observed the English gunners bringing their matchsticks to the touch holes. I swiftly clamped my palms against my ears, to try to stifle the ensuing din which exceeded the sound of a thunderclap. Both cannons lunged backwards amid huge puffs of blinding white smoke, as some of the troopers fell to their knees with their hands clasped tightly over their ears.

As the stinking haze cleared, Bingham kicked his steed towards the gate, roaring at his men to follow him, while the pockmarked Gilson and another lieutenant led their men after him. To a man we chased the sheriff's horse towards the gate, trampling stunned invaders who knelt in our path, as well as the severed corpses of their fellows. Our charge never faltered until we were through the smoking chasm, hacking at those natives who tarried before the walls while the rest beat a hasty retreat.

While the heretics around me hacked at the wounded who lay at our feet, I scanned my surroundings, despite my throbbing temples, to identify my best means of escape. A distant flash of lightning lit the sky, heralding a downpour that would clean the white pigment from my skin. In my panic I feigned fury, howling one of the cries I had heard from the heretics as I waved my sword above my head and made for the distant outline of forest.

'For Saint George!'

My eyes were closed with strain as an Atlantic sea breeze cleared the cannon smoke, and I resolved to put as much distance as possible between myself and the town. Despite my recent sufferings, I ran as though Satan himself were at my heels, with the onset of rain causing the white paint to drip off my hands and face. The cries of the butchered diminished as I veered away from the fleeing natives, so that it was soon clear to any onlooker that I was not in fact chasing anyone. Any hope that I might flee unnoticed was quickly dispelled as an arrow struck the ground near my foot.

'Christ's blood!'

A swift glance over my shoulder revealed archers atop the walls who fitted fresh shafts to their bows. Alongside them a trooper jumped up and down in a frenzy as he jerked the point of his sword in my direction, and distant trumpet blasts recalled some of the riders who chased the fleeing natives. I resumed my mad dash towards the forest ahead, falling over twice as my heart felt like it might burst. At least a bowshot's distance remained when I looked over my shoulder again, shocked to see a band of mounted troopers charging towards me. They were already close enough to draw their pistols, and I could also make out a dozen of their dreaded wolfhounds, snapping at the air as they ran alongside the horses.

I batted the awkward helmet off my head before also fling-ing off my loosely bound cuirass. My flight instantly became easier, and I never once looked back until I crashed through the cover of forest, my ears filled with barking close behind as the branches gouged my face and shoulders. The stolen scab-bard rattled at my hip, and I drew my sabre, hacking my way through the trees that grew more closely together, embedding myself ever deeper in the wood.

When the barking behind me grew louder I hurled the heavy sword into the trees to my right. As the blade crashed through the boughs, the pursuing hounds were diverted towards its loud rustles, which put further distance between us, while af-fording me precious moments to push on further through the growth. Heavy foliage shielded me from the sunlight, allowing me to drift from tree to tree like a shadow until I fell on all fours. Breath burned through me as I took a slight rest, yet it was clear that the enemy was fast closing in on me, with the forest full of the cries of beasts and men. Amid rasping gasps, I noticed a glimmer of light sparkling through the umbrage, which spurred me to resume my flight.

The baying of hounds was soon drowned out by the sound of a river. Yet I had hardly sighted the rushing watercourse when a look over my shoulder revealed the huge dogs only yards be-hind me. I crashed through the leaves and dived headlong into the freezing stream, shuddering all over as I came up for air. One of the hounds also hurled itself into the torrent, snarling wildly as it gained on me with a furious paddle, its tongue the size of a pig's ear and lolling between fangs the size of newly burnished pike heads.

It snatched my raised forearm between crushing teeth, and, with a groan of pain, I exhaled deeply and sank beneath the water. As the dog was pulled in after me, its claws tore up the wounds on my breast and shoulder, and my lips were parted in a silent scream until the beast at last released its grip. No sooner had I returned to the surface than the hound could be seen splashing away like a scared water rat, barking in distress after having nearly drowned.

I abandoned myself to the fierce surge of water, holding my throbbing shoulder and realising that I was being dragged back towards the ocean. The strength of the river was such that I was powerless to emerge from its current. I therefore chose to float on my back with my feet raised in front of me, thereby sparing my head from being battered against the low-lying rocks and boulders which littered the river. At least a half-mile must have been covered until my feet struck a rock which I clung to in fear, having noticed the distant silhouettes of troopers gathered along the rain-swollen banks of the watercourse.

My days spent hunting down fugitives in the Low Countries quickly returned to my memory, and I fumbled in the mud for one of the reeds which grew on a bank of dead leaves to my right. With a desperate lunge, I managed to snap off one of the stalks, only to lose hold of the rock as I drifted downstream again. Before my head sank beneath the murky water I took a large breath through the stalk, which dislodged silt into my throat, causing me to splutter and gag. Spots grew in front of my eyes as I clawed and kicked like a fiend, as the river hurtled me through a curving bight whilst the last few strokes of my arms had me burst through the water surface.

I coughed up the remaining mud in my throat as my good ear made out the distant patrols calling out to each other, then sank shoulder-deep into the swirl with a grunt. The din of the river masked my sounds as hounds crashed alongside it to pick up my lost scent, leaving me to float along with the current for a few minutes more. I next grasped a log which lay athwart the river and hauled myself onto it.

I shivered long thereafter upon its scrubby bark, which bit into the raw welts on my back until I turned over onto my stomach. The Spanish spider's claw marks on my breast still burned, while my shoulder felt like a throbbing ball of agony. Yet I ignored the pain in other parts of my body, merely grateful to have fled Sligo Town with my life as I turned sideways, trying my best to recover my breath once more.

'I'm alive,' I gasped in disbelief, as my face rested upon the rough wood, 'I'm alive.'

The memories of the torture chamber returned to me then, leaving me to cringe in horror at the end I had almost met while in Burke's power. Hurtado's last cry also flashed through my mind, as did the desperate struggle with the trooper in the wench's bedchamber. I also remembered the whore I had thrown into the cupboard, and I trembled again with unease at what I had done.

'If Bingham were to catch me now,' I uttered, feeling like I should move again although I still couldn't.

Finally, I thought of the prince's ring that I bore inside me. It seemed hardly possible, I told myself, that I had stumbled across such a gift amid so much setback. Despite finding myself wet and wretched, I could not help thinking that I had perhaps secured both wealth and freedom, and that my fortunes might have turned beyond expectation. For the first time in years, it seemed like all was not lost.

'We're not out of the woods yet,' I could almost hear Maerten saying, and a rueful grimace spread across my face, when I thought of how much I had endured without him.

As my breath was regained and my alarm somewhat lessened, I noticed the rustle of wind and the low hum of the current during the tranquil lull which was only disturbed by other forest sounds. I lingered upon the bark a while longer despite the freezing cold, and after resting for a few minutes more I slowly rose to my feet, crossing the log to the opposite bank and striking a path through the oaken woodland.

Due to my miserable condition, I resorted to stealth once more. I was constantly watchful since my environs were unknown to me. At all times I only trusted my eyes and good ear, knowing that capture by the enemy meant certain death. I marched on unhindered until I saw the great, flat-topped mountain to my left. The thought of hostile natives often stopped me dead in my tracks, but the words of Grian's wartynosed lover spurred me onwards, since I could still recall his mention of rebel Irish tribes in the north.

After almost an hour of walking, I knelt beside a rain puddle in a rock, lowering my face towards it to drink. Before disturbing the brown water, I was met by the reflection of a haggard and feral wretch, albeit one possessed of a prize which was worth a king's ransom.

'A prize that shall bear me to America,' I said defiantly, 'with Pieter.'

I ventured on past sunset, when luminous specks sprinkled the growing dark, leaving me in no doubt as to the identity of my new stalkers. Within an instant I climbed into the overhead boughs of an old oak, with its musky smell filling my nostrils, while rats and birds to scuttle away from me. The tree afforded me more sleeping room than I had enjoyed in months, and as I stretched out my aching limbs, the rustle of leaves lulled me into a dreamless sleep.

The rasp of heavy breathing woke me with a start, and I could hear men tearing through the thicket. I had slumbered for many hours, since I could make out wisps of black cloud fleeting across the new moon which cast strange shadows. I turned slowly onto my chest, as alert as a startled squirrel, then heard cries in Italian among other different tongues. Dreaded hoof beats were also heard as a band of fugitives were rounded up by their pursuers, amid cries of fear and the rustle of twigs. I curled up into a trembling ball as ropes were hurled over the branches around me, with one of the captors barking commands. A captive squealed in broken Latin, before he was gibbeted with the others.

'I am Venetian! Spare me, I beg you, for I too hate Spain!'

I recoiled from the light of the flaming torches below me, and when the captives had stopped kicking, the heretics could be heard searching through their clothes. When their deathly work was finished, the troopers finally made off again on horseback, leaving me to heave a huge sigh of relief. Yet I could not sleep again thereafter, for horrible sounds rose from the ground beneath me, as ravenous wolves growled viciously while they feasted on the hanging corpses.

The morning found me even colder and more wretched than before, and I was still drowsy when light filtered through branches to the deafening chirp of birds. It was almost noon when I at last mustered enough courage to attempt a careful descent towards the forest floor, my eyes averted from the grisly remains of the hanging captives. A wolf runt tarried at the foot of the tree, jerking its head wildly as it dug its small teeth into a severed ankle. It barely turned its head towards me when I landed behind it, but a hard kick in its backside caused the cur to issue a loud yelp before it ran off to rejoin its ravenous pack.

After the horrors of the previous night, I was driven in terror towards an unknown destination, my senses alert for the slightest hint of wolves or riders. A midafternoon sunburst cut through the grey clouds when at last I emerged from the woodland, watching the plains and hillocks which spread out ahead of me, with the flat-topped spur reappearing behind them astride its mist-shrouded peaks. I crouched low as I kept to a short uphill path, which brought me to a stalk-fringed lake.

The water's placid surface was only disturbed by mallard and teal, and a small settlement could be seen along its bank. This village was shrouded in morose, sullen colours, with a breeze from the east bearing a slight stench of the rubbish pits at its periphery. Despite the stink I did not stir from my hiding place for over two hours, since the sight of the settlement left me hoping that I might be able to scavenge or steal some food at night.

A growing hunger plagued me, for I had not eaten in over a day, so I lay on my belly between some low bushes. As the day wore on, I could hear the sound of harps and powerful voices coming from the huts, followed by the odd cheer and pounding of spear butts which hinted at some festival taking place. It left me wondering if I might attempt to rob some food, while the tribesmen were distracted.

'Should I risk it?' I asked myself as dusk descended, dreading recapture after what had befallen me at Sligo.

I could almost imagine Maerten running ahead of me as a slight breeze rippled the lake water, which somehow reminded me of our ill-fated chase of Gabri through the streets of Seville. The grumbling in my stomach only worsened when the wind bore the smell of cooked meat towards me, as the distant herdsmen gathered around their peat fires and readied their dinner.

With renewed resolve, I crept against the wind for fear that the natives' dogs might pick up my scent, with the wafts of braised beef being too much to bear and causing my stomach to rumble again. When the nearest sentry turned to talk to someone from his settlement, I ran over to the hut which was closest to the rubbish pits, then peered through the spaces in its timbered wall.

A faint smokiness filled the air within, caused by a low flame which was encircled by small rocks. Through the haze I could make out some stools standing alongside a pile of skin which served as bedding, and a blob of wet dough was rising upon a heated stone. Not a soul was seen inside, so that I dared to venture into the cabin, where I found a small sack of oatmeal bread. I snatched two buns out of it before running away from the hut, intent on eating the stolen food in a safe place.

My cheeks bulged with fare once the cover of high grass was reached, and as I gobbled up the bread I heard a rumble of hooves behind me. I turned in horror, making out the distant outline of horsemen against the setting sun. It was a large body of troopers, who rode at a canter with their hands on their weapons, with each face drawn into a deathly grimace. Any doubts I had about the loyalties of the tribesmen in the settlement were instantly dispelled at he sight of a such a heavily armoured yet stealthy force of mounted Sassanas.

'Holy host!' I exclaimed, upon realising that I stood directly in their path, so that I sprang to my feet and ran back towards the huts, crouching low and keeping to the cover of grass.

I rushed through the town, making towards a group of men and women with fearful faces who had gathered around their cooking pits with swords and spears. Some of the natives cast me befuddled glances while others noticed the bread in my hands. To a man, they appeared ignorant as to how close the enemy already was, so that I spat a gob of food onto the soil and blurted my warning aloud.

'Sassanas!'

Tribesmen looked to one another in fear as a cry was heard, followed by a distant trumpet blast which announced the enemy's charge. Women ran to their huts and called to their children while their husbands spread themselves around the fires with their crude weapons held up before them. I made my way past a herdsman who led his cow away when the first mailed heretic tore through the cabins and kicked over a campfire. A thickset Irishman was brained by the mace of a passing enemy as I fled through the settlement, ever wary of any immediate danger and hardly believing that I was fleeing troopers yet again.

Riders flooded the settlement as I ran past another hut, where a petrified woman brandished a dagger as she spread an arm in front of her wide-eyed brood. With a curse, I left the settlement behind, jabbering in fear as I hurled myself behind a bank of land which ran along its periphery, to conceal myself from the raging fight.

To my dismay the hiding place was a rubbish pit that was filled with all of the village's offal, yet my disgust was swiftly forgotten when a rider appeared but a few paces away from me. From his high-crowned hat I recognised the evil, pockmarked lieutenant, John Gilson. The sight of him left me burying my face against the entrails, bones and other excrement beneath me, until the loathsome officer and his troopers had clanked past me. No sooner did they ride off than I rose on my knees and elbows, trying not to gag. A clash of steel returned my attentions to the settlement, where I noticed a spirited sally by six natives in yellow tunics. The men drew their weapons to a loud war cry as they charged out of a flaming hut whose wattled rafters were blackened by smoke.

'MacGlannagh Abú!'

The foremost gallant was a head taller than his fellows, and his red beard was the longest I had yet seen among the natives. It fluttered over his chest as he delivered huge sword strokes, each of which felled a heretic that stood in his path. Upon noticing him, Lieutenant Gilson beckoned to another band of troopers to join in the fray. Yet they too were also slain by the half-dozen natives, who still howled their battle whoop as they cut down the troopers.

'MacGlannagh Abù!'

My spirits were roused at the sight, and for a moment it seemed that the night raid might even be repelled by the warriors in saffron. A piercing whinny was heard to the left, and I turned to see Gilson and his officers sliding off their horses. Together they assaulted the saffron swordsmen who turned to meet their charge. A fierce hand to hand melee ensued, as sparks flew off blades to swift thrusts and parries.

From where I lay, the Irishmen appeared to be having the better of the fray, until Gilson surprised everyone by whisking a pistol from his belt. A gunshot was closely followed by an agonised roar, as the redhaired gallant was seen whirling around, spurts of blood bursting through his fingers from a wound in his midriff. The man's yellow tunic turned scarlet, and his knees buckled as he fell to the ground. His stricken men hurled themselves in front of him, desperate to spare their leader from further injury. Other firearms were also used by Gilson's men to kill or wound the natives in saffron, so that their brave resistance was quickly quelled.

With the saffron kerns being finally subdued, the lieutenant beckoned to his troopers, who followed him into the settlement to quell what resistance remained. Only one of them tarried to finish off the brave redhead's last two surviving men, one of whom bled freely from a wound in his neck, while the other bent over the body of their fallen leader. This last native was smaller in stature than his fellows and wept aloud like a woman as he shook the redhead by the shoulders amid shrieks of despair.

'Aengus! Aengus!'

While witnessing the pitiful sight, it soon struck me that a better opportunity to flee north would not soon present itself, since the steeds of Gilson and his subordinates were being watched by a single scrawny horseboy. So I slowly hauled myself out of the filthy sludge into which I had landed and crawled towards the horses. I closed in on them rapidly and positioned myself directly behind the youth. The cruel horseboy giggled at the torment unleashed by the troopers within the village, for some of them could be seen raping women against huts, while others bound up natives and cattle in halters.

I bent over and silently picked a rock off the ground. The horseboy's laughter was quickly stemmed as the hefty stone crashed into the back of his head. As the youth tumbled to the grass, I stepped towards the pockmarked lieutenant's own mount, which was a sightly black destrier that pounded the earth, while standing a shoulder above the other horses alongside it.

When I seized its reins, a piercing howl left me jerking my head towards Gilson's remaining trooper, who had already slayed one of the last two saffron natives and readied to also kill the smaller one. This last rebel drew a dagger and aimed a stab at the stunned trooper, who beat the native away with his sword butt. The short rebel dropped his dagger and fell to the ground holding his face, while issuing a groan of pain.

At first I turned my back on them, full knowing that I needed to hasten away, before other troopers turned up. Yet I quickly realised that beyond a general understanding that I should make north, I had no real idea of where I was headed. I therefore decided to take the small rebel with me, that I might be able to use him as a guide. So I picked up a fallen spear and stole behind the howling trooper, then skewered him through the throat.

As he fell over, the snub nosed native I had just rescued stared up at me in disbelief, blood smeared across his face. He appeared to be but a petrified lad, who scurried back to his dead leader, holding the man's scarlet locks in one hand and beating his own grime-encrusted forehead with the other. Through the huts I could make out Gilson returning with his troopers, and a panic seized me. I ran over towards the small native, seized him by his mouse-coloured hair and dragged him behind me kicking and screaming.

The lad scratched and bit at my arm, until I finally turned around and buried my knee in his stomach. The blow ended all protest, and with a strength born of despair, I hurled him across the horse's saddle and climbed up after him. Our mount shook its head nervously as I wondered whether I should click my tongue or dig my heels into its flanks. Both actions were attempted while I planted my hand firmly upon the native's back, forcing his bruised belly upon the saddle and winding him further.

I could already make out the whites of Gilson's eyes through the distant huts. He flashed me a mocking smile as his fair hair fluttered against his jaw, leaving my heart to pound relentlessly against my breast as the rescued native groaned aloud. My attempt at escape already appeared to have been foiled when the lieutenant paused a few paces before me, calmly ramming a ball down his pistol as his band of troopers gathered around him, laughing at my frantic efforts to move his mount.

'For the love of the Virgin,' I howled, overcome by a mad desperation, 'flee, you whoreson!'

I reached over and punched the horse in its buttocks, causing it to issue a high-pitched whinny. Then it turned and bolted towards the open country, charging ahead with the speed of a fired cannonball. A loud cry from Gilson reached my good ear, yet I cared not for its meaning as the native rolled back onto me, leaving me to grasp the reins to keep from falling. Together we abandoned madness for mountains, fleeing the ravaged settlement as my new mount tore off at a frenzied gallop over glen and dale. As the crack of a pistol was heard far behind us, we made towards the distant, twilit peaks. A rueful grimace clouded my face at another growl from my stomach, which sounded a crude plaint to the memory of the oaten bread.

XIV

County Sligo to County Leitrim, Ireland

17-18 September 1588

We swiftly covered yard after yard, through each thrust of our steed's strained sinews. I clutched desperately at the mount's reins, struggling to somehow keep two runaways on horseback while the lofty mountaintops ahead revealed the way north, the sky above them darkened by dusk as the destrier charged through trees beyond count. Before long, the trunks of the growing forest drew too tightly together, forbidding further passage through the woods ahead. The horse lurched madly leftwards when it was met by this closing wall of bark, all but hurling us off its back as I tugged madly at its reins to bring it to a halt.

I threw myself off the mount with a snort of frustration, aware of the growing darkness about us. My ignorance of our whereabouts left me biting my lip in frustration, when a sniffle had me turn on my heel to glare at my fellow rider. When he lifted his head, a beardless face appeared which was the first I had seen on a grown native in Ireland. There was not a single hair of manhood above his lips, though there did emerge a babble of words in the Irish tongue.

Despite my ignorance of the language, I was taken aback by the high pitch of the lad's tone. Slender legs sprouted from beneath his knee-length tunic, and I issued a loud exclamation when unbound hair fell over his jacket shoulder.

'Why, you are a lass!'

The lad-turned-lass wiped her red-rimmed eyes with raw knuckles, then regarded me with a confused expression.

'Cad é sin arís?'

Her voice was indeed high and feminine, although the words she uttered remained unintelligible to me. At the memory of Burke's exchange with Grian's lover, I thought to hazard some conversation in Latin.

'Why, thou art a lass...' I repeated slowly.

In the growing nightfall, the native was being fast reduced to a grey outline, and although I could barely see her face, her bafflement was at once clear in her own reply in the ancient Roman tongue.

'Thou hath taken me for a lad?'

A small chortle was heard from the native as she stifled a sob, then she whirled our mount around with a sudden urgency to her voice.

'Aengus! Where is he? I hath abandoned him to the enemy!'

She sounded stricken by grief and was about to ride back towards the Sassanas' clutches before I rushed to her side and grabbed the horse by its reins.

'I entreat thee to flee with me, my lady! None of your party could have survived the raid!'

'But what of Aengus *mac an rí*? I shall not leave him to the Sassenachs!'

My memory of the fatal pistol shot suffered by the red-headed brave was still strong, and I was reluctant to be abandoned to the wood again. I blurted out my next thoughts, fearful that I might be rent from a civilised native, one with whom I could converse freely.

'I entreat thee to tarry, my lady! None could have survived his wound!'

This plea led to more distress than solace, for my listener's jaw dropped as confusion clouded her darkening face, as she leant over and spat furious words in my face.

'And thou knowest that for a certainty, grey wolf? Didst thou see him perish with thine own eyes?'

''Twas a mortal wound, my lady,' I replied, being unsure what she meant by grey wolf, 'he could not have been taken alive.'

'Then I shall see it for myself!'

Before I could protest, her heel struck me in the chest, sending me sprawling over the wet heather beneath us. Gilson's horse whinnied but once as the native coaxed it into a fast trot, followed by a gallop. With an oath, I beheld the shrinking quiver of the destrier's buttocks, which left me resolved to attempt a final plea.

'And what of thy kin?' I shouted. 'What shall become of them if thou shouldst also perish?'

The cry echoed across the plains that surrounded us, as horse and rider charged down a small descent until they were hidden from view. With a groan I rolled over onto my side, cursing my luck at having found myself alone and lost in the alien land yet again. After heaving myself onto my feet, I resolved to strike a path into the large forest ahead of me, before the cloak of nightfall was fully unfurled.

As I took my first steps towards the foliage, a loud wolf howl hit me like a gauntleted fist in the guts, with the sound being a stark reminder of my faint chances of surviving the night in the wild. I attempted another two paces, then started in fright upon hearing a faint jingle behind me and made out the obscure image of a fast-approaching rider. The sight left me rooted to the spot in dread, until I recognised the woman I had rescued atop Gilson's steed. My tongue was bridled as the horse made for me at a canter, for it was also clear from the woman's hunched, throbbing form that she was weeping and plagued by grief.

When she reined the destrier in alongside me the native lifted herself from the horse's mane and turned towards me. In the growing dimness, I could make out the tears on her cheeks, which slid off her chin as her shoulders shook from more sobs. Throughout her weeping I said nothing, for many years spent fighting had taught me that there was no use in assigning meaning to the death of those fallen in battle.

I held my silence until night set in, when our surroundings could only be gleaned by the wan light of the moon. The air had also grown colder, nipping me all over until I could not refrain from greater shivering. As her sobbing persisted, I eventually thought it fit to at least attempt some words of comfort.

'I entreat thee to find thy strength, my lady, for thou must honour his memory. He would not wish the enemy to also claim thee. Of this we can be certain.'

The woman's weeping continued a while longer before she finally raised her head. When she spoke again, it was if she beheld me for the first time.

'Thou art so thin...'

As if in reply to her words, an almighty grumble was heard from my stomach. At the sound, the woman dismounted from the charger, then strode along the tightly bunched trees until she made through a gap which I had not seen. The horse followed her with a snort, its reins dangling freely around its throat, and she led it through the slight hollow with a gentle hand rested upon its muzzle, leaving me to stagger after them in relief.

Although I had often been despatched on night raids and skirmishing parties, it was an effort for me not to trip over the roots of trees. Yet the native seemed to know the wood like the back of her hand, and after a few twists and turns we reached a small glade, which was sheltered from the ensuing rain by a roof of intertwined boughs.

The woman tethered the horse's reins to a bough and set about collecting firewood. I tried to be of assistance, knowing that the flames would provide us with warmth as well as protection. My search for branches and faggots was frustrated by the sores upon the soles of my feet, which ached terribly in the torn shoes I had stolen from Sligo. Yet within a few minutes a small pile of wood was gathered before the kneeling woman, whose brow was creased with effort as she drew a small blade and flint from her pouch, striking them against one another to unleash a shower of sparks.

I staggered off to gather more lightwood and returned to find a low flame already kindled. Were it not for the danger we were in I would have cried for joy, and as the small flame smouldered into a ball of fire, I eagerly fanned it with the palms of my hands, which startled the native and had her vanishing into the wood. In an instant she returned with handfuls of evergreen leaves plucked from the ground, which produced thick tendrils of smoke when she threw them onto the blaze.

'To make it smaller,' she explained to me, in a tone that suggested that I should not fan it again.

We kept watch in turns, with smouldering brands kept within close range to fend off wild beasts. My arms were wrapped tightly around me, for although the fire was but an arm's length away, the bite of the cold was unforgiving. After a time, I was able to ignore the glowing eyes of the creatures surrounding us as sleep finally claimed me. The night brought a fitful rest, which was often interrupted by the relentless howling of wolves and the frenzied whinnies of our mount.

Upon stirring, I snatched glances at the woman leading the horse close to the fire. For a while she mouthed soothing nothings into its ear and patted its back, until it had settled enough to spend the night alongside us. My sleep was only broken a handful of times thereafter, when I glimpsed the native sitting across the fire with her elbows upon the knees of her crossed legs, her fists held tightly to her face as her body quaked with silent sobs.

The dawn was met with the cry of birds, and chatter of squirrels heralded the first shards of daylight through the cover of branches. My heavy eyelids parted as I rolled over towards the low fire. I beheld its dying embers with a twinge of disappointment, for they had provided me with more warmth than I had enjoyed in weeks. The spells of unbroken sleep at night had left me feeling somewhat restored, yet my belly was torn by the unbearable ache of hunger within it.

At last, I could no longer stand my starvation, so that I staggered towards the foot of a tree, my fingers frantically tearing up the soil as I searched for a root to shove into my mouth. My furious burrowing had hardly started when I was startled by the appearance of the native at my shoulder, who proffered a handful of berries before my face. I snatched up the fruit and shoved it in my mouth, while I noticed her ochre eyes studying me from within finely chiselled features. As I swallowed the last of the food, she spoke in a voice that trembled with sorrow.

'Spain?'

'Aye.'

She nodded at my reply as I found myself taken aback by her handsome face, despite the purple blemish at the side of her forehead. The native's skin was as white as alabaster, after her kind, and her brown fringe and dimples were complemented by the slightest tip of a canine that peeked out from beneath her upper lip.

The torrid events of the previous night had left their mark on her, for blood and grime streaked her cheeks, and her broken lower lip gave her a vulnerable cast. As if sensing my scrutiny, she turned her face away from me, but I had already glimpsed that from almost boyish features sprung a beauty I had not observed before.

Having spent over a year at sea, I found her proximity overwhelming. It was hard not to recall those scenes of mistreatment I had witnessed all too often in the Spanish Netherlands, when depraved Spanish troops stormed a town and helped themselves to its womenfolk. Yet despite my own longing, I banished the temptation which gnawed at my consciousness, choosing instead to grit my teeth and force a smile on my face.

The native's startled expression turned severe when she beheld the burns around my left nipple. She stood tall and slender above me, a winsome lady of almost feline bearing, who dropped stealthily to one knee as she gently passed her fingertips over my breast. Her piteous gaze left me feeling uneasy, and I rose to my feet and walked away from her, turning towards the trees to shield my wounds from view.

Yet when I opened my mouth to speak, I was surprised to find that she had crept upon me again, before swiftly clamping her hand over my mouth and hauling me towards the ground. A low rustling could be heard through the trees, and for a few moments we lay motionless upon the earth, wary of alerting any pursuers to our presence. After these foreign sounds had subsided, the woman quietly watched our surroundings, then sprang to her feet and hurried over to the horse.

I swiftly made after her, hastening towards stolen charger whose size could be better appreciated in the light of day. The stallion was possessed of robust quarters, which could be launched towards enemy footmen at a steady, unstoppable gait. It was a destrier bred for impact rather than swiftness and agility, although its speed the previous day had left me in no doubt that the horse remained our best chance of eluding the Sassanas.

My wonderment at the beast's qualities seemed to be shared by the Irishwoman, who stroked its mane while whispering gently into its ear. She next took up its straps and gave them the slightest of tugs, before leading us out of the clearing and deeper into the forest. Her assured presence left me feeling greatly heartened, for she was evidently someone who knew her way through the wilds. As we pushed on into the wood our direction appeared to be the northward range of lesser heights behind the flat-topped mountain, which loomed tall and grey like the sky above us.

Along the way the native only paused to study the trees in our path, and to bend over to the grass and pick what appeared to be bits of three-leaved clover. I waited until she ate them first, after which I felt safe accepting the ones which she offered me. The plant had a sharp taste but was quite edible, and further curbed the ache in my belly before we ventured on. As the cover of trees about us thinned, we progressed over peat hags through ebony marsh, drawing ever nearer to the two heights ahead of us, until we finally ascended the slopes to our right, where the ridges and rubble were obscured by the morning mist.

Throughout our climb, we could see a far-off stump of mountain to our left, alongside the sea, which stood beyond an enemy garrison which I instantly recognised as Sligo Town. The ominous sight of the stronghold spurred me to hasten my pace, but by the time level ground was reached, the stallion was already limping and would not walk any further. I tugged at its reins to no avail, which left me feeling even more frustrated, yet the horse's obstinacy rivalled the stubbornness of the most hard-headed Spanish ass. I burst into a barrage of swear words, gesturing madly at our mount and searching the ground for a branch with which to beat it.

'Double-dyed whoreson of a heretical nag, I'll teach you to delay us!'

All throughout the woman had seated herself on a rock in front of us, watching me with her chin rested upon her knees with her upper lip curled disdainfully. When I stared at her askance, she stood up and walked towards the distressed horse, whispering into its ear and gently rubbing its muzzle with a frown of concern.

At her words, the creature nickered softly and flailed at the air with its tail, as it slowly refrained from its incessant stamping. Its anguished whinnying also subsided, while it allowed the native to bend over and lift one of the creature's front legs, grimacing with effort as she dislodged a pebble from its hoof. The effort led her tunic to slightly part from her chest, which allowed me to steal a glance of her bosom.

When at last the small stone was extracted, native threw it at my feet with a look of scorn. To my astonishment, she next shoved the saddle from the mount's back to the ground, then grabbed the horse's left ear and climbed onto its back. I was perplexed by this manner of mounting the horse, and it slowly occurred to me that in a land where everything was different, the heretic's ways were more familiar to me than the ones used by those of the faith. My awe at her actions was replaced by shock when the horse's canter broke into a downhill gallop. The native showed no sign of slowing the mount's pace, leaving me to issue a cry of protest as I flailed my arms madly above my head.

'Wait...wait!'

I slipped upon the dew-soaked heather and fell onto my face, then pushed myself back onto my feet to give her chase. Yet she was already charging towards the grasslands and tree clusters that stretched around us, so that I was soon surrounded by a disturbing silence, broken only by the odd billow of wind or the cry of a bird. A stream of profanity left my lips again as I fell to my knees and howled after the distant speck.

'Treacherous whoooooooooooooore!'

My bunched fists pounded the ground in a mad rage, and my spirits were crushed at finding myself alone again. When the pain in my knuckles became too much to bear, I buried my face into the ground with my arms stretched out before me, resembling the Mohammedans I had seen at prayer in African garrisons. The dew soaked my face as I groaned in despair, and I lay upon the grass for far longer than I should have.

The palms of my hands had turned as cold as ice when a clop of hooves was heard again. I lift myself off the ground at the sound and looked about me in fear, overcome by astonishment when the native reappeared upon the stallion. Her hair fell over her shoulders as she patted the stallion's neck and watched me with a steely glint in her eyes.

'*Muc*,' she said curtly.

'What?' I muttered softly, wary of scaring her off again.

'Pig,' she repeated in Latin, so that I knew that she was referring to the glances that I had stolen of her breast, when she had succoured the distressed horse.

My scowl eased as I forced a pathetic smile, amazed by her sense of awareness and knowing full well that in my situation I had little choice but to humour her. I also murmured an apology through my gritted teeth, to best ensure that she did not turn tail once more.

'My apologies, good woman, if I have offended thee.'

I had hardly spoken when tears welled up in her eyes again, and she bent over the horse amid muffled sobs. I rolled my eyes but kept myself from sighing in resignation, then made my way over towards the barebacked stallion. My failed repeated attempts to hoist myself onto it left me to finally grab it by the tail, an act that greatly upset the charger, which attempted to kick me. After I had somehow climbed onto its back, the steed issued a high-pitched whinny to a sharp shake of its hindquarters, tossing me face first into the mud at its hooves.

The mount whimpered aloud before my companion leant over towards its ear, stroking its fringe and using words and gestures to calm it again. After she had extended a palm and helped me to climb back up behind her, I warily placed my hands upon her hips, to which the native showed no objection. She then kicked the horse forward as we resumed our northward flight, with the woman locked in grief throughout. A near half-hour of weeping passed until I heard her voice again, as she pointed east of the mountains ahead of us.

'Those are the lands of O'Rourke, grey wolf. He is loyal to thy king.'

'Truly?' I asked, scarcely believing that we were so close to the lands of a vassal of Spain.

'Aye. The king of Spain oft sends him gold with which to resist the heretics.'

Feeling heartened by her words I prodded the horse's flanks in earnest, which did nothing to alter its pace as it grunted aloud and carefully continued its descent towards the valley. We were halfway through our downhill journey, with the scree barely visible at the end of the descent, when the lass spoke up again.

'Halt.'

'Halt?' I asked.

She tugged at the reins and brought our mount's trot to an abrupt end, leaving the horse to exhale spurts of mist as she gestured at the ground in front of us. The muddy earth was chequered with fresh spoor, and the curved dints of several hooves. When the native spoke again, her voice was both firm and decisive.

'Those tracks are less than a day old.'

I beheld the prints with a deep unease.

'The enemy?'

Her lip was curled again in disgust when she replied.

'Or the O'Reillys.'

At the sound of the Irish name, my jaw hung open in puzzlement.

'Are they not also rebels?'

'Nay,' spat the native, 'they are a tribe that lusts for power, and one which has long been in league with the Sassenachs.'

'How many passed through?'

'At least a score,' was her reply. 'We must hasten away from this place and make for the valley.'

Her decision to stray from the domains of a declared subject of Spain dismayed me, since I was yearning for shelter and refuge. My disappointment was further aggravated by my being unused to riding without a saddle, which had rendered my thighs red raw, so that the prospect of further riding was less than appealing.

'Is there no other course?'

'We have no choice. The way is too perilous.'

Our mount returned the way we had come, bearing us in the direction of the crests to our left before we rounded their craggy feet. I gasped in awe at the valley spread out ahead of us, which held a huge body of water at its base. A river curled like a hog's tail as it emerged from the right bank of the lake and cut across the lowland.

The other side of the vale was flanked by sheer mountain walls, where waterfalls sparkled upon distant cliff edges. It was a breathtaking sight, which left me feeling as dizzy as I was entranced. As we made towards it, the horse struggled to keep its footing over the treacherous scree, which ran all the way down to the valley floor below us. We were soon left with no choice but to continue our journey over the rubble on foot.

Once the descent was tackled, we passed into heavy foliage, then crossed the river at a shallow ford before approaching the banks of the lake. When we reached them, my guide chose to pause for a rest, since we had travelled for over an hour. I welcomed her decision, since the uneven ground we had covered had required a great exertion from me just to keep up with her. I seized the chance to dip both of my throbbing feet into the lake, with the native resting an arm on the horse's neck while it drank to stoop over and collect watercress, which she shared with me.

I had just eaten my fill of these plants that filled my mouth with a hot, peppery taste, when my guide uttered a sharp warning in her tongue. She jerked her chin at a band of men along the lake's northern bank, prompting me to stand on my numbed feet to prepare for the inevitable onslaught. Yet my fears subsided when her breathing eased, for it was clear that the approaching band consisted of a dozen barefoot natives, who wore white tunics beneath their embroidered jackets and cloaks. The men were of a wild cast and armed to the teeth, forming a protective ring around a man who was evidently of some importance.

This curious specimen differed from his fellows in that he wore a tonsure, with a slight stubble on his cheeks in place of a beard. A leather satchel that hung from his shoulder bounced on his thigh as he walked, and unlike the barefoot guards alongside him, he also wore trews and brogues. For the rest, his dress was not extraordinary, since like most Irish natives he wore a pleated white tunic, with a thick frieze cloak fluttering behind his gaunt shoulders.

With a cry my guide ran towards him, and I was surprised to feel the slightest prick of envy, when the man shoved his guards away and wrapped her in a lengthy embrace. As they drew away from each other, he gestured to the woman to calm down when she stammered broken phrases to him. He next held her by the shoulders as she rambled on, and his face was soon crinkled by grief as he pressed his eyes with thumb and forefinger in an attempt to hold back his tears.

After he had collected himself, the man held the woman in another embrace, in which they remained locked long after I had given my back to their unrestrained display of emotion. When at last their sharp and lilting tongue was resumed, I turned to find them trading further conversation, before the man turned to the tribesmen and issued what sounded like a frantic order. At this brisk command, the youngest member of the band immediately darted off in the direction from which they had appeared.

The other tribesmen's shields and small sacks of belongings bobbed upon their shoulders as they followed the man, who made towards me with my guide. At closer distance, his appearance was almost comical, with his green eyes being both heavy-lidded and close to the sides of his head. Wiry, copper curls wavered over the bald patch on his crown, which gave him an uncouth bearing that was clearly deceiving, for he addressed me in perfect Spanish.

'Hail, Spaniard. I am Redmond O'Ronayne, of the Cross of Tipperary.'

A rank odour hit me when his lips parted, which I recognised as stale mead. I did my best to ignore it, hoping that he would find my deep bow respectful. As I lowered my head to Redmond, I caught a glimpse of him out of the corner of my eye and found him to be serving me with a suspicious look. He may well have been left unimpressed by the tattered garments I wore, and his frown deepened when he spoke.

'How do you fare, Spaniard?'

'My feet are an agony, friend. But pray tell, what is your relation to the woman?'

A gust of wind blew past us in that instant, scattering his hair in all directions, and revealing a small pink patch on his forehead. All the while he studied me carefully, trying to discern the quality of the man who stood before him.

'I am her confessor. The woman, as you so crudely put it, is none other than Lady Muireann Mac an Bhaird, a highborn and celebrated *ollamh* among our people. You would do well to remember it, friend.'

His description of my companion left me feeling ill at ease, given the forceful treatment which I had dealt her the previous day.

'What is the meaning of this word, ollave?' I asked nervously.

My question drew a sigh of resignation from O'Ronayne, and I wondered if he was annoyed at my poor pronunciation of Muireann's title, as a result of my Latin ear.

'An *ollamh* is a master of learning, the equivalent of a professor from one of your Spanish universities. Muireann is a woman of many gifts and received the highest education in her early years.'

I listened to his words in stunned disbelief, while Lady Mac an Bhaird served me with a stare that bordered on the indignant. I cleared my throat awkwardly as I sought to change subject, as I queried after the man's status.

'If you are a priest, then where is your habit?'

'In this land, my friend, the life of a Catholic clergyman is not worth a single blade of grass to our enemy. But I do not believe that you require any convincing as to the necessity of my disguise?'

I nodded my understanding of his words when he addressed me again.

'You must gather your strength, Spaniard, and move on swiftly.'

'Where to?'

O'Ronayne signalled to the looming wall of mountain behind him.

'Rosclogher, a keep of my Lord MacGlannagh. Lady Mac an Bhaird will lead you there, for her knowledge of the secret passes in this land is unrivalled. I will also assign half of my kerns to her service. They are brave fighters, who will protect her with their lives.'

I met his words with a grunt of gratitude.

'My thanks, Father. Will you not join us?'

He shook his head swiftly.

'No. I am summoned to a small village to deliver last rites, for the dying do not wait. Yet I shall warn all folk I meet along the way that Breifne is no longer safe from the Bingham devils. The whole of Connacht is in tumult, for the land has never seen such times. It seems that Spain has finally heeded our call and come to our aid. Once more men dare to speak of a freedom which terrifies our enemies. It is why the heretics are raiding all of our settlements.'

The Jesuit's face shone with a righteous fervour while mine paled at his mention of the enemy, and upon noticing this he addressed me in a calmer tone, seeking to allay my fears.

'Once you are past those mountains, you should be safe. I have never known the enemy to venture so far north. They will surely know better than to venture into Dartry, for the Sheriff of Sligo himself fears to enter the land of the MacGlannaghs.'

As he spoke my teeth chattered from cold, and upon noticing me shiver, O'Ronayne surprised me by whisking his five-folded mantle off his back and wrapping it around my shoulders. When I tried to refuse it, he waved away my objections.

''Tis but a brat. I shall obtain another in the village I am approaching. Now be gone, and steer away from the lake. If you observe my lady's guidance, you may yet find safety. Godspeed, Spaniard, and may we meet again by the best hearth in Rosclogher.'

He embraced my guide a last time, before resuming his progress with his reduced band of men who quickly disappeared amongst the surrounding trees. When they had vanished from our sight, the native who the Jesuit had referred to as both ollave and Lady Muireann Mac an Bhaird gathered the reins of our mount. In silence we veered away from the water towards a deep cleft in the heart of the mountains, which closely resembled a curled lip of foreboding.

Muireann seemed to have regained some composure following her conversation with the priest, so that she snapped commands at the six tribesmen assigned to us, who each heeded her orders as if she were a man. Their swords were whipped from their scabbards, with two spears clenched in their other hands as they flanked us, closely surveying the surrounding terrain at all times. Meanwhile the ollave took up a nettle-strewn trail which twisted and turned into the mountains, while I limped as quickly as I could after her and her band, silently mouthing obscenities at the pains that afflicted me.

It was a path so abandoned that only the native goatherds could have known of it, for it was rugged in the extreme, and it took many tugs on the reins and much cajoling by the natives to get the stallion to follow them. These delays allowed me to keep within step of them, while the stinging hairs on certain plants brushed my legs, adding to my discomfort amid my wincing and heavy huffing, which were caused by the steep ascent.

As we rose ever higher, we soon caught sight of the high silvery waterfalls overhead, which caused us to draw our cloaks tightly around us whenever we passed beneath them and were sprinkled by their ice-cold water. For the rest of the afternoon, our ears were filled with the sounds of their rushing descent, which only grew with the frequent onset of rain. We would have been soaked through were it not for our thick mantles, which were pulled over our heads to serve as hoods. Lady Muireann led the way throughout our endless march uphill, pausing only to whisper to the horse in order to stem its nervous whinnying.

Our guards never once tarried, their stoic strength on the march similar to that of the Spanish tercios. We soon reached places where curious flowering plants clung to the lofty mountain walls, climbing ever higher along the scarped slopes, so that when we finally reached the summit of our rise, my head felt light from the staggering view of the valley below us. A falcon could be seen wheeling over our heads, and the air was so keen that it felt like my lungs were ablaze.

The lake below us had been reduced to nearly half its actual size, and after a few moments spent gazing at it, I fell back onto the ground, heedless of a wild sparrowhawk that flew past us with a shrill cry. Gilson's stallion was coated in sweat as it stooped over to chomp at some heather, a few feet away from what appeared to be a mound of grey stones. Muireann slowly drew away from the cliff edge as she studied the ground before us, then turned around and called out to me.

'Do no tarry, grey wolf! Dangerous beasts lurk here at night.'

With a huge effort I turned myself onto my back, feeling entirely drained of strength as I somehow managed a reply.

'But the horse needs a rest...'

When I regained my breath, one of the kerns stepped over with an extended forearm and helped me return to my feet, then hurried after the ollave as she led the stallion away towards a cloud-strewn skyline. The other men encircled her protectively, turning their heads towards the slightest sound while swiftly raising their weapons to defend themselves. Yet no trouble was encountered during the remainder of our journey, and we made our way down a tricky bridlepath in the last light of the setting sun, soon reaching a small cave in which we retired for the night. At the ollave's order, two of our number left to seek firewood in our rocky environs, while I lay in a corner of the grotto wrapped tightly in O'Ronayne's brat mantle, grateful that I had not been asked to brave the howling winds outside.

Almost an hour later, two respectable armfuls of fuel were brought to the cave by the returning kerns, and shadows played against the walls of our retreat when a fire was finally started. The relief was plain on the men's faces as we held our hands out towards the growing flames, for the frosty bluster throughout our climb had rivalled the worst Protestant bone-chiller in the Spanish Netherlands. Meanwhile our guide stood a few feet away from us, covering the horse with two blankets taken from the kerns, before proceeding to pluck the blackthorns out of its tail.

As the night set in, the kerns drew strips of dried cowflesh from their small sacks and shared them with me and Muireann. Thereafter they wrapped themselves in sheepskin blankets and huddled closely together, beckoning to me to lie alongside them. I raised my hand in polite refusal, for my sufferings in the previous days had made me more wary than usual of others. I remained lying against a rock far removed from the puddles of rainwater between us, attempting to forget the horrors of recent days and ignoring the pains which beset my whole body.

After a time, my attentions returned to the native, who also sat apart from the shivering kerns, but a few paces away from me. Although she gave me her back, I somehow sensed that she observed me in that unique manner of women, with the glimpses from the corners of her eyes quickly withdrawn whenever I looked at her. My mind eventually turned to pulling my mantle more closely about my shoulders, since the wind blew a constant swirl of hail and frost towards the mouth of our cave.

The cold only worsened when the fire died down, leading one of the men to valiantly remove himself from his fellows, long enough to hurl more brushwood upon the dying flames. His efforts led to a growing heat from the flames, yet it did not last for long, so that I was soon shuddering relentlessly while fearing that my fingers and toes would soon be claimed by the bite of the frost.

Before long, the icy gales became so relentless that the solitary guard at the grotto's mouth abandoned his post and dived among the shivering mass of his fellows. When all feeling was lost from my hands, I prayed to the blessed Virgin that I might survive the night through some miracle. Just when it seemed like the weather could not worsen, a furious wind blast tore through our shelter and snuffed out what flames remained. Gilson's horse shrieked and thrashed against its reins, which had been secured to a rock near the back wall of our quarters.

A low snarl was next heard ahead of me, and the quivering shadow of Muireann rose from the ground before she stumbled in my direction. My bafflement only increased when she hurled herself upon me, wrapping her arms and legs around me and burrowing her head into my chest. Such was the cold that my only immediate thoughts were of warming my hands and feet, so that we rubbed our limbs against each other to loud gasps, although our frenzied efforts only made for some very scant relief. I had all but given up on any warmth, when I felt a desperate tugging against my left arm. Before I knew it, she had pulled me over her to force the first of a number of rolling movements which had us splash through a puddle of rainwater. Its iciness caused me to howl out once, before we landed upon the dying embers that singed our frozen flesh, with the sudden heat allowing us to ease our grip on each other, which was finally released when the wind changed again.

For almost an hour thereafter, I gasped in disbelief at the ferocity of the gale which had all but claimed our lives. Then my thoughts turned to the native who was huddled against me, as I realised that I had not been so close to a woman since that ill-starred day in Willebroek, when I had marched off to the ambush. Almost as if moving of its own accord, my hand slowly slid along the woman's back, and despite myself my fingers found themselves curling around a stiff buttock.

There seemed to be no resistance to my gesture, so I lifted my head enough to nuzzle my nose against her neck, when the sharp edge of a cold blade met my throat. It was at once clear to me that the lady had drawn the long dagger at her belt, and her piercing eyes reflected the faint gleam of the dying embers as if she were some nightly vixen. I carefully removed my hand from her behind, slowly exhaling my relief when the blade was gently withdrawn from my gullet a few moments later.

'*Muc*!', she hissed, then returned to her feet and staggered away.

Towards dawn the restored warmth of my body made my head sag backwards from broken sleep, and my eyes closed until daybreak. The prod of a stick in my side had me stir with a start, and I noticed the slender figure of Muireann walking into the haze of daylight that streamed through the grotto, leading Gilson's horse after her. With a grunt I shuffled to my feet and hurried out after the kerns behind her. My subsequent attempts at conversation went ignored as we descended towards yet another valley which spread out before us.

Although she retained a mournful expression, Lady Muireann finally acknowledged my presence when she saw me staring open-mouthed at the huge peaks which rose to our left. She described them to me in Latin, as she gestured towards the rises as if they were prized possessions.

'That is the crest of *Gortnagara*, grey wolf, and that is *Trosc Mór*. Thou canst see its peak, although most of it is obscured by cloud.'

'Why dost thou call me grey wolf?' I asked, in genuine puzzlement.

''Tis our word for aliens from beyond *Éirinn*,' she replied, although I was still unsure what to make of this.

We ventured down the grassy slopes of the rise which the natives called *Taobh Bán*, nearing the green and brown blankets of woodland and moor ahead of us. The gnarled boughs of oaks pierced the thick furze and bracken, where clusters of other trees barred passage to all but those who knew of the concealed paths between them. In the distance a large body of water shimmered along the horizon where the grass met the sky.

'Yonder lies lough Melvin,' said Muireann.

Her words brought new vigour to my step, and throughout our journey towards the lake we met not a soul, save for the odd herdsman who minded a few soggy sheep which grazed in the shadow of the heights before us. At the sight of them, our guard of kerns whistled aloud, which prompted the shepherds to quickly round up their livestock and return to the uplands, all the while issuing shrill whistles of their own which carried across the plain.

When the pain in my feet became too much to bear, I implored Muireann to let me mount the horse for the remainder of our descent. After she agreed, we quickly reached the foot of the mountain, then made for a distant edifice. Upon sighting it, the other kerns ran ahead, leaving only one of their fellows behind with us.

'What is astir?' I asked the ollave.

'We are to repair to the abbey, while they scout our surrounds for signs of the enemy.'

I nodded my understanding as we ventured on towards the building, the kern keeping ahead of us while I rode Gilson's stallion which Muireann led by the bridle. As we drew nearer to the edifice, our pace slackened when we made out an abbey. It had long been defiled by the enemy, for its windows were all smashed, and one of its walls was blackened by flames. Sharp breaths escaped us at the sight, which soon turned into loud exclamations when we approached the bodies of the dead soldiers which were strewn in front of the ravaged building. When we trod through them the sun's reflection in their armour half-blinded us, so that we were spared some of the horror and misery which abounded between us and the desecrated abbey.

'What happened here?' whispered Muireann.

There were countless corpses in the mud around us, and I cringed with dread when I recognised the Castilian dress of the butchered soldiers who lay in our path. A fair few Italians and Germans could also be seen lying upon the grass, among men of other nations.

'So many men,' I muttered as we passed through them, thinking of the numerous cries in various tongues that must have been issued to distant mothers.

The sight of the dead left me recalling the grey stretch of beach where I had been shipwrecked, so that my insides were soon clenched in a tight grip of fear, with my palms turning moist in spite of the cold. My mind wrestled to allay the piercing panic which had seized me, and I flung myself off the mount when I heard faint, strained breaths from the grass below me.

Crows scattered and fled when I hobbled towards a man who lay motionless before us, and I flinched upon seeing a pool of blood gathered behind his cracked skull, not to mention the wretch's eyes which had been pecked clean. As I beheld him in pity, a slow murmur left his cracked lips, which was almost inaudible. I felt shocked by the helplessness of his condition, falling onto one knee and resting my hand upon his shoulder.

'What happened to you, soldier?'

After a few moments, a rasp resembling a chuckle left the wretch's lips, and the hair rose upon the back of my neck when he replied.

'Santiago...'

My blood ran cold as I recoiled from the voice, then suddenly recognised the once handsome features of Captain Arturo Fernández.

'Captain! It is you!'

Overcoming my revulsion, I gently placed my hands on his shoulders, drawing a gasp of pain from him when I tried to lift his head towards me.

'Aye Santiago... I pray, do not move me.'

I loosened my hold on him, letting the captain's broken skull lie back against the grass. The hopelessness of his condition both angered and dismayed me.

'What happened here?'

A wheeze was heard in Fernández's throat, as another hoarse reply left his lips.

'The heretics...they promised safe passage...they gave their word...we gave up...our weapons...'

My breath quickened in outrage at the enemy's deceit, as I observed Fernández's tattered clothes, which had been rifled and searched by the Sassanas who had abandoned my former officer without even bothering to end his misery. Behind him I could see the corpse of *El Perro*, who had been slain while faithfully fighting alongside his captain, when a sudden fear overcame me that the Sassanas might also have robbed me of my vengeance.

'And Ramos? And Salva? What of them?'

The wrinkles around the captain's eyes and forehead grew as he groaned in discomfort, and I shook him slightly while trying not to bare my teeth.

'I entreat you to tell me!'

Fernández struggled for breath, and the empty scarlet sockets in his face seemed fixed upon me.

'I know not for certain...Santi...we were attacked at...the dead of night...they fled to the woods...enemies on their tail...'

It was a great effort for him to speak, since he had long tarried at death's door and was in a terrible condition. While his body shook violently as he fought for breath, a sudden pang of emptiness ran through me at his mention of the enemy's pursuit of Ramos and Salva, which threatened the entire scope of my existence. A bitter taste filled my mouth, almost as if it were filled with ash from the van der Molens' house. For a few moments there seemed no reason to exist any more, and I almost wondered why I should even bother fleeing capture and death.

Then a gurgle from Fernández's stomach somehow reminded me of the bauble borne within me. Despite all my setbacks, I remembered that I had in my possession a precious ring. A trinket of such value that it would be a passport to America for me and Elsien's youngest brother Pieter, as well as other members of her long-suffering family, like her aunt Margareta.

'Your brother-in-law?' asked the captain, interrupting my thoughts.

'Perished in the shipwreck.'

'I am sorry...he...he was a good lad...'

The captain's words moved me, and I thought of Maerten and what he would have made of my plight.

'He was,' I managed, wiping away the warm tears gathering on my eyelids.

When I struggled back to my feet, O'Ronayne's kern wordlessly held out his sword to me, as I stood over the captain's body, pondering how best to make a clean thrust. Almost as if reading my thoughts, Fernández whispered at my feet, anxious to unburden himself before I despatched him.

'Forgive me...Abel...the fire-tax..I should... I should have been stronger...'

A deep sigh left me when I held the native's sword high over his head.

'Peace, Captain.'

A deep intake of breath was heard from Fernández, and I mistook his efforts at speech for last prayers as his words reached my good ear.

'I pray you Santiago...the sword, not the gun...'

His request left me feeling slightly irked, although I knew that he meant no offence, for the sword was still perceived as the honourable weapon of choice. I then looked at Muireann who stood in front of me. Her eyes were misted although not a tear lined her cheeks, even when she stared at the ground. I raised my arms and held the sword as high up as I could, despite my injured shoulder.

'Despatched by...Abel...de Santiago...' muttered Fernández almost reverently, '....Alba's...very own...Lynx of Haarlem...'

A last look at the captain's face revealed a picture of serenity, since he was finally about to meet the end he had craved. Blood was spattered everywhere when I brought the blade down hard, then flung the redsoaked weapon to the turf and fell onto my knees, my face held in my hands. The tears welled up in my eyes as I whispered a prayer beneath my breath, dedicating it to his passing. Then a vision of Elsien's face came to me, laughing and alive beneath the Empress tree, teasing me joyfully as I pulled her close towards me.

'For the love of God,' I whispered, 'will you never be avenged?'

Behind me I heard someone pick something off the ground, and drops were felt on my head, which I mistook for the onset of rain. My fingertips moved to my dampened crown, then I absently brought them to rest on my lips. The ensuing taste of blood had me jerking my head in horror towards the boughs overhead. I looked up to see more Spaniards hanging from the branches of the trees, men who had met with summary execution at the hand of the heretic. They swayed in the breeze with fingers curled like talons and naked as they were born, their blue tongues splayed upon their chests.

'Let us await the men in the church,' said Muireann, gently taking my arm.

I flinched at the ollave's touch, then cast her a bewildered gaze as she returned a hurt look which soon turned into a hard stare. At a slight nod of my head we hitched the horse to a tree, then walked in silence towards the blackened abbey. As we drew nearer, I suddenly froze in my tracks, for voices could be heard from inside it, which made the hair rise upon the back of my neck. I waved at the ollave and kern to gain their attention, then raised my finger to my lips in a gesture for them to keep silent as I crouched down low and crept behind a tussock which was close to the building.

'I'm starving, Curro,' said the first voice, which was both nasal and high-pitched, 'shall we move on?'

'Not yet,' grunted another. 'After that narrow escape, this has to be the safest place for now.'

'Perhaps, but we can't survive on clover and snails for much longer. And tonight this place will be choked with wolves. And should we not seek out any men outside who may still be alive? I swear I heard one calling from the ground.'

'Forget them,' snapped Ramos, 'we'll be fortunate if we don't perish with them soon.'

My blood boiled at the sergeant's open disloyalty to his own comrades, which I had experienced first hand.

'By the Virgin,' I whispered, beneath my breath, 'they are both here.'

A burning rage seared through my limbs as I held up my bloodstained blade. All weariness and pain were instantly forgotten as my heart beat ever faster, when Muireann spoke behind me in the lowest voice possible.

'What is the matter? Are they not thy comrades?'

Once again, I gestured at her to keep silent as I whispered a last request.

'Stay here with the horse and guard. There are evil souls about. If I call out to thee, thou must flee this place.'

Her hand fell to my shoulder again as I took my first step towards the abbey.

'Stay, why wouldst thou venture on? The other wood-kern shall soon be here.'

I sighed aloud before gently taking her hand and removing it.

'I must settle this now, or die trying.'

As I stepped towards the church, the kern moved alongside me. I gestured to him to remain behind, when Muireann hissed at me.

'Conall goes with thee!'

Her words sounded like an order, and I did not wish to argue with her and alert my former comrades to our presence. With a slight nod of my head I ventured on with the Irishman, treading as lightly as I could as I approached the entrance to the abbey's chapel. My teeth were instantly gritted as the door creaked aloud at my touch, which silenced the low muttering inside.

I held the sword out in front of me as we entered the church, thirstier than ever to claim my longawaited revenge. On my right, Conall held his spear above his head, glaring from side to side as we were greeted by the sight of yet more death and destruction. At least twenty dead Spaniards swung from the rafters above us, obscuring our view of the desecrated chapel as we slowly stepped towards them. The grotesque sight looked like some chamber of hell, with the dead soldiers' wrists bound and their heads curled unnaturally over the nooses around their necks. I then noticed a few of them gently swaying at the back, prompting me to raise my sword.

'Have a care,' echoed a familiar voice, 'you who come bearing arms in a house of worship.'

'Show yourself!' I snapped angrily. 'Let us end this here and now.'

My words were met with a lengthy and disturbing silence, and I suppressed a shiver as another tremor ran through the hanging bodies to my right.

'So much anger, brother,' said Ramos from the back of the church, in a tone that sounded sympathetic. 'Even now you would not put aside our quarrel? Have we not all suffered the same tragedy? Are we not all true believers, gathered in a house of God?'

'I can think of no better place to end our quarrel,' I snapped back, pushing aside the twisted legs and hands in my path, and being ever watchful for the first sign of my former comrades.

There was no further attempt made at conciliation, and I knew I had to be at my most vigilant. As another charred body swayed before me, I kept my eyes peeled for any other movements, watching for the slightest twitch of another corpse. My stomach squirmed when a number of bodies bobbed sideways to our right, and as we turned to face them, a cracking sound was heard behind me, followed by a loud groan.

'What in hell?'

As I turned on my heel, I saw Conall landing at my feet in a heap, with the crown of his head bloodied by a heavy blow. As I beheld the kern's fall, a pole end landed heavily upon my wounded shoulder, causing me to twist sideways in pain. A hefty arm then burst through the dangling corpses, wrapping itself around my neck and pulling me to the ground.

'Release me!' I roared, as the sword was knocked out of my hand and I was dragged towards the altar.

Upon reaching it a heavy heel landed upon my neck, pinning me to the ground as I angrily strove to push it away.

'Why it really is him.'

The voice belonged to my former sergeant, who appeared half amused as he leant over me, bringing his boot down harder upon my throat. In the scant daylight within the building I could also see Salva's twitching face staring down at me, until the two men's heads almost touched. In their torn vestments and rusted armour, they cut a leaner and more wretched sight than when I had last met them in Seville.

'He doesn't look much better off than us,' mused Salva, with his yellowed plait dangling alongside his head, 'Shall I finish him?'

The corporal walked over to a small stack of firearms and weapons which they had collected at the altar, then bent over to pick up his *partesana*.

'Always so hasty, man,' said Ramos, waving Salva's words away in annoyance. 'Put it down, for I would talk to him first.'

So saying the sergeant withdrew his foot, then grabbed me by the scruff of the neck and hauled me to my feet. As I shook furiously in his grasp, I was awed by the power of his grip, which was as strong as it had always been.

'Stop wriggling like a whore,' he snapped, slapping me hard across the face. 'What are you doing here, Abelito?'

'Trying to kill you,' I snarled, seizing his hairy arms and trying in vain to force them away from me.

He issued a low chuckle at my resistance, then shoved me against the wall behind the altar, slamming me into it a few times until I all but passed out. Ramos next pressed me against the sharp bricks by thrusting the pole of his halberd under my chin and pushed it hard against my neck with his outstretched hands.

'Speak whoreson,' he growled, with his face inching closer towards mine. 'What are you doing here?'

I stared back at him helplessly, with blood flooding my mouth from my nose. As my senses were slowly regained, it occurred to me then that both Ramos and Salva's cocksure bearing was betrayed by a slight cast of desperation. The intensity of their gaze hinted at them hanging on my every word, for they were clearly fearful of finding themselves in a land where Catholics were the oppressed minority. As soon as I made this realisation, I sought to compensate for my lack of strength with my wits.

'Flee, my lady,' I roared in Latin, 'flee! They have overpowered us and wounded thy kinsman!'

'What are you playing at?' snarled Ramos, as he squeezed the pole of his weapon ever more tightly against my throat. 'What are you saying?!'

'Latin,' hissed Salva, his eyes wide with fear in his twitching face, 'it was something in Latin.'

Ramos jerked his head towards the shattered windows to his right.

'Who else is there outside?' he said. 'Quick, tell me what you see!'

The corporal ran over to the side wall, being ever the faithful lackey, then rested the palm of his hand over his eyes as he peered outside,

'I see only dead bodies,' he said, before exclaiming, 'and a horse!'

'A horse?' said Ramos, his eyes narrowing in keen interest.

'Yes sergeant! A fine, black stallion, hitched to a tree!'

Upon hearing this, Ramos was instantly overwhelmed by thought, so that I seized on his moment of distraction, grabbing the pole and shoving it back into his face. It was a blow which would have felled most men, yet the sergeant's grip on the halberd barely slackened as he stared back at me in bafflement, so I rammed my knee into his groin, then ducked beneath the pole and caught him again in the crotch with an upward punch.

As he fell onto all fours I held my hands together in a tight grip, then swung them into his cheek. He fell over sideways with a loud roar, which brought Salva running towards us, as I rolled over sideways and fled the chancel, tearing off down the aisle and shoving dead bodies aside before the corporal could reach me.

'Finish him!' yelled Ramos behind us, 'I'll fetch us the horse.'

No sooner had he said this than I came upon the body of Conall, pausing long enough to draw his sword from its scabbard, before running on towards the abbey's entrance. When I reached the doorway, I turned to find the hanging bodies of the Spaniards swinging violently as Salva burst through them and hurried over towards me, brandishing his dreaded *partesana* spear. Its long blade and cruel edges glinted wickedly as he twirled it in the daylight, and I swallowed tightly and restrained a shiver at the sight of it, for I had often witnessed the Corporal's deadly work with it in battle.

'Let's finish this,' he said.

We circled each other like rabid dogs for a few moments, before he flew at me like a fiend. I parried his opening flurry of lightning-quick strokes which were as fast as he was agile, coming both from the side and above as I staved them off with difficulty. The corporal beat me back against a wall, then nicked my left shoulder and beat me back again. His height gave him an added advantage, yet I somehow drew myself away, just as the spear point sliced my kneecap, then was beaten back again.

Each time I managed to dodge a fatal blow, with my sword left ringing until it almost flew from my hands. He still came at me, ripping the side of my shirt open with another swing that I somehow sidestepped, with my sword held out before me again. I tried to think of a way to unnerve him, resorting to the cheap goading I had often heard among brawlers.

'Come on then, corporal, let's have you rejoin Gabri and Cristó.'

At my taunting, the devil's eyes all but bulged out of his twisting face as he charged forward again, landing a series of swings like hammer blows which left the sword barely dangling from my hand. I knew that my blade would soon be lost, and the ferocity of his onslaught had left me too breathless even to goad him. Then a distant memory flashed through my mind, of a feint I had seen during my childhood in Malta, in one of the many duels alongside the harbour. Yet I instantly abandoned the idea, for I knew I would have to be as fast as a snake to carry it out.

Salva charged me again, chopping swathes of air but a hair's breadth from my cheeks, as I shifted from side to side. My throat was just nicked before my thigh was struck by the butt of his pole arm, which thwarted my withdrawal. Another gash appeared at my hip, when I brought my blade up to fend off a crushing blow which was about to be landed against my forehead. The *partesana* was then swiftly withdrawn as I seized his shoulder and shoved him away.

'Have to try it,' I whispered to myself, utterly short of breath and feeling incensed that he would soon prevail.

I feigned weakness as I parried his next thrusts, pretending to have almost lost my footing as I assumed a look of fear. He was emboldened at the sight of this, as another swing of his pole arm was barely staved off, but I had watched him fight too many times before so that I knew what would come next. At any moment I expected one of his next thrusts to go straight through my chest, and when the mortal blow was aimed I resorted to the memory from my childhood. With a cry of effort, I shifted myself sideways with what remained of my strength, then slammed my elbow downwards, catching the pole of his weapon between my arm and side.

It was the cheap move from the dock, yet it did the trick. Salva appeared baffled as he tried to wrench his weapon away from me, his face torn by a deep frown in the time it took me to spring forward with a roar and kick his knee in sideways. It bent unnaturally with a loud crack as he sagged sideways with a shriek, just as I landed a crunching blow of my bleeding forehead against his nose. The corporal howled yet again before he was felled with a blow to the chin from my sword pommel. As he regained his senses, he stared back at me in disbelief from the ground, as my sword point was rested upon his throat.

'When Ramos gets back...' he snarled, recovering his defiance in the face of death.

'You fool,' I gasped at him, also struggling to regain my breath, 'he's already flown.'

'Stay your forked tongue, Santi,' he replied with bared teeth.

A loud whinny from the stallion was heard outside, and doubt clouded the corporal's twitching face as I lunged forward, shoving the sword through his throat and leaving him to thrash wildly upon the straw underfoot. I took in his wild movements for a few moments as I staggered backwards, then stepped forward again and kicked him off the blade before crashing through the abbey's door, battered and bleeding. Despite my weariness I quickly studied my surroundings, fearful that I had once again lost the bigger prize.

Muireann and her returned kerns were already running over towards me, and together we looked on in dismay as Ramos thundered past us upon the black destrier. He leant forward as a spear throw from one of the natives flew past him, with another dart catching the back of his rusted breastplate.

'Farewell Abelito!' he called out to me with a mocking laugh, until our next meeting!'

The horse grew smaller as it thundered off, leaving me to growl in frustration as I threw my sword to the ground. My mind raced to think of a way to stop him, and for a moment I wished that I had a rifle. I then remembered the small pile of arms I had seen at the back of the church, and I raced back into the chapel, jumping over the corporal's still corpse and flinging hanging bodies aside until I reached the altar. I could make out a belt of powder charges amongst the small pile of arms collected by Ramos and Salva, as well as a ball bag and a musket. I seized up all three and tore back through the church, batting the hanging bodies away until I was back with Muireann and her group of kerns.

'Thou lackest all the tools,' she observed as I flung everything onto the ground before me.

'Draw thy knife and flint!' I gasped, spitting a ball down the musket, before also uncapping a powder charge and shoving its contents into the pan and then down the bore.

The ollave stared back at me in puzzlement and then did as I said.

'I need sparks on the pan,' I snapped at her, leaving her frowning in puzzlement, before she nodded slightly and quickly drew her knife and flint.

'At my order then!' I snapped, then slammed the butt of the musket against the ground to compensate for my lack of a ramrod, as I stared fearfully after the shrinking sight of the mounted Ramos.

The sergeant had already covered the slight descent and was fast charging up a gentle bluff. When the musket was loaded, I fell to one knee, aiming it after him. As Ramos grew smaller, I captured his form within the length of my thumb, estimating the distance before swinging back the doghead and barking at the ollave.

'Now!'

She already held the flint a few inches away from my face, before striking it hard with her dagger. The first shower of sparks singed my cheek as they landed upon the rifle's breech, yet I did not budge a fraction of an inch as I shouted at her once more.

'Again!'

Muireann struck the rock a second time with all her strength, landing sparks on both my face and the musket. I closed my eye, ignoring the burning upon my forehead and cheek as a plume of smoke emerged from the pan. My heart quickened as the musket was fired, leaving me to hope that I had not moved too suddenly. Yet as the smoke cleared, I was dismayed to see Ramos atop the horse, and I groaned aloud in disappointment as it charged on, then dropped my gun with my head hung low.

'Grey wolf!' exclaimed Muireann, quickly sheathing her knife and drawing her bow, and I looked up and saw the distant figure of the sergeant toppling off the horse, which slowed to a canter and then to a halt.

The kerns cheered aloud at the sight, and one laughed aloud in disbelief. I ignored their mirth and was already racing towards the distant steed, desperate to reach Ramos.

'Grey wolf!' screeched the ollave again, and I looked behind me to see her gesturing to the hills behind us, where distant riders had appeared in domed helmets.

Her kerns quickly dispersed at her order while she growled in annoyance and then hurried after me, so that we both raced towards the horse, which was our only hope of escape upon the open plain.

'Faster,' she cried after me, 'they will soon be upon us.'

My lungs were aflame by the time we raced uphill and reached the horse, where Ramos could be seen gasping for breath as blood burst from his back and chest.

'Abelito!' he gasped, 'Abelito!'

I whirled upon him with my knife drawn, before Muireann seized me by the shoulder and pulled me towards the stallion.

'Is he even worth thy life?!' she cried.

'What life?!' I howled at her, shoving her away as I ran over towards the sergeant and kicked him across the face, sending him rolling away downhill.

I was blind with anger and meant to slay him by my own hand, when the first crack of a pistol was heard behind us. Several riders could be seen making towards us, having already reached the end of the descent. With gritted teeth I stared after the bleeding figure of Ramos, feeling enraged that I had not the time to finish him. For a moment I stood rooted to the spot with the growing thunder of hooves in my ears, uncertain what to do as the sergeant noticed the approaching troopers and somehow rose to one knee.

'Abel,' he shrieked, 'do not abandon me...'

A vein in my temple bristled with mad rage, that he still had the temerity to assume that I might help him.

'As you did at Willebroek?!' I roared in outrage.

I suddenly realised that he had sealed my doom by delaying me, and he flashed me a smirk as I made out the troopers' pistols being aimed in my direction, as one rider stood in his stirrups to take his shot. Then hoof beats pounded the turf behind me, and a hand snatched my shirt and dragged me away from both Ramos and the ascending riders. Muireann's hand never relinquished its grip as she slowed the horse long enough for me to somehow haul myself onto its back.

'Climb up, grey wolf,' she cried, 'we must flee.'

Muireann insisting that she sit behind me, as a pistol shot was fired by one of the troopers.

'For thy protection,' she snapped.

Feeling too shocked to argue, I snatched up the horse's reins and slashed them across its withers, and it instantly bolted towards the open country at a furious gallop. A backward glance revealed Ramos raising his hands towards a trooper who rode at him with a drawn blade. There followed by the frantic yelling of men, when of a sudden the horse jolted sideways, and I looked ahead again to regain my balance, as our mount thundered on towards a growing wood. When I looked back again, I could see our pursuers spurring their mounts with gritted teeth, led by a man who looked all too familiar while his mantle fluttered around him.

'Burke,' I gasped in despair, as the hair rose upon the back of my neck.

Muireann beheld me in puzzlement as her windswept brown hair rippled through the air about her. Beneath us the destrier charged on past alders and yews along a curved path, soon reaching the browning stretch of untamed country which lay ahead of us. Before long, the boggy moorland slowed our progress to a quick canter, which was broken by sudden charges whenever the marsh became firmer.

Sidelong glances over my shoulder revealed a score of troopers riding hard behind us, some of them close enough to attempt pistol shots at us. Our horse twisted and turned in different directions with great vigour, yet with two riders upon its back, it was gradually starting to lose ground. Another glimpse over my shoulder revealed Muireann lifting her bow, aiming a fitted shaft at one of our pursuers.

'Nay!' I cried, knowing that the difficulty of such a shot might cause her to lose her balance.

Yet her audacity was undeterred, and she executed a perfect Parthian shot when she released the back of her bolt that instantly struck home, flinging a trooper onto the ground. Pistol shots were fired by the other pursuing riders, who were so close that we could make out the mud being flicked off their mounts' hooves as they drew ever closer to us.

In that moment, the heavens opened, rendering all firearms useless. Yet Muireann had barely just issued a sigh of relief when the last crack of a pistol unsettled our mount, which slipped on the mire and hurled us sideways. The rest was but a painful blur as we flew off the shrieking stallion's back, with the ollave rolling over the dirt ahead of me. My arm took the brunt of my tumble, when I saw our writhing mount catch Muireann's forehead with the edge of its hoof.

This blow rendered her a lifeless heap, and I turned to make out the whites of Sergeant Burke's eyes which glared at us, as he drew ever nearer, so that I readied to join Ramos in the next world. The closest trooper was barely two yards away when an ear-splitting yell could be heard from the thick bracken around us, followed by the whistle of javelins and darts.

'MacGlannagh Abù!'

At this cry tens of knobby knees sprang from the surrounding brush as kerns in white tunics raced at the enemy. With their leather shields held before them, these bearded natives hurled themselves at their mounted foes and dragged them upon the ground, jabbing their long blades into our enemies' faces and throats. They were closely followed by a score of bare-backed horsemen in saffron linen, who galloped forth in their steel caps and mail shirts, wielding spears and fletched darts.

I hauled myself away from our whinnying stallion whose hindquarters bounced against my ankle, then crawled over towards the ollave and seized the sword of a slain heretic. A trooper bore down on me with a raised demi-lance when a black-haired Irishman rode up behind him, unhorsing the Sassana with a thrust of his javelin. I had hardly reached the sword when I saw Treasach Burke whirling towards me, his scarred face wracked with fury as he raised his bloodied mace above him. I rose to one knee and parried the sergeant's first thrust, with his second swing aimed between my shoulders. When I raised my sword to meet the vicious strike, the flat of my blade crashed into my forehead, turning all to black.

XV

ROSCLOGHER, DARTRY, COUNTY
LEITRIM, IRELAND

20 September 1588

My head throbbed like a war drum, and the raw welts on my back scraped a harsh cloth when I stirred. It felt as though I lay upon a bale of hay, with its prickly straws leaving me to groan in discomfort. When my eyes opened, a shifting glow reduced my sight to quick blinking, until I could see that I was surrounded by the crude boarding of a cabin. My nostrils twitched at the scent of the sods between the planks, which sent a quiver of pain up the bridge of my nose.

I lifted my head at a clacking sound and made out the blurry image of a man seated ahead of me upon a stool. Behind him burned a small fire which produced the blinding glare, and its smoke trailed towards the hole in the thatched roof above us. The man was the immediate subject of my attention, for I could see that rough-hewn beads of a rosary were curled around his right hand, which struck one another to a faint mumbling. I was instantly flooded with relief, as I realised that my minder was not a heretic. He must also have been at my bedside for a long time, since his eyes were shut and he gently swayed like a pendulum.

His movements were also accompanied by the faint lapping of water against a bank of land, a sound that, together with the musty smell of moss from the cabin's walls, hinted at the nearby presence of a lake or river. In my struggle to comprehend these new lodgings, I produced a slurred whisper.

'Where am I?'

In the flickering firelight I could see that he bore the familiar garb of the Jesuit fathers, for his black cassock was bound by a girdle of the same colour. Three peaks arose from the square cap on his head, which also confirmed him to be one of those zealous upstarts that followed Ignatius of Loyola, the founder of the Society of Jesus. A deep unease seized me upon recognising his vestments, for throughout my army years I had come across all manner of charlatans who posed as priests, with the sole intention of stealing money from weak and dying soldiers.

The Jesuit's eyes shot open as I attempted to rise from my litter, and a scrape was heard from his seat when he wobbled to his feet. I had almost raised myself up when a bony forearm fell across my chest, shoving my raw back against the harsh sackcloth on which I lay, causing little bits of dried grass to fill the air as they rose from my litter, glinting in the faint sunlight which streamed through the cabin's boards.

'Be still, Spaniard! You are in the town of Lord MacGlannagh!'

A hellish pain pierced my ribs when I tried to resist his wild shoving, and an anguished whisper left my lips.

'Who?'

'My Lord MacGlannagh! He is the master of Dartry, and commands all lands from Grange to Ballyshannon!'

The fellow's breath reeked of stale mead, and as I beheld his raw-boned figure, I recognised the priest whom I had met when fleeing the enemy with the ollave Muireann. The mantle he had given me during our escape through the valley had probably saved my life in the mountains, and I remembered that he called himself O'Ronayne of the Cross of some place or other.

Low whispers could be heard from behind the Jesuit, which drew my attentions towards the shadows that shifted in the doorway, of two men in long tunics, as well as the unmistakable outline of their spears. Snatches of conversation could also be heard from them, marking them out as kerns who were posted outside our cabin.

'Are you holding me captive?'

The priest appeared baffled by my question. He made no reply as he walked towards a flagon beside his stool, then took a long swig from it and wiped his sleeve against his mouth. When at last he replied to me, his voice was deep and brusque, unlike the highpitched tone of most clergymen I had met before.

'Whatever makes you think that, Spaniard?'

With a grunt of effort, I raised my arm, pointing at the rugged shadows on the ground behind him.

'Are they not guards?'

The Jesuit beheld me carefully, without ever once looking in the direction of my gesture.

'Very observant,' he said quietly, 'although given your present condition, even a child could restrict your movements.'

A small smile appeared on his face, and he took another swig before explaining himself further.

'They are indeed guards, friend Spaniard. But they have been tasked with protecting and not restraining you. Your arrival in Dartry has stirred the passions of its folk, many of whom have been overcome by the desire to steal a glimpse of you and to learn more about the Spanish landings. Those men at the door are worthy kerns, who have been posted to the infirmary so that you may recover in peace. I have attended to your wounds for the last three days, in which you have mumbled an endless stream of nonsense.'

'What sort of nonsense?' I exclaimed, suddenly recalling the ring and fearing any dark secrets which I may have revealed to him.

'Oh, all sorts of gabble,' replied the Jesuit, 'mutterings of miller's daughters and a sheriff's catch, Flemish night raids and an Iron Duke, silver fleets and Sassana stones...'

At his last words I swiftly sought to change the subject of our discussion, by blurting out the first question I could form in my mind.

'By the Virgin, what nonsense I have gabbled! Yet I pray you tell me, Father, do you also have skill in the art of healing?'

O'Ronayne cleared his throat awkwardly, seemingly surprised by the question.

'Indeed, Spaniard, I am not merely a man of the cloth but also one of healing. Did I not tell you that I tended to -'

'Ah, a barber surgeon?' I cut in enthusiastically and inno-
cently enough, but I could see at once that my words had irked
him.

At his flustering I realised that he was not only gaunt, but of
a countenance that was both hard and severe, and when at last
he spoke again, his voice was terse.

'I am a student of the *Hôtel-Dieu*, a school which has produced, physicians of the calibre of Ambroise Paré.'

His riposte left me stunned, for the *Hôtel-Dieu* was known
far beyond Paris, and was said to be without equal in the art
of healing. His claims of being a qualified physician were reinforced by the trestle tables behind him, which bore all manner
of herbs and implements, so that I watched the Jesuit warily
thereafter, and carefully minded my words. He was clearly a
learned man and not one to be slighted, being no doubt autho-
rised to wield the blade on my person.

'Forgive me, Father, if my question has caused you offence.
But what is a learned man of your skill doing in this far-flung
corner of the world?'

The priest's brow further darkened at these words, and his
reply seethed with indignation.

'I could ask the same of you, Spaniard. Yet where else would
we rather be? Connacht is a key battleground of the one true
faith, full of sons ready to die for the teachings of Rome.'

His talk of death left me feeling ill at ease, although I had
spent years courting it as a soldier. My unease was also caused
by the memories of recent days, in which all manner of perilous events had been endured since my landing upon the beach.
It swiftly occurred to me that I was indeed fortunate to somehow find myself in the ramshackle cabin, despite its stench of

blood and piss. Meanwhile O'Ronayne held up the beads in his hand, staring at them as if he was discerning some deep truth which he alone could see, as he whispered beneath his breath.

'These people are my flock. They have more need of me now than anyone else in this world.'

'Your Spanish is flawless,' I remarked, seeking to flatter him. 'Your talents would be well received by the Army of Flanders.'

A muffled laugh was heard by way of reply, as he took a loud slurp from his vessel before mocking my suggestion.

'The Army of Flanders is where I learnt your tongue!'

His revelation left me startled, and made me see him in a different light, for despite my mistrust of men of the cloth, it was impossible not to feel a sense of kinship with those who had endured the same sufferings. It also occurred to me that the Jesuit would understand my background better than most, and that much prudence would be required in my dealings with him.

'You served Spain in the Netherlands?'

'Yes, Spaniard,' he replied, with a forlorn expression, 'for five long years.'

'Paris... the Spanish Netherlands...' I remarked, 'you are indeed well travelled...'

'Indeed,' replied the Jesuit, 'and in these parts they say that he who travels has stories to tell.'

A few wordless moments passed between us, as was typical of veterans of the raging conflict between the Spanish Crown and the heretical Netherlanders. Inevitably I thought of my former comrades, and a grim satisfaction overcame me, when I recalled the end met by Salva and Ramos. It was hardly possible for me to believe that I had at last avenged both Elsien and Reynier, as well as Maerten. For it had taken years for me to accomplish, although I knew that there was one oath I was still sworn to fulfil.

My thoughts were interrupted by a loud burst of hoarse coughing, which revealed another convalescent in the infirmary across the hut. In the cabin's poor light I could see a young apprentice in an apron but a few feet away from us, holding a bowl to the face of an elderly tribesman. The Jesuit ignored the sounds of the only other invalid in the hut, as he spoke to me again.

'And now it appears that I am to serve with Spaniards again. The Lord has answered our prayers, for Spain has seen fit to answer our pleas for aid!'

His expectant grin soon turned into a worried frown when I hesitated to confirm his declaration. I had never heard of any plans by the Armada's commanders to assist the Irish rebels in their plight, and O'Ronayne's suspicious look returned when he addressed me again.

'But we have talked enough about me, Spaniard. There are some questions that I would ask of you.'

His eyes narrowed when he said this, and I tried not to fidget as his inquiring began.

'What is your name, my son?'

He had not yet finished speaking, and I was already fumbling in my mind for some alias to go by in days to come. For although the Jesuit knew of my lightheadedness, to keep him waiting too long could confirm any suspicions he had of me. For a moment I almost blurted my true name of Abelardo de Santiago, with the name on the tip of my tongue when I suddenly hesitated. For I was reluctant to use the name of a soldier who was wanted by the Spanish Army for murder, and who was renowned as a deadly sniper among the heretics.

'Juan de los Hospitalarios, Father,' I replied, using my childhood name.

A frown spread across O'Ronayne's face when I said this, and one of his eyebrows was raised in apparent disbelief. He rose to his feet with a pout and placed his hands behind his back, slowly pacing from side to side in front of my bed.

'And what is your rank, friend Juan?'

'Shot,' I said without hesitation, which drew a look of disdain from the Jesuit.

'Under whose command?' he said sharply.

'Don Jaime de Guzman' was my next swift response, for after my narrow escape at Sligo, I made sure to only make stories up about people who could not deny them, and I knew full well that the worthy lieutenant Guzman had been felled in an exchange of fire off the coast of Calais, having last been seen disappearing beneath the waters of the English Channel.

Far from appearing appeased by my answers, O'Ronayne shook his head in annoyance, muttering something beneath his breath as his pacing grew faster. I felt like a mouse encircled by a cat, for my exchange with him had of a sudden come to resemble an interrogation. I looked around me for some weapon with which to defend myself, as well as the best means of escape.

'The scars on your back,' he snapped, with barely disguised irritation, 'they are only a few days old. What was your crime?'

This last inquiry caused me to scowl back at him, and the fierceness of my retort all but had me rise from the sackcloth.

'I was captured and tortured by the English enemy! Who *also* sought to interrogate me!'

My scarcely veiled implication did little to throw the resolute Jesuit off my scent, as he pressed on with his questioning.

'And the scar on your ankle? Was that also inflicted by the heretic?'

He almost had me then, for in my anger I stuttered, just as I was about to confirm his question, which would have marked me out as a liar. For O'Ronayne would have known that the chain marks around my ankle were not as recent as the ones on my back, so I instead quickly blamed the infidels for it, given that all good Christians blamed them for everything.

'I was captured by corsairs in my youth. They bound me to the rowing bench for well over a year.'

Upon hearing this claim, a triumphant grin grew on the Jesuit's face, leaving me fearful that my slave status had been discovered.

'It is indeed most curious that this occurred so long ago, friend Juan. Especially when one considers that your hair, whiskers and beard appear most short. Almost as if you were recently shaved in the manner of a galley slave.'

In that instant I thanked the Lord that I had cut the forelock off my head at Calais. I was also fortunate that my cheeks had not been tattooed in Seville, in Salva's haste to sell me to the demented overseer of the Santa Maria de Visión. After a moment's uncertainty, I was saved by a terrible itch in my nether regions, which I had refrained from scratching out of good manners. Yet at the Jesuit's remark I scraped at the sore bites around my crotch without mercy, leaving him to look at me askance. My eyes rolled at him as a sign that he was slow on the uptake, as I provided an answer to his last query.

'All kinds of vermin were to be found aboard our ship, which greatly frustrated the captain, a fastidious Venetian. He unleashed the barber surgeons on all members of the crew regardless of rank, until all of their razors were blunted.'

O'Ronayne fell silent at my last claim as he continued to pace about but refrained from asking me anything further. In seeking to break the awkward silence between us, I asked a question which had nagged at me throughout our discussion, yet which I had not yet had the opportunity to ask.

'Lady Muireann, does she still live?'

O'Ronayne appeared suspicious at my interest in the ollave's welfare, but he finally replied after helping himself to a long draught from his flagon.

'She received a strong blow to the head, but it will take more than a horse's hoof to disable Lady Mac an Bhaird. She is mending well, and my bloodletting helped her to recover from her drowsiness. The Lord be praised for, as they say in this land, health is better than wealth.'

A deep foreboding grew within me at his mention of his bleeding the ollave, and I stared back at him in horror. From my earliest days I had harboured a deep mistrust of the methods of healers, and the death of several comrades at the hands of surgeons had done little to allay this concern, leaving me to regard the common practice of bloodletting with nothing less than contempt. Upon noticing my drawn features, the Jesuit's black robe swirled around his ankles when he stooped towards me, clenching my chin between thumb and forefinger. His grip was as hard as iron, and his eyes passed carefully over my face as he held it up to the light of the fire.

'Of a sudden, you appear rather pale, Spaniard. Perhaps some bleeding might also aid your own recovery.'

He released his hold and trudged over to one of the trestle tables behind him, then picked up a red-and-white-striped pole, as well as a bandage to serve as a tourniquet. I beheld the coloured stick in stunned disbelief and was soon flailing my arms around me and shouting in protest, causing the Jesuit to observe my movements in surprise, as two of his apprentices appeared behind him wearing the same startled expression. Just when I feared that they might seek to restrain me, O'Ronayne quickly acted to allay my unease.

'Peace, Spaniard, do not stir! I shall return these implements to their bench, for in any event you seem sprightly enough!'

When the vile objects were put away, I fell back upon the sackcloth with a loud sigh of relief, while the apprentices returned to the other side of the cabin, and the Jesuit took up his seat again on the stool by the fire. My relief at his gesture was followed by renewed concern for Muireann, and at the treatment she had received after the savage kick to her head.

'And where is Lady Mac an Bhaird now?' I asked in exasperation.

'She is presently recovering in the quarters of Lady Dervila Bourke, the wife of Lord MacGlannagh. In her own way, the chieftain's wife is also a devoted student of medicine, or should I say potions. It is through her patronage that this house of healing is kept, and my medicine chest amply stocked.'

At his reference to this second woman, I looked aghast once more, so that the Jesuit appeared concerned as he quickly leant forward and shook my forearm.

'Whatever is the matter, Spaniard? You look like you have seen a troop of mounted heretics!'

'That name – Burke,' I stuttered. 'It belongs to that devil who gave us chase.'

O'Ronayne looked confused as he slowly drew away from me, with a flicker of understanding in his eyes.

'You mean that devil of the sergeant?' he asked. 'You mean Treasach?'

My nod of affirmation made him cross himself.

'That cur!' he growled, as his fists trembled with indignation. 'I cannot believe that he escaped our ambush! But fear not, my son, for although he derives from the same tribe as Lady Dervila, her people are a God-fearing tribe who also resist the enemy. Treasach fled their lands as an outlaw many years ago, before he embraced the cause of the Saxon devils. He is a merciless, avaricious monster, albeit a very skilled tracker. He has been responsible for countless atrocities, and a raging bonfire awaits him in the lowest depths of hell. You were most fortunate to escape his grasp.'

I shuddered when I recalled the treatment I had received at the hands of the merciless sergeant, and how close I had come to oblivion. When I regained my composure, I asked O'Ronayne another question, since he had referred to Lady Bourke by her maiden name, while also stating that she was the wife of a lord.

'Why do you refer to Lady Dervila by a different name from your lord that you call Manglana?' I asked. 'You speak of her as if she were some courtesan.'

A burst of mead spurted through the Jesuit's lips as his green eyes widened like those of a toad's, leaving him to gasp desperately for breath. Upon hearing his master's violent coughing, one of the youthful charges reappeared at O'Ronayne's side out of the smoke, proceeding to slap him heartily upon the back. It took well over a minute of this lusty beating until the Jesuit appeared to recover, waving the young man away and hissing his reproof at me.

'Have a care for your words, Spaniard! Have a care! Had those guards outside understood your tongue, they would have led you away for the dishonour that you cast upon their queen!'

After coughing again into his clenched fist, the Jesuit wiped his forearm across his lips, beholding me as if I were a madman.

'You are fortunate that I know you to be an alien, a grey wolf who is ignorant of the ways of the Gaels. But you would do well to remember that among my people a woman always retains the name of her sept. She never assumes that of her husband. Not even in part.'

I sighed in resignation, for the ways of the Irish seemed well beyond my reckoning. Although I was familiar with the frank and independent manners of women in the Spanish Netherlands, which exceeded those of females from other nations, the Irish women's right to never assume their husbands' names baffled me.

'Forgive me, Father, since that practice is identical to the Spanish custom, and is not one that is typical of northerners.'

'And yet that is the way of the Irish, friend Juan. And only part of the status that is accorded to womenfolk here. Long gone are the days when our highborn daughters could become chieftains or bards, but the Brehon law still grants them all other rights which are accorded to men.'

He took another swig from his vessel, before further explaining his people's custom.

'The *ollamh* Muireann, in particular, is held in higher regard by Lord MacGlannagh than most of his male subordinates. But then she was always his preferred foster child, and is also beloved by his wife.'

'Foster child?'

'Yes, Spaniard,' said the Jesuit, 'among the tribes of Ireland, fosterage forges alliances which are stronger than blood. Muireann was sent here by her late father when she was but a child, for he was a powerful vassal to MacSweeney, Lord of Banagh, which borders Dartry to the northwest. My lord and lady dote on her more than they do on most of their own kin, for she is possessed of many talents. They gratefully accepted her into their household, when she was married to their son Aengus *Cliste*.'

O'Ronayne's eyes misted at his mention of the ollave's husband, as I recalled the powerful redhead who was so formidable with the blade. I could still see him being felled by a shot from Gilson's pistol, before I had somehow dragged Muireann away.

'In the Glenade Valley, Lady Mac an Bhaird told me that you spirited her away from the Sassenachs. Tell me, Spaniard, did you see Lord Aengus fall? How did he meet his end?'

It was clear that the ollave's husband meant much to the Jesuit, for his voice had turned soft and was barely audible.

'He fought like a lion,' I said.

At my reply the Jesuit's long sleeves fell over his knees like sails, as he bent forward and set his flagon upon the ground. His hands trembled when his palms were rested upon his cheeks, and his lips quivered when he repeated his last question.

'How did he perish?'

'It was a shot to the stomach,' I said tersely, knowing that the meaning of such a wound would not be lost on him.

A muffled groan left O'Ronayne when his hands covered his face, and it was clear from the throbbing of his shoulders that he wrestled with a deep sorrow and struggled to restrain his outrage.

'Oh woe!' he rasped. 'Woe that our *Tánaiste* should have met such an end! Will Providence grant us no respite? He was our salmon of wisdom, who saw the path through all manner of strife!'

Upon sharing this lament with me, the Jesuit's eyes were reddened and raw as he pulled his face away from his arms.

'Aengus *Cliste* was a prince among goodly men, ever keen to defend Dartry and serve his lord-father. He was both learned and noble, but above all, a friend.'

Another gasp left him before his bemoaning was resumed, leaving me to wonder what sort of man I had abandoned. I finally understood why the ollave risked capture and death, while being reluctant to leave the body of her husband behind.

'What grief shall my lord endure upon receiving these tidings,' O'Ronayne continued, 'to learn that he has lost his son and best servant to the most cowardly of arms? Tell me, Spaniard, what kind of low-born hound slew our *Tánaiste* with so base a weapon?'

The Jesuit's reference to firearms left me feeling even more ill at ease. For in a land where everything was different, I had half-hoped that my skills as a sharpshooter might serve to enhance my host's opinion of me. My thoughts turned to the identity of the redhead's killer, bringing back memories of the renegade Lieutenant Gilson, who like Burke raised his sword against his own people.

'It was an officer. He was fair-haired and wears a high-crowned hat.'

'Gilson,' snarled the Jesuit.

His fists throbbed and he bared his teeth at me as though I were myself the renegade.

'John Gilson. That other bloodthirsty, profiteering traitor! But how did he discover our *Tánaiste*'s whereabouts?'

I had no reply to this, and O'Ronayne bit his lip as his face turned a hue of violet. One of his eyes widened, and he smacked his thigh with his palm.

'There is an Iscariot in our fold. Of this I am certain! One of Sinon's trade who must be in league with the Sassenachs!'

The assertion was disturbing, and I jolted upright in fear when the fire popped loudly behind him. With a curse the Jesuit shot to his feet and stepped towards a small pile of pine cones beside the kindling and logs, which were heaped a few feet away from the fire. Holding one of them up before his nose, he snarled angrily and hurled it in the direction of his apprentices, narrowly missing one's head.

'Too many men have I trained in the art of healing,' he said, returning to his seat, 'only to lose them to some detachment of Sassenachs during their journey to a neighbouring village. Most have lost their lives to that whoreson Sergeant Burke. Too many for it to be purely down to chance.'

I heard his concerns with growing unease, watching him carefully until he met my stare with a low rant, while nodding in the direction of his attendants.

'Now I am reduced to imparting my knowledge to these sons of low-born oafs, a pair of empty-headed louts who cannot tell a young cone full of sap from an old dry one!

He glared at the men who cowered behind him, then sighed aloud and resumed his rant.

'In truth I would prefer to hurl lavender upon the flames, to help dispel the stink of rotting flesh that gives way to bad humours. Yet the means that my lord once accorded me are now reduced due to the cost of our struggle with the heretic. These days most of Lord MacGlannagh's wealth goes towards paying his militia of armed mercenaries, which largely consist of all the blaspheming, low-born filth that the wilds of Scotland have to offer!'

When his grumbling had ceased, he turned again towards the fire. Upon seeing that its flames had all but burned out, he summoned one of the apprentices he had just insulted to hurl more logs upon the hearth, which was encircled by a ring of jagged rocks. No sooner was his bidding done, than O'Ronayne picked up a stick and poked at the growing flames, before patting his hands against his garb and bending over to reach for his drink. When he proffered it towards me, I raised my arm in refusal. After all, I had only just regained consciousness, and I desired my wits to remain undimmed. The Jesuit did not appear to mind, as he threw himself back on the stool.

'You are a wise man, Spaniard. This is one foul brew.'

'Do you drink throughout the day or only in the evenings?'

The note of sarcasm in my voice had O'Ronayne slowly pulling the vessel away from his lips.

'Our laws allow me three pints of drink a day, Spaniard. And I can drink them whenever I like.'

In emphasis of this right, he ended his riposte with a spirited burp, which was as loud as it was unbefitting of a former charge of the *Hôtel-Dieu*. The sound of his discharge was more telling of a whole hogshead of ale than a mere three pints, but the Jesuit took issue when I remarked upon it.

'I am owed drink in arrears,' he retorted with a deep scowl, 'which I am claiming during my hours of leisure! When my lord chieftain is returned from battle, you shall see that this time is but the calm before the storm. The Lord alone knows what his men have endured at the hands of the Sassenach.'

The subject of drink was subsequently avoided, as I returned our discussion to the subject of our common enemy.

'I pray you, Father, to tell me the meaning of this word Sassana? Is it used in reference to all heretics?'

He frowned at my last utterance, annoyed by my hapless pronunciation.

'The word you heard was Sassenach, which is our word for Saxon. Saxons, Sassenachs, they are but different words to describe the same devils locked behind their garrison walls, who only appear to unleash merry hell among us. For too long now have they put innocents to the sword, while they tear down our forests and set us against one another.'

When the Jesuit spoke, his bunched fists trembled again with rage, so that the cross on the end of his rosary swung from side to side.

'They are a terrible enemy. After supplanting the faithful among them, they now seek to destroy our own places of worship. The monasteries and the ancient schools lie in ruins, and priests of all orders are put to the sword.'

O'Ronayne hung his head and shut his eyes for a few moments, visibly trying to recollect himself. When at last he had stopped bristling, he returned his attentions to me.

'How does your head feel?'

As I gently stroked the bulbous welt on my forehead, the tips of my fingers passed over two rows of fine stitches alongside it. The sutures were as far apart as the width of a sword blade, which sparked memories of my last confrontation with Burke.

'It feels well enough, Father, when one considers that it was almost split open. Were it not for your kin, I would be dead. When the horse slipped, I was sure that our end was nigh.'

The Jesuit pulled the mead away from his lips and nodded his agreement.

'Yes, you certainly were done for. Cathal *Dubh's* ambush saved your hides.'

'Cathal who?' I asked, frustrated at being met with so many new words.

'*Dubh*. It means black. 'Tis our name for Cathal the black, the marshal of Lord MacGlannagh's horse. It was Cathal *Dubh* who requested that I personally tend to your wounds, for my skills are often sought by the *derbfine*.'

He uttered the last word with a certain reverence, which left me to conclude that it might be best to pursue its meaning at a later date.

'Then I am much indebted to him.' O'Ronayne smiled.

'As are the whole tribe, Spaniard. The marshal's forays against the enemy are famous among us. For aside from leading the chieftain's horse, he is also our exalted champion cattle-raider. Braver men are not easy to find, and he tracked your pursuers for miles while planning the ambush.'

'Then may God protect him, for delivering me from torment and death.'

'You are indeed fortunate to still be alive. The enemy is desperate to catch all Spaniards, and there is even talk of troopers hunting them down as far as Breifne O'Rourke.'

He turned his head towards the direction of the doorway where the dusk was gathering.

'Who knows how many of your kinsmen are still out there, left to the mercy of wild beasts and Saxons.'

He had hardly uttered these words when a strident wolf howl was heard outside, which was as loud as an ocean gale. I shuddered as I recalled the perils I had escaped, soon wondering what other dangers lay in store for me.

'What shall become of me, Father?'

O'Ronayne cleared his throat awkwardly, without meeting my plaintive gaze.

'It is Lord MacGlannagh and not I who shall decide your fate. He and his allies have long sworn fealty to the King of Spain, causing the Saxons to refer to them as the 'northern rebels'. This should bode well for you, although the intentions of rulers are about as predictable as their alliances.'

His reply did nothing to relieve my distress, and I could not resist pressing him further on the matter.

'Yet if your Lord Manglana is an ally of Spain, then surely he would protect us?'

'As I said, it remains to be seen. For I know that there are those who counsel him against harbouring Spaniards, given the horrors inflicted by the Saxons on those who dared to do this. It is said that the English Viceroy in Dublin has pronounced the death sentence on all those who would afford you shelter and aid. It was all that the common folk needed, in a year when they have endured all manner of sufferings, not least the unnaturally cold and fitful weather. I fear that their misery shall only worsen, for all the signs point to a terrible winter ahead.'

'Then what should I do?' I asked helplessly, fearing that no place was safe for me in Ireland.

The Jesuit observed me silently, then spoke again.

'Do what I do, Spaniard, and commend your soul to the Lord. Ultimately He alone can accord you eternal salvation.'

'Yes,' I said with a slight nod of my head, trying to appear outwardly convinced by his words.

O'Ronayne took another long gulp from his seemingly bottomless decanter before addressing me again.

'I should also attend to your spiritual needs, Spaniard. Do you wish to confess?'

I was about to decline this offer, when the snorting and whinnying of horses was heard outside the cabin, followed by the sound of jingling reins and loud salutations. There was also a clinking noise, and then the thud of feet landing upon grass. With a grunt of outrage, the Jesuit sprang to his feet and turned to face the figures who had appeared in the doorway of the infirmary. He gestured at them to leave, while snapping threats like a guard dog. His frantic movements caused the hazy smoke to swirl through the hut, obscuring my line of sight.

Yet upon recognising the entrants, O'Ronayne fell silent and took a few steps back, serving them with a deep bow. Through the smoke that filled the cabin, there stepped forth a man of short height and haughty bearing, with two taller companions at his back. They each held domed helmets and short lances, which marked them out as a select band of fighting men.

When they drew closer to my litter, I recognised them as some of the valiant horsemen who had rescued me from the clutches of the renegade sergeant Burke. They cut a fine sight in their short-sleeved mail shirts which reached down to their knees, glistening like snake scales in the glow of the hearth. The shield straps that crossed their chests and the swords at their hips also revealed them to be warriors of highborn means.

Their leader greeted me with the slightest of nods, causing his long beard to sway from side to side. Its tip reached beyond his breast and was one of the longest I had seen among the natives. When he next returned a bow to the Jesuit, I caught a waft of burnished leather and oiled steel, which was mingled with the rank odour of sweat from hard riding. While this visitor exchanged words with O'Ronayne in Irish, my eyes fell upon the pommel of his sword, noting that its hilt was curiously bound by a leather thong and crafted by a swordsmith I did not know of. My study of the curious blade was broken when the rider turned to address me in heavily accented Latin.

'Greetings, grey wolf. I am Cathal *Dubh,* my Lord MacGlannagh's marshal.'

Cathal the Black's voice was hoarse and barely discernible, sounding more like the last whisper of a dying man. His appearance was also subdued, for although I recognised his raven locks from the attack which had rescued my life, they also covered his face like a curtain so that little of it could be seen. The man seemed intent on concealing his appearance from others, since he stood away from the flames, so that he was concealed by the umbrage along the wall of the cabin.

'I owe thee my life, Lord Cathal,' I said, 'for thy swords delivered me from a cruel end.'

The marshal observed me at length, then addressed the Jesuit with a wave of his hand in my direction.

'Behold one of the sons of Golam. The Lord be praised, for the Milesians have returned in our hour of greatest need.'

I was uncertain what the marshal meant by these words, though O'Ronayne nodded back to him, shifting his speech from Spanish to Latin.

'So it doth appear, Lord Marshal.'

Another loud pop was heard from the fire, due to the young pine cones which had vexed the Jesuit. In that moment a flash of firelight lit up the room, and I almost gasped with shock. For it was in that instant of unexpected brightness that the marshal turned his head away from O'Ronayne, causing his hair to fall away from the right side of his face.

In those fleeting moments of revelation, I could see that his once-handsome features had been riddled with more nicks and marks than a whetstone. My surprise was at once tinged with sympathy, as I realised that my rescuer had been afflicted by smallpox in his youth. His grin also filled me with dread rather than confidence, for despite his bushy beard I could see that his thin lips barely reached his gums, rendering his smile similar to that of a death's head.

'Thou must wish that thou had stayed on thy ship,' he whispered from the growing dimness.

I carefully cleared my throat while I decided on my reply, realising that he had not yet learned of the defeat of the Armada by the English.

'I had no choice,' I said. 'We were shipwrecked.'

O'Ronayne spoke up in a sombre tone.

'One of many unfortunates cast upon Streedagh, my lord. A terrible tragedy. Had the Spanish captains journeyed but two hours south, they wouldst have reached the river Gilty.'

The marshal proceeded to question my status and experience, and I repeated many of the same falsehoods I had told O'Ronayne, as the Jesuit scowled at me suspiciously once more. When asked what rank I had held in the army, I again said the word 'shot', albeit much more hesitantly, knowing that I was addressing a highborn cavalryman who would inevitably hold a low opinion of firearms. Indeed, at my revelation the marshal exchanged a look with the Jesuit before he asked what had befallen me following my shipwreck.

At his request, I recounted my misadventures from when I had found myself washed up on the beach, taking care to exclude any mention of Don Gaspar de Hurtado and the precious ring from my tale. Both the Jesuit and the marshal listened intently to my account, only interrupting me to give names to the landmarks in each part of my story. From them I learned that the flat-topped mountain behind the beach was Ben Bulben, and that the coastal abbey was named Sta-ad. The defiled abbey where I had despatched Salva was that of Keeloges, and Cathal referred to the river I had dived into as the same Gilty which O'Ronayne had already mentioned. When I described the events which had unfolded in Sligo, the marshal spoke up in awe.

'No one has ever fled the town... and yet that would explain the marks on thy wrists.'

'And breast,' added the Jesuit.

O'Ronayne nodded once at my reference to the attack of the Irish tribesmen on the garrison town, which had allowed me to escape the fort. He attributed it to an Irish lord named O'Connor.

'Lord O'Connor rightfully attempted to reclaim his town from the enemy. He was once their ally, yet he shall pay a hefty price for it. Verily do they say in these parts, that he who lies down with dogs, gets up with fleas.'

At my references to Treasach Burke and John Gilson, the Jesuit appeared stunned, while the marshal spat on the ground in anger.

'Those men are demons. They fought for Spain years ago before returning to Ireland. Profiteers to their core, they are slaves to the power that stems from the Sassenachs' queen, Elizabeth Tudor. Now they are but a pair of blackguards who serve the heretic cause.'

'Thou also met with Bingham?' whispered O'Ronayne.

'Aye,' I nodded.

'Broke thy bonds and laid hands on his whore?' said Cathal.

'Aye.'

They regarded me without speaking a word, then both trad-ed a glance and shook their heads in disbelief.

Finally the marshal piped up again in his low voice.

'Thou fledst from the jaws of certain death.'

'And made some powerful enemies in the bargain,' added the Jesuit. 'Little wonder then, that they threw caution to the wind when they gave thee chase.'

I shivered slightly at the memory of it before the marshal spoke again.

'Do not fear, grey wolf, for we are the avowed enemies of the Bingham brothers and friends to all their foes. Were it up to them, they would have long crushed us and all of our allies.'

Cathal grimaced when I sought more information about the Binghams, for I was curious to learn where the devils hailed from and the extent of their power.

'They are the second sons of a Saxon house,' he replied, 'En-glish heretics who butcher us far from the eye of their heretic queen. Even her viceroy in Dublin has sought to curb their ex-cesses against us many a time. But 'tis said that they have the support of their queen's secretary, that devil of all heretics, Sir Francis Walsingham.'

I instantly felt uneasy at the mention of this name, for the notoriety of the English queen's spymaster was such that I had even heard of him when serving in the Spanish Netherlands. O'Ronayne snorted in wholehearted agreement.

'The worst of them is Richard, the Governor of Connacht. Although his younger brother George, the Sheriff of Sligo, is not far behind him when it comes to cruelty. Alack, he is the man who had thee tortured at Sligo.'

Cathal next asked me about Aengus's passing, so I retold the same episode I had recounted to O'Ronayne. My narration was followed by another long silence, interrupted only by the crackle of burning fuel and the odd cough of the other invalid in the cabin. During this time I noticed that the marshal's head had dropped, and that one of his hands had risen to his face. His companions also appeared deeply aggrieved, while the Jesuit did his best to stifle a sob.

'Then it is true,' he said in a faltering voice, 'that Aengus *mac an rí* is dead. Who will guide us now?'

None present offered him a reply, until he spoke again.

'The shame of it. And to think that he was abroad on a peaceful errand, escorting Lady Mac an Bhaird to an *ollamh* gathering, one hosted by our foster father the O'Connor Sligo. He was himself also keen to attend, for our *Tánaiste*... our *Tánaiste* was always enamoured of learning.'

'What is the meaning of this word, tanist?' I asked, after the marshal had again drawn his hand to his face in sorrow.

'The *Tánaiste* is our second elect,' managed O'Ronayne, between sniffles, 'an heir to the chieftain who is elected by the highest assembly of freemen.'

I grappled with the concept of an heir who was elected and not necessarily the first born son of the chieftain, while O'Ronayne wiped his tears in his sleeve. He then stole another swig of mead, as if punishing himself for the loss of Muireann's husband.

'At least we have our *ollamh* back,' he croaked.

He had hardly spoken, when a muffled cry was heard in the doorway, followed by loud protests. The two kerns charged with guarding the cabin's entrance stepped in front of us with a worried look, while the Jesuit beheld them askance. Then a young lad with a head of red curls strode through them with tear-streaked cheeks and a pair of blazing eyes, crying out to us in his heavily accented Latin.

'What has become of my father, grey wolf? Why shall none tell me where he is?'

Both marshal and Jesuit beheld each other in concern, until O'Ronayne walked over to the young intruder. With a gentle but firm rebuke, he wrapped an arm around the boy's shoulders and ushered him towards the entrance into the infirmary. Yet before he left us, the stripling cast me a longing gaze so anguished and plaintive, that even my hardened heart was stirred by the sight of his distress.

'Who is the lad?' I asked, when the boy was gone.

'Another blameless victim of the heretics,' rasped Cathal from the shadows, 'for he is Lochlain, the son of our *Tánaiste* and Lady Mac an Bhaird.'

The revelation came as little surprise, for the boy's complexion was the same as that of his late father's. A silence lingered after the lad was led away, until the marshal cleared his throat and rested his hand upon the hilt of his sword.

'Until our next meeting, Spaniard. I bid thee farewell and a hasty recovery. On my part I must retire early, for tomorrow shall find me leaving again at dawn, guarding our western borders in my lord chieftain's absence. Yet it is heartening to learn that we have the presence of true bravery in our midst. We are always in need of worthy soldiers, men who can aid us in our constant struggle against the Sassenach.'

I was unsure how to respond to his compliment, for many a noble officer had told me during my army career that all sharpshooters were cowards and not true fighters. I had seen enough fearsome swordsmen in the Spanish Army to accept this as truth, yet I sought to humour the marshal with a wry smile.

'My sword is thine for as long as thou requirest it, Lord Cathal.'

A flash of yellowed teeth could be seen as the marshal grinned in the flickering firelight.

'Thy service shall be gladly received, grey wolf, at least by me. For our enemies are as bountiful as the wolves in the hills. We also resist a tribe that is unmatched by any previous foe for strength and cruelty, and one which wants the heads of all shipwrecked Spaniards. Thou hath no choice but to join with us, if it be Lord MacGlannagh's will.'

'Better to join you,' I replied, 'than to be an outlaw condemned to death.'

'But are they not the same thing?' asked O'Ronayne, as he reappeared through the shroud of smoke.

'Perhaps they are,' I declared, 'except that now I need not run all the time.'

The marshal cleared his throat awkwardly, seeming almost reluctant to enlighten me otherwise.

'Do not speak too soon, grey wolf. Few places in Ireland are safe from the Sassenachs.'

O'Ronayne sighed wearily as he nodded his agreement with the marshal's words. Then his head fell back again, as he helped himself to another swig from his flagon.

Here ends THE SHERIFF'S CATCH, *being the* first part of THE SASSANA STONE PENTALOGY.

The second part is called A REBEL NORTH, *for its events recount the further trials of Abel de Santiago in the rebel kingdom of Dartry.*

Thank you from all of us at Tearaway Press for reading The Sheriff's Catch by James Vella-Bardon.

We've worked really hard to get this title published and we hope you've enjoyed this award-winning, critically acclaimed, bestselling read.

If you'd like to support James' work, you could post a review about The Sheriff's Catch on Amazon, Goodreads or elsewhere, if you get half a minute. Doesn't have to be anything too long, just pick a rating and then add a line or two about what you made of his debut. This will help alert other readers who may also be interested in James' work.

If you need a hand with this, just contact us at:

info@jamesvellabardon.com

And you're interested in receiving the occasional email update about James' books, you can sign up to his mailing list on:

www.jamesvellabardon.com

All the best!

Historical Note

Even today, the word 'armada' still conjures up the image of a great fleet in the Anglosphere. In fact, in 2017, then US President Trump declared that he would be sending an 'armada' against North Korean dictator Kim Jong Un. I think few would disagree that this is mainly due to the Grand Armada 1588 which was despatched by King Philip II of Spain to help conquer England.

And yet most of us English speakers still know little about it. The popular myth is as follows: a David vs Goliath story in which a lesser English fleet beat the big bad bully Spain. The Armada's defeat has given rise to a legend which is a foundational keystone in the English psyche: the first time England took on first of many nasty Continental powers and won. During the Battle of Britain, Winston Churchill said:

'We must regard the next week or so as a very important period in our history. It ranks with the days when the Spanish Armada was approaching the Channel, and Drake was finishing his game of bowls.

I can still remember reading about the famous Sir Francis Drake episode, when I was a boy. With the Armada sighted off the coast of England while he played on Plymouth Hoe, Sir Francis is supposed to have famously said:

'We have time enough to finish the game and beat the Spaniards too.'

An account which further reinforces the myth that the English prevailed against a powerful and much larger invading fleet, through dashing derring-do and the clever use of the fireships.

Little if any of all this is actually true. Few people know, for example, that the English fleet had more ships than the Armada itself. Less know that – far from the cocky, arrogant air assigned across the board to all things Spanish – that the Spaniards were in fact travelling to England with much anxiety, led by a reluctant admiral who constantly implored his King to abandon the venture. All of which is a far cry from the spooky, sinister representations of 16th C Spaniards in screen dramatisations which conveniently tap into the 'black legend' of Imperial Spain which still endures in the Anglosphere, to score a quick win.

Professor Gareth Mattingly, a Yank who won 1960's Pulitzer Prize for 'The Defeat of the Spanish Armada', has also shown that this representation of 16th Spaniards is not accurate. His book recounts how an emissary of Pope Sixtus V visited Lisbon and struck up a conversation about the Armada's impending sea battle with the English with 'one of the most experienced officers of the Spanish fleet' (Recalde?), who told the Pope's man:

'...unless God helps us by a miracle the English, who have faster and handier ships than ours, and many more long-range guns,

*and who know their advantage just as well as we do, will never
close with us at all, but stand aloof and knock us to pieces with
their culverins, without our being able to do them any serious
hurt. So, we are sailing against England in the confident hope of
a miracle.'*

I don't detect any of the hubris that's often popularly repre-
sented in that reply.

So anyway, back in 2008 I thought that it would be inter-
esting to tell the Spanish Armada event from the other side's
perspective, a view that has never been presented in English
fiction. I tried to be as historically accurate as I could, to show
the pros and cons of all the cultures which form part of the
Sassana Stone Pentalogy, namely: the early modern Counter-
Reformist Spaniards and Reformist 'New English', and the
'late medieval' Gaelic Irish.

The backdrop to all this is 16th century Europe, with the
16th century being the century (as previously also observed
by Salman Rushdie) in which man experienced the greatest
amount of seismic change on every level: religious, scientific,
the arts, medical etc. Which is probably why the French call
it 'Le Grande Siècle', meaning 'the Great Century', with the
two superpowers of the time being Catholic Spain and Otto-
man Turkey. Truly a fantastic canvas to use for my storytelling.
What's perhaps less known is that the 16th C is also called the
'Iron Century', due to the significant military developments
which occurred during it.

The battle of Gravelines, between the Spanish Armada and
the English fleet, was a watermark moment in the history of
naval warfare, with the English fleet relying on speed and firepower instead of the age-old grappling and boarding. This was

the fruit of an astute policy to invest in and upgrade the Royal Navy, which was commenced by Elizabeth's father Henry VIII.

To my mind, it is somewhat ironic that the English so successfully employed tactics at sea in 1588 which the Spaniards used on land to crush the French army at Pavia 1525. Pavia, where the groundbreaking Spanish 'pike and shot' tactics – also involving a high degree of mobility and firepower – utterly devastated the fearsome French cavalry, so that the French king himself was taken prisoner by the Spanish.

But back to the Armada: Philip II being uncharacteristically hellbent on deploying his troops to invade England is recorded. What is less known is that the Armada was not sailing directly to England. For it was in effect a big taxi service which was meant to pick up the Duke of Parma's veterans from Calais – veterans of the Army of Flanders who were probably the toughest and best troops around back then - to next drop them off in England. Except, and this is also lesser known: Parma (often listed alongside Alexander the Great and Napoleon as one of history's greatest military leaders and strategists) had absolutely no intention of sending his troops to board the Armada's ships. To him the plan to invade England was all a needless caper dreamed up by a monarch who was detached from reality, and he had enough to contend with in Flanders.

The anecdote about the Prince of Ascoli being sent to urge Parma to send his men to Calais is also documented in the sources. As is Parma ordering his men to make a big act of boarding barges in order to appease the departing Ascoli, before ordering them to disembark and return to their previous duties.

What's also documented is the incredible bad luck endured by the Armada before and following its departure: the dire prophecy of the astrologer Regiomontanus is recorded, which resulted in Philip working the Admiral Santa Cruz to death to try get the fleet to leave in 1587, in order to avoid the many defections which did happen at year end. This rush also led to many deals being struck between the Spanish crown and dishonest contractors, so that the water casks being defective, food going off and many other unexpected problems encountered along the way are also all documented.

As was the ridiculously bad weather encountered by the great fleet, storms so bad that they would have been notable in winter - except they were incredibly happening in summer. Never did one speak more idly than when one referred to the Armada as 'great & most fortunate navy' since I cannot think of much else that could have gone wrong during its voyage.

As for the rest: the use of the fire-tax by disgruntled Spanish troops is also recorded in the sources, as was the Spanish tendency to refer to all provinces in the Low Countries as 'Flanders', even though Flanders was but one of these many provinces. So that a Brabantian from Willebroek would have inevitably found himself referred to as being Flemish by the Spanish soldier. Which of course presented me with a challenge, early on in this book, as to how various characters would refer to Elsien and Maerten.

As for Seville being 'the Great Babylon of Spain', this is described in fascinating detail in Mary Elizabeth Perry's 'Crime And Society In Early Modern Seville', in which we learn that Seville's 1580 population was estimated to be 90,000 people – the largest in Europe after Naples, Venice and Paris. In her equally brilliant 'Aristocrats And Traders, Sevillan Society In The Sixteenth Century', Ruth Pike describes how plague often afflicted the city, referring to the collective measures advised in 1579 to address the plague, which she says returned to Seville in 1587 and continued for three or more years. I think that following the incredible events of 2020, we can all now appreciate the disruption that that would have caused.

Finally I want to address a question which many readers have asked since Sheriff was published in the UK: were people back then really that tough?

I'll share a brief anecdote about Miguel de Cervantes, famous author of Don Quixote. Suffice to say that prior to the great sea battle against the Turk, Cervantes was half prostrate with fever so that he was ordered below decks. Yet as battle commenced, he begged for a post of danger, so that he was sent into the thick of combat and suffered three gunshot wounds: two in the chest and one in the left hand (which he subsequently lost). Cervantes incredibly went on to survive these wounds, and I also invite doubters to read up on what he subsequently endured after being captured by North African corsairs, before managing to come out the other end, relatively in one piece. People were tough above all else back then, and anyone that's read the riveting biography 'The Adventures of Captain Alonso de Contreras' knows that in early modern Spain, children never left home without a dagger, and sometimes also killed each other in the street during brawls.

Oh and women were made of sterner stuff too. It's also recorded that barely a few hours after giving birth at sea, the legendary 16th C Gaelic heroine Gráinne Ní Mháille (anglicised as Grace O'Malley) realised that her ship was being attacked and boarded by North African corsairs. After grabbing her sword, she rallied her men to repel the attack, before also capturing the pirate ship for herself.

Acknowledgements

Being a writer means that I mostly enjoy being hidden away with my books, tapping away on my laptop. I don't actively seek out DIY jobs around the house, nor do I lead the charge in domestic matters. My long-suffering wife will attest to this.

But when a dirty bunch of possums caused our bedroom ceiling to come crashing down in early 2019, I knew that progressing with my writing was going to be a little bit trickier than first anticipated.

My close friends may recall that our house at the time was nicknamed 'Bag End' by yours truly. This was because it had something of the hobbit hole about it, particularly since it was fast becoming too small for us following the birth of our second kid. So when the broken ceiling was repaired after a cramped two months without the use of two rooms, we instantly readied to put Bag End on the market.

There followed much disruption, as well as back and forth, with two young children in tow. We had to move in and out of a crummy flat in Lindfield twice to get Bag End painted and then styled. Which is not to mention the time sinks caused by us trying to find another place to move into. It took almost six months to get everything ready, and all in all it was practically impossible to get any writing done.

After the huge hassle of finally moving into our new place (which I nicknamed Rivendell) at the end of '19, we did not anticipate the next Biblical challenges around the corner. The infamous 'Black Summer' kicked off within the very same week, essentially the start of NSW's worst bushfires on record. Which meant we had to pack everything and move out of our new place for a while. Upon returning to Rivendell, our new suburb was hit by a mini tornado which also went on to wreak havoc across most of the lower north shore. It also meant that we were without power for over a week. This was followed by bad flooding and a winged termite invasion, so that my friend Mark Nees laughed aloud at our bad run and asked me: 'what next? The plague?'

And then we got Covid.

I need not describe the home-schooling havoc caused during the first half of 2020. We were left dazed and confused after things returned back to normal, before a Covid panic blew up in our area again towards the end of the year, effectively scrapping our Xmas and NYE plans.

All throughout this trying time, in which I was constantly tormented by my lack of progress with my writing (there's a first world problem for you right there), I was supported by some good friends who helped me get through it all while retaining some degree of sanity. I'd like to thank my cousin Pierre Fenech, Jorge Perez y Asenjo, Nicky Valenzia, Virginia Ball, Kristian Bonnici, Dery Sultana and Steven Gatt for putting up with all my moaning. My thanks also go to my parents Frank and Josanne, as well as anyone else I forgot to mention.

Once again, I'd also like to extend my gratitude to all those people that helped create or improve the text of Sheriff first edition, which was published in the UK by Unbound during a magical 2018, who include:

Anton Tagliaferro, the late Harry Calleia, Martin Pisani, Donna Madden, Dr Anton Caruana-Galizia, Anthony Vella Gera, Scott Cross, Brien McLaughlin, Seamus McCanny, Marguerite Cousins, structural editor and acclaimed author Dexter Petley, structural and copy editor Jessica Hatch, Jim Gill, structural editor CM Taylor, copy editor Andrew Chapman, Xander Cansell, John Vella Bardon, Alfred Tagliaferro, Katharina Ohman, Klaus & Susan Vella Bardon, Eylem Kamerakkas, Godfrey Callus, Godwin Fernandez, Richard Campbell, Eddie Ripard, Cerena Moses, Mark Oastler, Steve Conlon, Tina Case, Isabella 'Iris' Bleszynski, the late David Busvine, Margaret Kennedy, Kevin Lowe, Dianne Ashcroft, Eddie O'Gorman and John Cunningham.

I'd also like to thank all those wonderful people who understood the significance of Sheriff and helped to promote or stocked it post-publication: Malcolm Miller and Michael Vella de Fremeaux at Agenda Bookshop, Amanda Agius at Merlin Library, Audrey Cassar at BDL Books, Matthew Xuereb and Stephanie Fsadni at Times Of Malta, David Lindsay at The Malta Independent, David Grech and Jean Paul Azzopardi at Lovin' Malta, Laura Calleja at MaltaToday, Trudy Kerr and the guys at XFM, Teresa Quinn at Bookline, Maltese Cultural Ambassador Joseph Calleja, Mary Samut-Tagliaferro at UM Library, Claire Busuttil, Former President of Malta: Marie-Louise Coleiro Preca, the guys at Abbeys Bookshop and Better Read Than Dead in Sydney, Gill Woodhouse, Ron Briffa at TeaRoom, Peppi Azzopardi, Edward Mercieca, Vanessa

Dorahy, Alison Riseley, Maria Micallef, Bec Kelly, Dr Joseph Camilleri and Prof Ivan Callus, amongst others.

A big shout also goes to Dr Nicholas Valenzia and his colleague Dr Antoine Camilleri at MamoTCV, who kindly used some of their valuable time in 2019 to help ensure that I was truly unbound. And a nod also goes to my supportive writer mates the talented Steven A. McKay, Paula Constant, Craig A. McDonough, Rosanne Dingli and Liah Thorley, as well as the two worthy gatekeepers at the awesome Grimdark Magazine, Adrian Collins and James A. Tivendale, for giving my reviews a great home.

Finally a big cheers to the team at Tearaway Press for their backing, as well as the awesome Beta readers of this 2nd edition of The Sheriff's Catch - you know who you are.

About the Author

James lives in Sydney with his young family and a maniacal cavoodle.

The recipient of a few international literary awards and nominations, he enjoys reading gritty thrillers filled with moral dilemmas and a real sense of danger.

www.jamesvellabardon.com

Special Thanks

Heartfelt thanks to each of the following patrons in the redoubt-able 'el tercio del patrón', who believed in this novel and backed the publication of its first edition by Unbound in the UK:

Simon Abela, Maryanne Abela Medici, Laurence Adams, Thomas Agius Ferrante, Lynn Allenby, Rachel Alt, Matthew Aquilina, Chiara Attard, Louis Attard, Barbara Azzopardi, Connie Azzopardi, James Azzopardi, Natasha Azzopardi, Roberta Azzopardi, Sergio Azzopardi, James Bannister, William Barella, Jonathan Beacom, Daniel Bianchi, Nicholas Bianchi, Isabella Bleszynski, Anna Maria Bonnici, Joseph Borg, Joseph F Borg, Adam and Melissa Bradford, Jillian Brand, Amarjot Brar, Malcolm Briffa, Mathew Broom, Lara Bugeja, Franz Buhagiar, Marco Burlo', Marco Buttigieg, Paul Cachia, Harry Calleia, Keith Callus, Richard Campbell, Stuart Campbell, Anton Caruana Galizia and Claudine van Hensbergen, Susan Case, Tina Case, Charlot Cassar, Diana Cassar, Patricia Cassar-Torreggiani, Laurette Cavanough, Tiziana Ceci, Ian Cilia Pisani, Steve Conlon, Mark Cordina, Marguerite Cousins, Paul Croci, Scott Cross, Milena Cupac, Ruza Cupac, Abi Curtis, Anton Dalli, David Darmanin, Robert Day, Ashley Dayman, Nicky de Battista, Melanie De Cressac, Elizabeth De Gaetano, Oliver Degabriele, Mark Degiorgio, Paul Degiorgio, Steph Demarco, Karl DePasquale, Edward Despott, Arun Devendran,

Ben Di Qual, Caroline Dingli-Attard Inguanez Brown, Lesley Dudzicki, Wyn Edwards, Rokhsareh Elledge, Patrick Ellul, Rhys Evans, Daniel Falzon, Malcolm Falzon, Lorraine Farrugia, Paul Farrugia, Peter Paul Farrugia, Kathrina Farrugia-Kriel, Herb Fava, Noel Fava, Pierre and Jennifer Fenech, Godwin Fernandez, Mark Fiorentino, Julian Fleri Soler, Stijn Floridor, Angela Forbes-Siegner, Gabriela Freire, Margaret Frendo, David Galea, Martin Galea, Andrew Galea Debono, Alice and Stephen Gatt, Craig Gay, Ingrid German, Matt Githens, Sabin Gnawali, Mark Grech, B H, Ewan Hall, Gerhard Hambusch, Gladiene Harverye, David Herrera, Richard Jenkins, Lanneke Jones, Eylem Kamerakkas, Dan Kieran, Carolyn Kiffin, Nathalie Kinnear, Virginia Koch, Anton Komarov, Olga Komarova, Sheridane Kumanidis, James Lai, Richard Lee, Joyce Li, Tina Lombardi, Slum Lord, John Ma, Nicole MacDonald, Amelia Madden, Colin Madden, Donna Madden, Glaze Madden, Tom Madden, Anne Marie Magri, Dorota Maj, Joanna Malinowska, Nikki Mallia, Simon Mamo, Steve Mamo, Kevin Manicolo, Leong Mar, Brigitte Martin, Patrick Lionel Martin Maney, Carl Marx, Gordon McCann, Dani McCartney, John A C McGowan, Mark McKendry, Ray Mercieca, Chris Mifsud, Chris Mifsud Bonnici, John Mitchinson, Cerena Moses, Jan Muscat, Mireille Muscat, Sergio Muscat, Rae Ni Corraidh, Marcus O'Neill, Tara O'Shea, K P, Joseph Pace, Liz Parsons, Di Paterson, Stefano Pellegrini, Jorge Perez y Asenjo, Ian Perry, Martin Pisani, Steve Pisani, Justin Pollard, Mike Portanier, Martin Puchert, Ross Pulido, Faye Purdon, Anne Raffel, Mirko and Kristina Rapa Manche', Ashley Reid, Eddie Ripard, Caroline Risiott, George Robson, Liz Saliba, Peter Saliba, Edward Sammut, Frank Sapienza, Claudine Schembri,

Celine Schwarzenbach, Adrian Sciberras, Lara Scicluna, Jacqueline Scully, Ashish Sethi, Darren Sillato, Dhanesh Singh, Alison Smith, Tony Smith, David Spiteri, Matthew Spiteri, Ella Strickland and Dragan Avramovic, Gerald Strickland, Melissa Stutsel, Simon Sullivan, Dery Sultana, Matthew Tabone, Anton Tagliaferro, Leah Taylor, Sasha Taylor-East, Josh Terlich, Cynthia Thomson, Roger Tirazona, Catherine Todd, Melanie Toepfer, Dianne Trimble, Nick Valenzia, Astrid Van Steen, Maarten Van Steen, Ricardo Vasquez, Bernard Vella, Carla Vella, Doris Vella, Gege Vella, Luca Vella, Olivia Vella, Peter Vella, Suzanne Vella, Anna Vella Bardon, Frank Vella Bardon, John Vella Bardon, Josanne Vella Bardon, Klaus Vella-Bardon, Louisa Vella Bardon, Marcus Vella Bardon, Mark John Vella Bardon, Michael Vella Bardon, Susan Vella Bardon, Andre Vella Bonnici, Ian and Maria Vella Galea, Bernard von Brockdorff, Shelagh Wadman, Nik West, Adam White, Kathleen Williams, Matt Williams, Dusty Williamson, Matthew Xuereb, Matthew Zahra, Michael Zammit Maempel, John Zappia, Bruce Zhao and Nadine Zrinzo